Essays on Medieval Civilization

The Walter Prescott Webb Memorial Lectures: XII
Sponsored by the University of Texas at Arlington

The Walter Prescott Webb Memorial Lectures

Essays on Medieval Civilization

By

Richard E. Sullivan
Bernard McGinn
Bede Karl Lackner
David Herlihy
Fredric L. Cheyette

Introduction by Bryce Lyon
Edited by Bede Karl Lackner & Kenneth Roy Philp

University of Texas Press   Austin & London

Library of Congress Cataloging in Publication Data

Main entry under title:
Essays on medieval civilization.

(The Walter Prescott Webb memorial lectures; 12
ISSN 0083-713X)
  1. Civilization, Medieval–Addresses, essays,
lectures. I. Sullivan, Richard Eugene, 1921–
II. Lackner, Bede K. III. Philp, Kenneth R., 1941–
IV. Series: The Walter Prescott Webb memorial lectures;
12.
CB351.E78   940.1'4   77-17068
ISBN 0-292-72023-8

Printed in the United States of America

Contents

Preface

On March 31, 1977, the Twelfth Annual Walter Prescott Webb Memorial Lectures were held at the University of Texas at Arlington. Three papers were presented during the morning session by a local historian and two distinguished guests, while a third visiting scholar delivered the evening lecture. Medieval civilization, the topic of this year's lectures, would have pleased Webb, who explored how the Great Frontier effected major changes on Western Europe since 1500. Webb would have also found these essays stimulating because they explore unfamiliar topics, reveal the vitality of the past, investigate the basic concerns of mankind, and reevaluate the meaning of medieval history for the modern world.

In order to honor Walter Prescott Webb's relish for historical debate, Professor Bryce Lyon, from Brown University, was asked to write an introduction that would challenge the new interpretations of medieval history that emerge from these essays. He has succeeded admirably in this task. The Webb Lectures Committee also requested that Professor Richard E. Sullivan, of Michigan State University, write a historiographical essay that would reassess the significance of the Middle Ages, rather than a more traditional piece of historical research. Webb would have enjoyed Sullivan's thought-provoking response which rejects the genetic approach to this historical epoch. Professor Sullivan provides us with a new paradigm that demonstrates how the dynamism of Western civilization derives from the thirteenth century when contradictory institutional and ideological elements were juxtaposed to create a vibrant social structure.

Professor Bernard McGinn, of the University of Chicago, sheds new light on the religious dimension of the Crusades. He describes the events surrounding the failure of the Holy Fire at Jerusalem in 1101 in order to show the unique piety of the first crusaders. The legacy of Hans Böhm, a lay preacher who championed the cause of the German peasants at Niklashausen, is examined by Professor Bede Karl Lackner of the University of Texas at Arlington. Böhm not only challenged the feudal system; he also established the first widespread protest movement in the German Empire. Professor David Herlihy, of Harvard University, presents a pioneering study of the history of medieval children. Shaped respectively by classical discipline, the Germanic world, and the teachings of the Christian church, adult attitudes evolved toward a fuller awareness of the potential of childhood.

In 1977, the University of Texas at Arlington sponsored its Third Webb-Smith Essay Competition. Funded by a generous grant from C. B. Smith of Austin, the award is given each year for the best paper submitted on the topic of the lectures. The current winner is Fredric L. Cheyette, of Amherst College, whose "The Invention of the State" examines how the concept of the state was devised in the last half of the eleventh century within the medieval church. Especially important was the role of a few clerical polemicists and Pope Gregory VII. They imposed a literate culture on a predominantly oral tradition based on custom, habit, and memory. Professor Cheyette's essay is included with the papers delivered during the lectures.

As usual, the Webb Lectures Committee would like to thank all participants in the series–speakers, students, faculty, and the staff of the Press–for their help and cooperation.

Bede Karl Lackner
Kenneth Roy Philp

Introduction

Bryce Lyon

Unlike previous Walter Prescott Webb Memorial Lectures, which focused on a theme concerned primarily with American history, such as "Essays on the American West," or "Essays on Walter Prescott Webb," the 1977 lectures, entitled "Essays on Medieval Civilization," are not circumscribed by a common theme but instead stretch across a historical period encompassing ten centuries. That only one medieval theme, the frontier, has any significant genetic connection with Webb's research is a measure of the many-splendored heterogeneity of history. And that the Department of History did not insist on this theme was wise, for to assemble four or five historians who could speak with authority on the exterior and interior frontier of medieval Europe would have been extremely difficult. The alternative was five essays, each on a different problem and with a different methodology. This diversity typifies the present broad spectrum of historical research on the Middle Ages which, though highly sensitive to new methodology and to the pertinence of related disciplines, has remained eclectic, not becoming the captive of any one of the bright new methodologies as have certain historical fields and most of the social sciences.

One connection between the essays of this volume and the writings of Webb is that Webb's research opened up a new perspective on the Great Plains, a thesis that at first received support but then came under attack by some who attempted to repudiate it. In American historiography, therefore, Webb is remembered as a pioneer who developed a fascinating and compelling interpretation of American history that sparked criticism from many fronts, which in turn modified the

Webb thesis and produced a new perspective on the Great Plains. All the essays in this volume challenge established interpretations of the Middle Ages in an effort to present a new view on a certain problem. Two of them are pioneering in what they do, by virtue of either the materials used or the questions asked that necessitate the reformulation of problems.

Since merely to summarize these essays and politely limit my comments to highlighting their admirable features seemed superfluous and bland, I decided to read and to react to them, to form opinions on their strengths and weaknesses as I would to those in any journal of medieval history. What follows are the meditations of a medievalist on the research and ideas of other medievalists. Obviously, they will not always be appreciated by the authors. Nor will the reader uniformly agree with them. But their purpose is to stimulate thought, to provoke response, even controversy, to what I consider the principal merits and failings of these essays.

In his essay, "The Middle Ages in the Western Tradition: Some Reconsiderations," Professor Sullivan makes an interesting attempt to reorder our traditional thinking about the Middle Ages and to challenge the classic conceptualizations of medieval civilization. Much of what he says strikes a responsive chord. I share his disillusionment with traditional and normal history and, like him, see throughout the Middle Ages discordant tendencies, a pluralism, a diversity, and a dynamism. No longer can historians speak of the "medieval mind," the "medieval synthesis," the "homogeneity of institutions and thought," and the "universal nature of the Holy Roman Empire." I am also sympathetic to Professor Sullivan's criticism of the paradigm of the thirteenth century as the synthesis of medieval civilization. He rightly warns historians of modern history not to regard the significant movements of Western European history as only beginning to percolate in the thirteenth century. Then, indeed, the church was not monolithic, as one can see by comparing St. Francis, St. Dominic, the popes, the canonists, the monastic orders, the local churches, and the heretics. Consider, too, the dichotomies among the scholastics. Professor Sullivan presents a convincing argument for dismantling the present paradigm of the thirteenth century and replacing it with a vaster paradigm encompassing most of the Middle Ages during which he sees creativity, flux, diversity, and dynamism. In the continuum of

Western history this means, I suppose, scrapping some of our favorite historical compartments, such as the age of Charlemagne, the age of chivalry, the renaissance of the twelfth century, and working instead to see the interconnection of the significant developments and how they collectively formed our Western civilization.

As Professor Sullivan well knows, the rearrangement of patterns of thought and the construction of different paradigms are not achieved without considerable debate among historians. He has, for example, made some generalizations about the thirteenth century that are unconvincing to me. We agree that stabilization did not come to all aspects of medieval society in the thirteenth century, but certainly by the last decade there is evidence of a stabilization that in the fourteenth century contributed to a plateau and a retrenchment in some areas of endeavor. Despite regional variations, in general this pattern of stabilization is revealed in loss of population, a slackening of economic activity, a temporary end to European expansion, a decline in institutional innovation, and a kind of ecclesiastical arteriosclerosis. Some historians see not simply stabilization but decline and waning in the fourteenth century. The point is that one must acknowledge some generalized stabilization which is already detectable late in the thirteenth century.

Professor Sullivan's generalization that political particularism did not triumph over the universalism of the Christian imperial idea in the thirteenth century seems unjustified. How can he say this when political particularism in Germany and Italy was rampant and when the emperors were nothing but figureheads? How can he say this when we know what Philip the Fair of France and Edward I of England did to Boniface VIII and when we see the bitter struggle between these two agressive monarchs of states rapidly assuming their peculiar political forms? How is it possible to speak of other than particularism throughout the Middle Ages? Some churchmen and theorists may have written about a universal Christian empire, but in the real world no such empire with a universal set of values existed. When I look at medieval Europe, I see instead a feudal particularism gradually replaced by a larger nonfeudal particularism embodied in such evolving states as France and England. In Germany and Italy, where such states did not emerge, there was nothing but particularism up to the nineteenth century.

So what are we to do about the thirteenth century? Professor Sullivan has torn gaping holes in its imposing Gothic edifice and has given it a different paradigm. For him "it was during the thirteenth century that the cultural plurality inherited from the prior centuries was successfully reckoned with in a way that set a unique course for the future of the Western world." He sees "the thirteenth century as the culminating period in medieval history . . . marked by the framing of a civilizational order that featured the juxtaposing of opposites into the total fabric of society." He would replace the paradigm of the thirteenth century as a century of synthesis with one of a century that digested and then made room for the diverse and dynamic elements of medieval civilization. This is a provocative thought, but it demands careful scrutiny before it becomes one of our medieval paradigms. The thirteenth century may well have been a period when pluralistic developments and forces consolidated themselves, but if we accept this paradigm we must then explain why it is *the* medieval century to account for in the continuum of Western history. Can we be so certain that it was such a special century?

The essay by Professor McGinn, "*Iter Sancti Sepulchri*: The Piety of the First Crusaders" plows no new furrow in research or interpretation of the First Crusade but argues from close examination of one event for a return to a more traditional interpretation of the First Crusade. On April 21, 1101, Jerusalem was shocked when the Holy Fire, the fire that for centuries had regularly and miraculously descended from heaven on that day to light the lamps in the tomb of the Lord, did not appear. Nor did it appear the following morning. When various interpretations of the fire's failure to appear did not allay the fears of the throngs in Jerusalem swelled by bands of pilgrims, and when prayer and a detailed confession of his sins by the patriarch Daimbert still evoked no fire, there was organized a penitential procession to Solomon's Temple to beg forgiveness for the human sins that apparently had caused God to keep the fire from descending. A crowd of nobles, clergy, pilgrims, populace, and even King Baldwin of Jerusalem marched barefooted in penance to Solomon's Temple with the happy result that when Daimbert returned to the Church of the Holy Sepulchre he found the miraculous fire burning brightly.

This event–the *iter sancti Sepulchri*–brought to all in Jerusalem a great sense of relief because, according to Professor McGinn, it symbolized the raison d'être of Jerusalem, the Kingdom of Jerusalem, and the First Crusade. The appearance of the fire confirmed the belief of all Christians that Jerusalem was the birthplace and center of their faith, that here Christ had lived, preached, performed miracles, been crucified, resurrected, and buried. It was for this that the First Crusade had been organized; for this that Western Christendom had made heroic efforts to take Jerusalem from the infidel and restore it to rightful Christian possession. The Kingdom of Jerusalem with its satellite crusader states had been erected to preserve Jerusalem and the Holy Land as Christian. Jerusalem and the kingdom symbolized the success of the First Crusade and the belief of Western Christendom that, were these places not in Christian hands, all would go badly.

On that Easter Sunday of 1101 the ritual of the *iter sancti Sepulchri* with its *confessio, concordia,* and *processio* reminded the participants that these elements underlay the First Crusade and accounted for its ultimate triumph. In other words, contends Professor McGinn, a basic piety and religious fervor of eleventh-century Europe were responsible for the First Crusade; it was a holy war. This interpretation, presented with compelling force by Carl Erdmann in 1935, has been a favorite of Crusader historians in one form or another since the second half of the nineteenth century. By comparing the elements of the First Crusade with those of the *iter* and placing strong emphasis on those religious forces and developments of the eleventh century that led to the First Crusade, Professor McGinn has reminded us that the cause and effect of faith in the Middle Ages, especially in the period up to the twelfth century, was paramount in the daily workings of men's lives, their aspirations, their successes, and their failures. He has given us a salutary reminder that at least in the Middle Ages many men were not motivated primarily by political and, above all, collective and impersonal economic and social forces.

Although Professor McGinn does not say so, the First Crusade is the only Crusade that will bear his interpretation; for it alone could he adduce evidence of the broad and pervasive faith that moved those who responded to Pope Urban II's eloquent appeal. This raises some questions. Even if one grants the piety and ritual of eleventh-century Europe as symbolized by the *iter*, is Professor McGinn justified in ascribing the First Crusade and its creations in Syria solely to religious forces?

I do not oppose returning to a more traditional interpretation of the First Crusade provided it concedes a role to other forces. That Europe in its religious development was finally ready in the late eleventh century for this great effort is well known, but equally well known is that it was also ready in other respects without which all the religious fervor in the world could not have restored Jerusalem to Christian possession. Europe finally had the military might, manpower, and economic resources to mount such an offensive. Many of the feudal aristocrats who went on the First Crusade did so from a desire and need for land. Christian forces could never have reached Syria without the Mediterranean having been opened up to Christian ships and without such places as southern Italy and Sicily having become secure Christian beachheads. The economic revival of Europe in the late tenth and eleventh centuries provided the resources and skills needed to contemplate such an undertaking. One must not forget that supplies had to be purchased and ships chartered, and that without the support of the Genoese and Pisans at critical junctures the First Crusade would have failed. While some Crusader leaders were devout believers, certainly the Normans were not; yet their military proficiency, previous crusading experience, familiarity with the infidel, cynicism, realism, and ambition account for most of the Christian victories.

These secular forces at work in the late eleventh century combined with a remarkable religious fervor to make possible the capture of Jerusalem. Because another essay in this volume refers often to paradigms, these questions and observations are to remind readers that for most medievalists the eleventh century is a paradigm of revival, recovery, and dynamism in most aspects of Western European life. It is generally recognized as the century when that vibrant movement and development characteristic of Western Europe began to appear.

Concerned also with religious history, Professor Lackner's essay, "Hans Böhm: Shepherd, Piper, Prophet," takes us in time to the later fifteenth century. Convinced by his study of Böhm that this unlettered and ignorant layman with a gift for making music has been unjustifiably relegated by historians to a minor role as social reformer and agitator, Professor Lackner attempts to demonstrate that Böhm occupies a significant place in later medieval German social and religious history. His brief appears to rebut the traditional view of Böhm, yet when one regards Böhm in the total context of the religious and social history of late medieval Europe, there is obviously little that is novel about him. His rustic and humble social position, his ideas and dreams of a better and more just society, the people he attracted to him as followers, and his unfortunate end have a familiar ring to anyone conversant with the peasant uprising in Maritime Flanders early in the fourteenth century, the Jacquerie of 1358 in France, the Great Revolt of 1381 in England, and the social and economic turmoil of the larger Flemish and Italian cities.

Böhm's ideas mirror those in the sermons of the Dominican preachers and religious reformers. To discover the specific source of Böhm's ideas is not possible. Illiterate, he was surely unaware that some of what he said at the village of Niklashausen had already been said by Huss and Wycliffe. But their ideas as well as those of heretics and of hundreds of anonymous reformers had in simplistic terms become familiar to peasants and urban dwellers. These ideas had become a part of oral lore known to most common men. Professor Lackner's essay suggests how intriguing would be an attempt to trace and account for the transmission of ideas among simple and illiterate people; it shows that the social and religious ideas of late medieval Europe were so widely dispersed that under propitious political, economic, social, or religious conditions they were an arsenal for social reform. We see this in Luther's time, particularly with the Peasant War of 1525. While justified in seeing Böhm as a champion of "the cause of the little man," Lackner does not convince me that Böhm "created the first nationwide movement in the German Empire" to further that cause or that he "overcame local particularism and was able to bring about an antifeudal mass movement." Where is the evidence that during Böhm's life he strayed out of the Tauber Valley where he was born or that he led or instigated any mass antifeudal movement? Lackner is claiming too much for Böhm. To me the use of "nationwide" in fifteenth-century Germany is anachronistic. A casual glance at a map of Germany in the late fifteenth century is enough to show that it was but a patchwork of numerous secular and ecclesiastical principalities and free cities.

The final two essays of this volume are more methodologically and conceptually innovative. That of Professor Herlihy, "Medieval Children," reflects his current interest in medieval demography and the secrets it has to reveal on some hitherto unknown aspects of population growth and decline and on the functions and occupations of class. Here he is primarily concerned with the attitudes and values of a society. According to him, those who have written on medieval childhood have concluded that in Western Europe childhood was not recognized as a distinct phase in human life and children only came to be appreciated and valued after the Middle Ages. While some scholars have credited Rousseau with calling attention to children, others believe that only now are children coming to be fully appreciated. Professor Herlihy attacks and attempts to dispel such opinion. Despite the sparse and disparate evidence available, he makes a convincing case that medieval people came to care about their children.

Although the classical world practiced infanticide, we know that members of the higher echelons of society were concerned for the welfare of their progeny. Besides providing a good education, they attempted to guide their children toward respectable careers and to provide inheritances. Apparently the Germans had affection for their young, but that the *leges barbarorum* indicate low wergelds for children and the elderly suggests that only physically competent and productive adults counted in early medieval society. This attitude seems prevalent down to the eleventh century when, according to Professor Herlihy, it was altered by social and economic developments of the eleventh and twelfth centuries, such as the rise of a commercialized economy and the proliferation of special skills which led urban inhabitants to invest in their children. They supported schools to make their children literate, encouraged training in various occupations and professions, and eventually established hospitals and orphanages. Treatises on the rearing of children appeared, concentrating upon what we would consider social and psychological development. During the thirteenth and fourteenth centuries the cult of the Christ Child reflected a growing appreciation for children and, artistically, the Christ Child began to assume the form of a very human and appealing baby. In the fourteenth century, when plague and other physical catastrophes took a brutal toll of the young, society became more concerned with the health and survival of its young. It would appear, therefore, that, before the humanism of the Renaissance, the Christian family of Martin Luther, and the affectionate romantic values of a Rousseau, people were caring about children.

Much of what Professor Herlihy has skillfully assembled from scattered demographic, urban, church, literary, and artistic sources has been known in different contexts. Urban historians, for example, have known about communal schools, about the bourgeois eagerness for literacy, about the training system of the guilds, and about the hospitals, orphanages, and charities. Art and church historians have long spoken of the growing humanization of the Christ Child. But Professor Herlihy has pulled these disparate strands together to make us realize that at least the feudal aristocracy and the bourgeoisie cared about their children and began to do so by the twelfth century. He is most convincing when citing evidence of a practical and human quality. When he cites statistical evidence, I am not persuaded that the impersonal numbers are convincing, particularly for the Carolingian period.

I hope that this volume of essays will somehow be wafted by a strong breeze out of the halls of history into those peopled by professors of education and child psychology. If such professors will then read this essay, they will learn that their bone has been gnawed for centuries and that what they have been presenting as new insights into the understanding of the child are actually only what medieval people, those people of the "Gothic Dark Ages," already knew and were putting into writing. They will read that in the thirteenth century Vincent of Beauvais wrote: "Children's minds break down under excessive severity of correction: they despair, and worry, and finally they hate." From Italian humanists they will learn that physical discipline is "contrary to nature," that it "induced servility and sowed resentment, which in later years might make the student hate the teacher and forget his lesson." Medieval people were even aware of the wide variation in the aptitudes and inclinations of the young. What the Florentine Giovanni Dominici wrote about matching aptitude and profession could well come from a textbook on career development and training written in 1977. "Nature aids art," he wrote, "and a skill chosen against nature will not be learned well." What a shame that these modern pedagogues never had a course on medieval history. We might then have been spared all their obvious and arid pontifications.

Professor Cheyette's "The Invention of the State" is not so much a quest after the origins of the typical European state as it is a search for the idea or concept of the state, its laws, and its institutions. He particularly wants to know how the modern West came to think of human law and the state as coercive. He does not find this coercive idea among the Greeks. Rather, they were convinced that good states and laws were the *sine qua non* for the good society and individual. He might well have found the modern view of the state and law in Roman history but he skips from the Greeks to the Middle Ages when, he contends, little if anything was said in the abstract about state, law, and authority until the eleventh century. Up to this time medieval Europe was mostly an oral society with its ideas reflecting those who uttered them and handed them down from one generation to another. These ideas expressed orally could not be abstract, according to Professor Cheyette, because they issued from a specific person, such as a king, a doomsman, an official, or a priest. It was Clovis or Charlemagne who uttered ideas and commands, not the king or emperor. Laws related to specific people and addressed themselves to specific crimes and differences. Charters referred to men granting and receiving land but not to feoffors, feoffees, vendors, and buyers. This interpretation of the thinking and oral expression of early medieval Europe is too frequently overlooked or unknown. It is not that early medieval institutions and laws were not coercive and not disliked, but that they were not speculated about and talked about in the abstract. Until the eleventh century men were little concerned with universals; what mattered was real persons and things.

Professor Cheyette sees this attitude changing in the eleventh century, a change related to the Investiture Controversy that forced spiritual and secular officers to think and write about the nature of their offices and their authority. Now such individuals as Pope Gregory VII or Henry IV came to be thought of as holders of an office. The powers and rights of the popes as enunciated by Gregory VII in the *Dictatus Papae* became the powers and rights of office and were considered vastly superior to the secular powers of the office of emperor, an office, Gregory argued in his famous letter to Bishop Hermann of Metz, that originated from men ignorant of God who secured their power by pride, plunder, and treachery. Professor Cheyette contends that in the act of assembling the *Dictatus Papae* Gregory in a sense initiated "the new imagining" about offices, laws, states, and power. Men began to "see office and property not as having character but as impersonal and abstract because derived from an impersonal and abstract body of rules." In appealing to rules in writing rather than to what men remembered, the Gregorian reformers initiated a process of thinking in the abstract about authority and law.

Assuredly the intellectual and religious revival of the eleventh century, what Professor Cheyette calls "the great medieval awakening after 1050," fomented this transformation. Henceforth, written records become sufficiently numerous to verify this change in modes of thought. Although records before 1050 are too scarce for a sure answer, it would still be challenging to ascertain whether the Investiture Controversy was such a watershed in this change. Interestingly, Professor Cheyette notes that Ivo of Chartres relied upon a text of St. Augustine when making a distinction between an office and the holder. If St. Augustine made such a distinction as early as the fourth century and if he was the favorite author of early medieval men, others under the influence of his political ideas must have used them just as did Ivo of Chartres. Unfortunately, we lack the evidence to substantiate this likelihood. What did Charlemagne really think about his authority, his office, his laws, and his vast possessions? Did not he or his advisers or his subjects ever get beyond their persons and the particular? What about the more literate Alfred the Great? It is inconceivable that these two and a few others prior to Gregory VII did not occasionally escape from their skins and look at themselves as wielders of law, as holders of an office with authority. Whether or not convincing, Professor Cheyette's thesis is novel and offers an alternative to the traditional institutional explanation of the concept of the state.

That three of these five essays—those by Professors McGinn, Herlihy, and Cheyette—deal with subjects that force the authors to confront the eleventh century is noteworthy and more than fortuitous. Whether the problems are social, economic, political, or religious, it is striking that these authors find in the eleventh century the beginnings, forces, and developments that contribute to their elucidation. These three essays are linked by a stream of historical tendencies important in Western history. Perhaps Professor Sullivan should take another look at his medieval centuries. He might well discern that the thirteenth was not all that consequential, that its paradigm might be overshadowed by that of the eleventh century as the period when the vital juices of the Western world first began to flow.

Essays on Medieval Civilization

The Middle Ages in the Western Tradition: Some Reconsiderations

Richard E. Sullivan

The selection of the topic of the Middle Ages as the subject for the 1977 Walter Prescott Webb Lectures has emboldened me to depart somewhat from what appears to be the tradition governing these lectures. Rather than presenting a paper directed toward either of my two rather narrow areas of specialization within the vast spectrum embraced by medieval history, early monasticism or Carolingian history, I have elected to address a broad historiographical issue. In part, I was led to this undertaking because of certain issues that have intrigued me for several years as I have taught and studied the Middle Ages.[1] The opportunity to serve as a Webb lecturer afforded a chance to collect and order my thoughts and to see if I could shape them into a meaningful statement about that long era. Beyond that, I feel that every specialized scholar, and particularly one who concentrates on a remote era or subject, has an obligation to make intelligible to all of his scholarly co-workers why he labors in his chosen vineyard. Without such efforts, the scholarly world, even in a single discipline, becomes Balkanized to the point where communication ceases and the fruits of learning grow sterile. By virtue of the fact that the Webb Lectures attract scholars representing many disciplines and, particularly, historians interested in various eras and subsections of the past, the occasion seemed ideal for a medievalist to articulate some ideas that would perhaps relate medieval studies to the larger realm of historical studies, thereby contributing to the unification of a discipline which very often appears on the verge of disintegration.

As already noted, I wish to focus this paper on a historiographical problem. I shall reflect on the problem of how we do and should look at the Middle Ages as a chapter in the total stream of the human experience. These reflections will, I hope, constitute a plausible case for fitting the Middle Ages into the historical continuum in a somewhat different fashion than has been the custom for both medievalists and those concerned with other historical eras. I shall offer my argument with humility, for it is indeed embryonic and tentative. What it now needs is vigorous scrutiny from as wide a spectrum of medievalists as possible, as well as a rigorous critique from historians knowledgeable about other segments of history that interrelate in any fashion with the medieval period.

Certainly someone has already asked what purpose can be served by posing once again the well-worn question: What were the Middle Ages? My defense is a simple one, but one that I think worthy of serious reflection. Although we seldom discuss it, I submit that historical inquiry into any segment of the past is directly and decisively related to conceptions shared by investigators at any particular moment about how that period fits into a larger historical continuum. For example, Greek history was investigated in one way by historians who saw the Greeks as progenitors of the democratic tradition that evolved through many post-Hellenic centuries and in an entirely different way by historians who viewed the Greeks as participants in the creation of a Mediterranean community that culminated in the Roman Empire. Or, again, American history has been treated much differently by historians who see the essence of modern history in terms of the democratization of the world than by those who see the same era in terms of the victory of capitalistic imperialism in a world setting.

These simple examples point to a profound truth: Historical inquiry is conditioned by paradigms that operate in much the same way in channeling the thrust of investigation and interpretation as do the paradigms in scientific inquiry so brilliantly described by Thomas Kuhn.[2] The conceptual and instrumental framework crucial to historical research centers in formulations shared by historians concerning the way in which a segment of time relates to what came before and after. Like the Kuhnian paradigms in science, these formulations about the basic relationship of a historical epoch relative to other epochs have sufficient substantive validity to persuade considerable numbers of historians that they supply a legitimate foundation for the practice of history and are sufficiently open-ended to leave all kinds of challenging problems for resolution. They therefore define "normal" history, providing a consensual framework within which research proceeds down determined lines to fill out the parameters implicit in the paradigm. Within this context, the answer to the question "What were the Middle Ages?" is obviously vital, for it determines the focus and thrust of research and teaching about every aspect of the Middle Ages and provides a common ground upon which a large community of researchers can articulate a generalized understanding of the Middle Ages.

If my argument that a shared view about how a particular period fits into the larger continuum delineates and directs research and interpretation about that period has validity, then it follows that changes in that consensus will alter the focus and thrust of investigation. Borrowing once more the Kuhnian idiom, a change in the paradigm will result in a historiographical "revolution." Again, the matter of "What were the Middle Ages?" takes on crucial importance, for, if a fresh answer to the question is postulated as a replacement for an accepted or "normal" response, the entire approach to the study and interpretation of the medieval period will be altered.

It is the purpose of this paper to explore a new definition of the place of the Middle Ages in the historical continuum. It will attempt to sketch a new paradigm that, if accepted, might refocus and redirect the study of and teaching about the Middle Ages and very likely alter the approach to much of Western European history since the medieval period.

As a first step in developing my case, let me define where we presently stand in terms of the placement of the Middle Ages in the total stream of history. In reflecting on the long tradition of medieval historiography, I believe our present paradigm is the product of four successive approaches to the era, each complementing its successor but each also solidly rooted in a particular and unique interpretation of the place of the era in the total stream of history.

First, there were the interpreters of the past who lived during the Middle Ages. In the main, medieval historians saw their age as a chapter of *Heilsgeschichte*, during which all that had transpired since the Incarnation was preparation for the day of final judgment, always immediately immanent. St. Augustine was the architect of this view; the vigor of the concept was dramatically demonstrated as late as Otto of Freising (d. 1158) and Joachim of Fiore (d. 1202). All medievalists know what fascinating interpretations of the actions of kings and saints, popes and paupers, knights and knaves this paradigm produced when applied by medieval chroniclers, annalists, and biographers. And all know how painfully difficult it is to educate students in the art of deciphering medieval historians in the face of the bias built into their writings as a result of their implicit assumption that their day might well stand at the end of time, their constant concern that everything they recorded and interpreted might well be the crucial harbinger of the day of judgment.[3]

Toward the end of the Middle Ages, perhaps as early as the *trecento* in some parts of Western Europe, the first signs of a new view of the place of the Middle Ages began to emerge. Observers began to see the era as a "dark age," characterized by assorted forms of barbarism. The earliest proponents of this view were the humanists, who found in the elegant language and literary style of the ancient world their model of civilized existence. The dim view taken toward the Middle Ages by these literati was reenforced by a wide-ranging group of religious reformers of whom Martin Luther serves as an archetype. They saw the Middle Ages as an era marked by the prostitution of the true spirit of primitive Christianity. The dark-age interpretation of the medieval period received its final and clinching impetus from the rationalists who conquered the intellectual world in the seventeenth and eighteenth centuries. Confident that man was capable of perfect rationality and that the world was awaiting a perfectly rational ordering if superstition, faith, and ignorance could be expurgated, the historians of the Enlightenment saw in the Middle Ages the total embodiment of all that was antirational and therefore anticivilizational. The works of Voltaire and Gibbon stand to this day as impressive monuments of the genius of historians in delineating a totally consistent view of a millennium of human experience which proved Voltaire's advocacy of the study of the Middle Ages because "it is necessary to know the history of that age only to scorn it."[4] Knowing the history of the Middle Ages in Voltaire's perspective consisted of seeing it as a dismal dark age positioned between a glorious classical age and a new age of enlightenment. Telling the history of the Middle Ages was an exercise in collecting evidence of folly, superstition, violence, ignorance, blind faith, and so forth. Never was the investigation of medieval history more solidly secured in and shaped by an assumption of where the period fitted into a grander order of history.[5]

A third overarching view of the Middle Ages emerged in the late eighteenth and early nineteenth centuries, closely associated with Romanticism. Generated chiefly by an aversion to the sterile world of the rationalists, by a search for emotion and warmth in an overformalized world, by a sense of kinship with the stirring forces of democracy and nationalism, and by a newly discovered feel for nature, the view of the Romanticists toward the Middle Ages was basically nostalgic. With a reach somewhat longer than that of modern nostalgists, who have had to stretch to get back three or four decades to Chaplin movies, the big bands, and dime novels, the Romanticists leapt back to the Middle Ages to find an empathetic environment. In the era's simplicity of life, depth of religious feeling, solidarity of social organisms, and closeness to the soil, they caught a reflection of a noble life fully worth recapturing. Wordsworth at Tintern Abbey, the Grimm brothers gathering stories from the mouths of peasants, Sir Walter Scott and Lord Tennyson reconstructing the noble lives of gallant knights, Chateaubriand rapsodizing on the *Génie du christianisme*, and Victor Hugo recapturing the mysteries of medieval Paris–all played a role in recasting the Middle Ages in terms much more sympathetic than had been the interpretation of their predecessors. More artistic than scholarly, more given to feeling and intuitive insight than to thorough and systematic investigation, the Romanticists played only a small role in providing a solid basis for comprehending the real nature of the Middle Ages. However, because they saw the period as one in which certain kinds of legitimate human experiences blossomed, the Romanticists elicited a new appreciation for the Middle Ages in its entirety and drew attention to many of the era's features that had theretofore been neglected.[6]

In fact, the Romanticists set the stage for a fourth broad interpretation of the Middle Ages, which took shape in the nineteenth century and which still exercises a powerful imperium over medieval studies.

Like all historical paradigms, the view of the Middle Ages that took shape in the nineteenth century was a product of a general intellectual environment which permeated contemporary patterns of thought. Two particular ideas were crucial in shaping the new approach. First was the impact of the scientific spirit which insisted that all seekers for the truth, including historians, be objective. This posture demanded that all ages of the past be given equally neutral treatment, unmarred by preconceptions, assumptions, and prejudices. Leopold von Ranke defined the new terrain when he pronounced that all ages were immanent in the sight of God, by which he meant that no historian had a right to prejudge an era but rather an obligation to see it in its own dimension and time—even if that age was the "dark ages." Second, and much more important, was the genetic approach, insisting that the reality of things was defined by how they became what they are. Rooted in the scientific concepts canonized by Sir Charles Lyell and Charles Darwin, the genetic approach to the cosmos pretty generally captured the intellectual world of the nineteenth century. Accepted with alacrity by the historians, that approach soon elevated Clio's servants to the center of the stage in all matters pertaining to the study of human affairs. The key to understanding reality centered in the discovery of how things came to be. Like the geologist outlining the stratification of rocks to demonstrate how the physical environment evolved to be what it is or the biologists piecing together the fossil evidence that traced the evolutionary emergence of various animate species, the historian became the scientist of social experience fabricating an interconnected, cumulative narrative that showed how what exists today had evolved from something originating in the past. By virtue of his capacity to reveal the process of becoming, he joined the physical scientists and the biological scientists as possessors of indispensible keys to understanding reality in the human dimension of the cosmic order.[7]

The triumph of scientific history and of the genetic approach engendered a fresh place for the Middle Ages in the historical continuum and a new focus for all investigations of the period. To put the matter in somewhat simplified terms, the Middle Ages became at one stroke both the subject of objective investigations and the point of origin of most of the basic features of at least three major cultural communities of the modern era: the Western European, the Islamic, and the Byzantine–East European worlds. To the historical investigator, it became the period where one began inquiries in order to discover the origins and thus the nature of what now exists. The investigations of all features of the modern Western European world–nation-states, representative institutions, the class system, imperialism, capitalism, literary and artistic forms and motifs, educational patterns, science, and so forth–began to be pushed back into the Middle Ages. As the evidence piled up, the medieval period increasingly became a key element in the continuum that created the modern world, perhaps even *the* key element because, more often than not, the medievalist could demonstrate that his epoch was the age of genesis of the crucial ingredients of the modern civilizational order. The medievalist grew mighty in the tribe of historians, performing such feats as transporting the Renaissance back to the twelfth century, reducing the Reformation to but one more episode in a long succession of transfigurations of Christianity, greatly lengthening the age of European expansion and discovery, inventing parliaments long before the English revolution, discovering the genuinely authentic national spirits in the vernacular literatures of the Middle Ages, demonstrating that men were rational long before they had any right to be so, and even stealing the frontier from the cowboys and the ploughmen of the Western world.[8]

There is little doubt that the genetic approach still provides the paradigm that guides the mainstream enterprise of medieval history. It would require only a modest effort, I suspect, to extract from most teachers, researchers, and students of the Middle Ages a confession that their efforts were aimed at understanding the era more fully in order to comprehend more clearly how the present came to be.[9] And those historians who concern themselves with things "modern," that is, postmedieval, seldom fail to preface their treatment of the modern world with serious reflection on its medieval origins.[10]

Nor would anyone dare belittle the product of the genetic paradigm. The collective effort under the umbrella of the genetic approach has indeed borne magnificent fruit. I would venture that some of the most thorough and exciting scholarship produced over the last century has been the work of medievalists filling out the details of the genetic paradigm, work rivalling in its intellectual sweep and appeal even the revelations of the Marxists about class conflicts, or of the psychohistorians about the special problems of Luther or Hitler, or of the new leftists about the satanic character of Americans.[11] And I would further venture that the medievalist *qua* teacher has demonstrated a capacity for heightening historical consciousness surpassed by few other specialists. Indeed, medievalists have lived in a heady age; perhaps they have earned the right to be a little arrogant– or perhaps better, I should say, the genetic approach to history, laced with a strong shot of scientific objectivity, created a paradigmatic ambience extremely favorable to their temporal focus.

So much for "normal" medieval history, for the paradigm that delimits and defines our approach to the Middle Ages. Trusting that I have adequately acknowledged the rich harvest of knowledge and understanding that has flowed from that paradigm, I must now enter the caveat that lies at the center of my presentation. I find myself increasingly restive with the dominant thrust of medieval studies. What troubles me is the paradigm itself: I have increasing difficulty with the assumption implicit in the genetic approach which insists that the medieval period fits into the larger stream of human history as the unique epoch during which occurred the definition of patterns of institutions, ideas, and techniques that determined the basic configurations of at least one and possibly three living cultural communities. At this point, I make no claim that my discontent deserves to be elevated to a universal statement. My reflections on the problem have not revealed the sources of trouble with total clarity. But at least some possible causes of my disenchantment have emerged. Perhaps they deserve note because they pose some basic issues about the nature of medieval studies.

First, I find myself increasingly troubled on philosophical and experiential grounds with the basic proposition so central to modern historianship, namely, the concept that one can only explain and thus comprehend reality by discovering and revealing how things came to be. This is not the place to expose possible limitations on this fundamental canon of modern historiography. Let me only say that I find it almost impossible to give meaning to many phenomena bearing on my own life by reconstructing the narrative which shows how these conditions came to be what they are. The suspicion that there is indeed a genetic fallacy tends to breed doubts about my ability to relate in a meaningful fashion many medieval phenomena to the present world, as indeed I should be able to do if the genetic approach is valid.[12]

Second, I have always been disturbed by the inadequacy of the modern view toward the Middle Ages in coping with the totality of the Middle Ages. Try as hard as they might, most medievalists have found it impossible to push their search for the genesis of things modern back much earlier than the tenth century.[13] This leaves half a millennium–the early Middle Ages–either unaccounted for or open to bizarre interpretations. The effort of Henri Pirenne and his disciples to annex most of the early Middle Ages to classical history has involved some grave difficulties.[14] It has not been very enlightening to be asked to accept the early Middle Ages as the real dark age, a kind of truncated version of Gibbon's grander view of the Dark Ages.[15] Nor have I found much consolation in the efforts of some sociologically oriented historians to treat the early Middle Ages as a disembodied "model" of a backward society to be compared with analogues drawn randomly from the totality of time, space, and human experience. In short, the prevailing approach to the Middle Ages is flawed by its inability to account for the medieval period in its entirety; I see no way that this flaw can be mended as long as the genetic approach prevails.

Third, the genetic approach has failed to yield any insight clarifying from whence came the dynamism that has sustained continuous growth since the Middle Ages. It does not explain why institutions and ideas shaped in the Middle Ages as crucial components of Western European civilization demonstrated such vital capacities for development in succeeding centuries. In fretting about this lacuna in my historical perspective, I have ultimately concluded that the genetic approach to the past has a major limitation in that it accentuates the linear, temporal aspects of the human experience at the expense of the dynamic aspects. As a consequence, it produces a one-dimensional view of the Western European experience that provides no way of accounting for the movement, growth, and transformation that have been so patently present in the Western European world.

Finally, I have been increasingly troubled by some jarring dissonances between the genetic approach and the crisis in Western civilization that grips our generation. For the last half-century, intellectuals with a historical bent of mind have been tortured by a mounting uneasiness about the possible demise of Western civilization. These fears have been chillingly articulated in the writings of Oswald Spengler and Arnold Toynbee, whose admonitions have gained considerable credibility from such terror-laden events as the advent of fascism, the horror of modern warfare, the threat of nuclear annihilation, the dehumanization of life by mechanization and bureaucratization, the vision of an overpopulated world struggling to survive in a setting where resources have been squandered, and the prospect of dying in a polluted environment.

The source of our malaise is certainly not agreed upon. But I would propose that we shall ultimately come to agree that the root of the trouble in the contemporary Western world lies in a lack of congruence between ideology and institutions. In oversimplified terms, our times are out of joint because we believe one set of things about the essential nature of the cosmos while at the same time we are compelled to conduct the routine activities of our collective existence within a set of institutional patterns that emerged from another, quite different set of convictions about the fundamental order of things. In my judgment, the basic institutions prevailing in the modern Western world were formed within the context of a set of assumptions (or, perhaps better, convictions) about the cosmic order and the human condition rooted in the Judeo-Christian tradition as that tradition was articulated during the Middle Ages. We are, however, living in a situation where there has been a rejection of the Judeo-Christian concepts in favor of a world view composed of a concatenation of ideas drawn from Darwin, Freud, Marx, behavioral social scientists, and modern biologists. Despite considerable agitation over the last few decades, there has been only modest movement toward fundamental institutional changes that would accommodate the new world view. The consequence is a dissonance between institutions and ideology that breeds the cardinal afflictions of the age–alienation, meaninglessness, despair, hedonism, senseless violence, escapism.

This insight into the nature of the troubles in our world increasingly vitiates for me the utility of the genetic approach to the Middle Ages. If the burden of the present centers in reforming institutions framed in a medieval world view to fit a discordant postmedieval ideology, there seems little point to an effort to root out and describe the medieval origins of present institutions that appear doomed. One is tempted once again to cast the spell of darkness over the Middle Ages, to view it anew as an era that visited on its heirs a bitter heritage which they would do well to escape. It certainly seems fatuous to look to that distant age for the origins of what is the essence of the modern world. I fear, in fact, that this sense of the crisis of our age is leading many away from the study of history as the key to comprehending reality toward the dreary swamps of prophecy and futurology.

If it does not appear too immodest, perhaps these concerns can be made to yield a meaningful generalization that has a bearing on the current state of medieval studies. The long-agreed-upon, bounteously fruitful paradigm defining the place of the Middle Ages in the total stream of history is disintegrating. Its decomposition is not a consequence of its having produced wrong history. Rather, we are witnessing once again what has happened before: historians are being faced with a new range of basic questions about the state of the world and the condition of man to which the genetic paradigm does not seem to speak meaningfully. These anomalies, deriving in the main from the wisdom provided by "normal" history, are forcing a search for a new angle of vision on how the medieval period fits into the total stream of history. Like their predecessors who more than once radically redefined the place of the Middle Ages in the historical continuum, medievalists know instinctively that, if they do not discover a new paradigm congruent with their changing sense of what is significant about the period, they will begin to witness the atrophy of their own inquiries and the loss of interest among those whom they would instruct about the past.

If all of this has any validity, where do we go now? I would like to devote the rest of this paper to a possible answer which does no great violence to the present state of medieval studies but which defines more adequately the place of the period in the total stream of history. The amount of space that I can claim for this task in this essay requires that I paint with broad strokes, but I will risk superficiality in hope of planting a provocative idea.

As I have reflected in recent years on the total sweep of medieval history, utilizing at least a respectable portion of the vast knowledge produced by scholars animated and guided by the parameters imposed by the genetic approach to the past but at the same time troubled by the nagging concerns already outlined, I have been increasingly forced to the conclusion that the key to understanding the place of the Middle Ages in the historical continuum lies in one's interpretation of the thirteenth century. I suggest that the genetic approach has misread the essential character of the crucial segment of medieval history, bounded on one extreme by such events as the accession of Innocent III, the blasting of the Hohenstaufen dreams with the death of Emperor Henry VI, the Magna Carta, the Fourth Crusade, the triumphs of Philip Augustus, and the advent of the universities and at the other extreme by the beginning of the Avignon papacy, the opening of the Hundred Years' War, the appearance of the *Divine Comedy* and of Marsiglio of Padua's *Defensor Pacis*, the onslaught of the Mongols and the Ottoman Turks, and the preaching of Meister Eckhart. An alternate interpretation of this era points toward a new, challenging, and potentially fruitful paradigm that will redefine the place of the Middle Ages in the total stream of history.

It would, of course, be rash to argue that there is total agreement among medievalists about the essential nature of the thirteenth century as a discrete segment of the entire medieval period. This much-discussed century has been treated from innumerable perspectives and with infinitely varied emphases, all of which create the impression that the period has a fluid, unfixed place, both in the medieval period proper and in the total continuum of Western history. I have become convinced that such, in fact, is not the case. Reading from a perspective generated out of my already confessed discontent–or newly discovered bias, if you prefer–I am persuaded that, despite all the surface variety, there is a strikingly uniform approach to the thirteenth century shared by almost all medievalists. More significantly, that uniformity has, I am convinced, been imposed on medievalists by the demands of the genetic paradigm that has reigned over the historical enterprise during the last century. Thus, the imperatives of that paradigm for the thirteenth century must be clearly understood.

The genetic approach to the Western European tradition, demanding as it did that the Middle Ages be united with subsequent Western European history into a single continuity, posed a special problem for all historians, including the medievalists. They had to find a meaningful point in a temporal continuum that could be defined as a starting point from which they could proceed toward and ultimately to the present. The medievalist had to supply his fellow historians with a reference point from which the evolution of modern Western civilization could proceed. He had, as it were, to stop the rolling film to supply a still shot that would give investigators of subsequent ages a meaningful springboard from which to proceed with the construction of the narrative that would elucidate present reality by showing how it came to be what it is.

The medievalists—all breeds of them—responded by delineating the thirteenth century in a fashion that fit those specifications. It emerged as the culminating era in medieval history, an age characterized chiefly by stabilization and synthesis. These years, argued the great majority of medievalists, witnessed in Western Europe a process of putting into ultimate medieval form and into proper juxtaposition vis-à-vis each other a set of institutions, ideas, and techniques that established the roots of a unique Western European civilization. Out of that pattern of civilization, stabilized and synthesized in the thirteenth century, evolved the modern Western European world.

The thirteenth century was preceded by a period of rapid, diffuse, unstructured growth extending from the tenth through the twelfth century. This remarkable expansion had its origins in feudalism; manorialism; the debased, secularized religious establishment of the feudalized world; and the meager intellectual heritage deposited by the Carolingian renaissance in tenth-century monasteries. Change was stoked by population growth, new modes of economic exploitation, rapid social transformations, widening intellectual horizons, expanding aesthetic capacities, heightened spiritual awareness, and increasingly sophisticated managerial skills. But like all renaissances, the so-called twelfth-century renaissance eventually lost its growth thrust. As its dynamism ran out, creative men in the succeeding age —the thirteenth century—consolidated its best features into an ordered world containing basic features crucial to Western Europe's future history. The great popes of the thirteenth century set together the pieces of the Roman Catholic church in all its administrative, fiscal, legal, liturgical, dogmatic, and penitential elements. The feudal monarchs articulated their prerogatives, structured their administrative apparatus, and defined their ways of dealing with the communities that constituted their realms. The merchants and artisans formalized their productive practices into a definable system and fastened their domination on their urban places of abode. At the same time, the aristocracy assumed its position as a distinct class. The widely divergent facets of learning were consolidated in the great *summas* of the scholastics and the codes of the jurists, and the processes of learning became institutionalized in the universities. Diverse streams of artistic talent crystallized in the universalizing Gothic style, while burgeoning literary forces found focus in the magnificent vernacular romances. Even the frontiers of Europe stabilized as Western adventurers were compelled to abandon their footholds in Byzantium and the Near East and to draw iron boundaries against Mongols and Ottoman Turks.[16]

Indeed, elsewhere, according to the reigning interpretation of the thirteenth century, the keynote was stabilization, the fixing of the prime ingredients of a distinct Western European pattern of civilization. Equally important, the major elements of Western European civilization moving toward stabilization reenforced one another in a synthesis that created a societal order possessed of its own organic cohesion.[17] From that fixed basis, an almost programmed ordering of things, one could proceed to the present by narrating what happened to any or all of the key elements of the medieval synthesis—such as its national states, its church, its economic system, and its intellectual and artistic establishment.

Although this oversimplified sketch certainly involves a considerable degree of caricature, I think it comes close to epitomizing the predominating conceptual approach to the thirteenth century. Does the evidence, even in all its impressive array, sustain the overarching thesis that the century witnessed a process of consolidation and synthesis which produced stable and distinctive institutional patterns capable of generating an evolutionary thrust toward a future that would never escape a recognizable kinship with its thirteenth-century roots? I find it increasingly difficult to believe so; perhaps I have even come to suspect that the evidence has been arranged to support the demands of the paradigm rather than to reflect the essential nature of the period.

The ultimate validity of my argument, of course, must rest in a convincing demonstration that the basic nature of thirteenth-century history is ill-described by descriptive formulations emphasizing consolidation and synthesis. Such proof would require an ordering of evidence that lies far beyond the scope of this essay; as a consequence, this paper must claim no more than a tentative and unsubstantiated formulation of a new approach to the century. But at this point, I must at least suggest how, in selected aspects of the period, my reading of the evidence points away from the prevailing interpretation toward a different characterization of the century.

In the political realm, I find no convincing evidence–except for the wisdom of hindsight–that signals the victory of the political particularism of the protonational states over the universalism of the Christian imperial idea, of centralized royal government over privileged private political rights and powers, or of rational political techniques and legislation over customary practices and precedents. Rather, I see a massive and serious effort to assure that all of these political modes, techniques, and ideas were incorporated into actual institutions. It is difficult to proclaim the death of political universalism grounded in Christian ideology in the face of the virulence of the Ghibelline tradition in the most diverse circles or of the guiding political concepts of the later Capetians or of the almost bizarre ambitions of a Henry III or Edward I of England. Rather, it seems to me that there is hardly a political system in thirteenth-century Europe that did not incorporate significant elements of universalist ideology into its program and aspirations in close admixture with amazingly parochial views of the nature of the political order. Likewise, I see as a vital part of thirteenth-century political history the validation and institutionalization of localized feudal, municipal, ecclesiastical, and even private privileges into the rapidly maturing royal or "national" constitutional systems. Accommodations of this order, putting together a baffling array of contradictory prerogatives, rights, and privileges into a single political system, seem to me much closer to the essence of the political processes occurring under Henry III and Edward I or Louis IX and Philip the Fair or Frederick II or Alfonso X of Castille than does any clear line of development spelling the doom of local special privilege before monarchically imposed uniformity. I find it difficult to recognize in thirteenth-century events the triumph of rational political techniques and legal principles in the face of such "mixed" creations as the Capetian administrative system or the English common law or the Castilian Siete Partidas or the Hohenstaufen imperial constitution viewed *in toto* or even the communal government of almost any Italian or Flemish city. The intertwining of all of these diverse strands of political theory and practice seems to point straight to my central thesis: the juxtaposing of political opposites into living political systems as the essence of thirteenth-century political history. This dominant thrust, I would argue, vitiates the accepted view stressing the joining of various political trends into a synthesis institutionalized in the form of the dynastic, protonational states claiming a monopoly on political sovereignty.[18]

The world of religion presents a similar picture. Against the thrust for universal order represented by the imperial popes ran powerful currents seeking freedom of religious expression; both found a place in the living texture of religious life. It would be hard to find a thirteenth-century pope unwilling to make some concessions toward freedom or a proponent of freedom unready to recognize some realm of papal authority. For all the effort of the age to define dogmatic conformity, heterodoxy persisted and made its presence felt in dogmatic theology and legal prescription. Despite the massive effort at centralized organization and monarchical ecclesiology, an effort enshrined in the great canonical collections of the century and in the organs of the papal governance system, massive elements of nonconformist localism in organization and administrative practice were imbedded in the legal definitions and the sanctioned practices that regulated the governance of the ecclesiastical establishment. These discordant elements were accepted into that very body of law and were recognized in practice by the papal monarchs and their agents who interpreted and applied that law. The luxuriant formalism in religious practice that was spelled out in such abundance during the century mingled in actual usage with powerful currents of puritanical simplicity; right religion contained much of each, as was so dramatically played out in the history of those most sterling of all thirteenth-century Christians, the Franciscans. In the face of these rather well-known features of thirteenth-century religious life, one wonders how the conventional picture of the Church as monolithic, holistic, uniform, synthesized structure was ever fabricated.[19] Perhaps we all need to reread G. G. Coulton's *Life in the Middle Ages.*

Nor is the situation any different in intellectual and artistic history – the ultimate proving ground for all views of thirteenth-century history as the segment of the medieval period which witnessed the maturation, synthesis, and consolidation of an organic structure of thought, expression, and style and provided the starting point for Western *Kulturgeschichte*. My long-nourished reliance on Thomas

Aquinas as the examplar of a creative synthesis of discordant philo-sophical-theological positions has worn increasingly thin, especially when I attempt to use the works of the great doctor as pieces of his-torical evidence reflecting the intellectual temper of an age rather than as fixed points of origin from which modern philosophical and theo-logical positions have derived. His *summas* are, in the final analysis, an extraordinary conflation of contradictory ideas and concepts of di-verse provenance held together by a dialectical filigree which is pa-tently fragile and convoluted. In fact, I sometimes feel that his ulti-mate achievement, as well as that of all his scholastic compatriots, really rests on his dexterity in the use of dialectic to create an illusion that irrevocably contradictory ideas could be amalgamated into a sys-tem rather than in his ability to adjust opposites into a compatible synthesis that linked those opposites into a higher order of meaning. Perhaps we ought to trust Roger Bacon, with all his glaring intellec-tual contradictions, as the ultimate spokesman for an age that tried to have it all ways.

I am likewise struck by the abundance of dichotomies embroidered into the curriculum of thirteenth-century medieval universities to cre-ate a sanctioned educational program that seems to have even less or-ganic unity than does the curriculum at a modern university. The strands of mystical theology, biblical authority, patristic dogmatics, Aristotelianism, Platonism, Islamic science, classical rhetoric, and folk wisdom interwoven into the curriculum at Paris to constitute the *studium generale*, as well as the struggles to assure the predominance or even survival of any of these contradictory elements, serve well to illustrate how far synthesis, organic unity, and consolidation were from the minds of popes, rectors, faculties, and students. Even to al-low Thomas Aquinas, Bonaventura, William of St. Amour, Alexander of Hales, and Siger of Brabant to serve on a single faculty strongly suggests that the overpowering intellectual thrust of the thirteenth century was toward something other than synthesis and holism– or, as one authority has put it, "toward the policing of study."[20]

Particularly instructive to me in evolving a new sense of the essence of thirteenth-century culture has been the work of literary historians. Their skilled and perceptive analyses of the major literary pieces of the century reveal an amazing diversity and complexity of forms, motifs, language patterns, and themes woven together into almost every literary work of note. Even a modest venture into the scholarship relating to *The Romance of the Rose*, Wolfram von Eschenbach's *Parzival*, Gottfried von Strassburg's *Tristan und Isolde*, or Dante's *Divine Comedy* will go far to convince one that the artistic thrust of the century was toward the conscious incorporation of counterbalancing styles and ideas into the major forms of literary expression rather than toward the search for artistic synthesis. In short, literary history provides convincing evidence that thirteenth-century men were far less of one mind than they were of a mixed mind trying to find a legitimate place in thought and expression for everything under the sun, no matter how incompatible the mix might be. Literary history epitomizes the century's ruling passion: never to discard or to discredit anything.

I could continue in this vein to build my case that the essence of thirteenth-century history was the encasement of contradictory elements into every institution and value and belief. I would suggest that the essence of economic history in the period does not center in the triumph of an incipient capitalistic system but rather in the incorporation into the techniques and the ideology of every economically productive agency in society of an incongruous mixture of elements derived from protocapitalistic practices and from paternalistic, communal, corporate entrepreneurial experiences growing out of Europe's long agrarian past.[21] I find thirteenth-century social history ill-described by any general characterization that signals the emergence of the bourgeoisie at the cutting edge of societal development. I am more impressed by the evidence that suggests a definition of society which in practice and theory insisted on clear distinctions among classes but which allowed an immense range of social mobility and an amazing absorption into the ethos of one class of roles and virtues ascribable to another. All of which again adds up to the sanctification in the social structure of a confusing array of contradictions.[22] Even in the matter of the relationships between Western Europe and the non-Western world, where in the genetic scheme of things a Western march to dominance should have been prefigured, I discern the acceptance of contradictions– the passionate reaffirmation of the crusading spirit illustrated by Louis IX of France tempered by the drawing of defensive lines against the Turks and the Mongols, the intermixing of militant confidence in the inevitable triumph of Christianity with the

guarded trust of Franciscan missionaires or of Raymond Lull in per-
suasion as an effective weapon against the infidel "non-Westerners,"
the conflicting perceptions of a typical thirteenth-century ethnocen-
trist like Matthew Paris and of Marco Polo (who himself mirrored the
contradictions of which I speak).

These illustrations of the essential processes and developments of
the thirteenth century seem interconnected by a common bond that
provides a key to thirteenth-century history on all planes– a common
theme that has forced me into a new formulation of the basic nature
of the era. The thirteenth century was marked by the freezing of fundamentally contradictory elements into the fabric of institutions, into the basic processes of human interactions, and into patterns of
thought and expression. The keynote of the period is not found in the
skilled efforts made by the creative elements in society to consolidate
and synthesize a consistent pattern of institutions and ideas, the components of which complemented each other to create a harmoniously
organic civilization capable of sustained evolution into the future.
Rather, a common phenomenon that pervades every dimension of
thirteenth-century history is the incessant juxtaposing of contradictory institutional and ideological elements into a single system as a
means of establishing order and assuring stability.

That this particular segment of the Middle Ages would be dominated by efforts to accommodate contradictions should not be particularly surprising when one considers the thirteenth century from the
perspective of the eight medieval centuries that preceded it rather
than from the perspective of the present backward. A powerful case
can be made that the essence of history of the early Middle Ages lies
in the imbedding into the experiences of the peoples of the West of a
confusing array of contradictory cultural traditions. Put in terms of
provenance, Graeco-Roman, Celtic, Gallic, Germanic, Slavic, Viking,
Byzantine, and Muslim cultural elements were thrown together in a
totally bewildering fashion. These diverse traditions impinged on various areas of Western Europe at different times and with varying in-
tensity to compound the confusion already implicit in their coming together. Put in another context, these intermingling cultural strains
were widely divergent levels of sophistication. Interestingly enough,
many of these confluent cultural streams were in varying states of

decadence when they encountered one another, a sociological factor in determining the confusing shape of the early Middle Ages that needs more attention than has been given to it.

To the original mixture of cultural streams emptying on the West must be added new elements created by the early medieval Western Europeans themselves in their tortured effort to provide some basis of order in a disoriented world. Such things as feudalism, manorialism, customary law, monasticism, and vernacular languages come immediately to mind. Another factor contributing to the inorganic quality of early medieval life in the West was the absence of any overarching, directive force powerful enough to relate one cultural stream to another or to shape all to a common mode. The West lacked the integrative force supplied by the Byzantine theocracy or the Muslim religion as means of coping with cultural diversity. Perhaps the Carolingian effort represented a search for such a force; if so, it was largely abortive. On the whole, then, however one looks at medieval history down through the twelfth century, he is struck by the rampant cultural plurality that went into Western Europe's formation. It should hardly be a surprise that that experience produced a variety of deeply rooted contradictions and dichotomies in the institutional and ideological framework of emerging medieval society. Nor would it be strange to expect that eventually there would develop a heightened awareness of these contradictions and dichotomies as men in the West increased their capability and their need to communicate and interact. Many aspects of eleventh- and twelfth-century history suggest the growing consciousness of the glaring ambiguities firmly implanted in Western European society.[23]

In my reading of medieval history, it was during the thirteenth century that the cultural plurality inherited from the prior centuries was successfully reckoned with in a way that set a unique course for the future of the Western world. At first glance, this statement may seem to be nothing more than a reaffirmation of a very traditional interpretation of the thirteenth century as an era of synthesis and consolation of previous achievements into a holistic pattern of civilization that marked at one and the same time the culmination of medieval development and the starting point for the triumphant trek toward the modern world. But this, I insist, is where we must make a critical distinction. The fundamental developments of the century were not creative processes leading toward an organic, holistic, harmonious synthesis. Rather, what happened in this era was the fixing of a set of widely generalized institutional and ideological patterns that accommodated on a massive scale basically contradictory elements. The genuinely constructive and creative efforts of the century were aimed at coping with inherited cultural plurality by legitimizing dichotomous and discordant patterns of life and thought into a total system that had a place for everything comprising the ambiguous heritage of many centuries of random, undirected development. The energies of the era were not directed toward the construction of a balanced, harmonious, monolithic civilization in an Innocentian or Aquinian mode. Rather, they were consumed in the incorporation–often forced and tortured incorporation–of everything that was a part of the times into civilizational structures that took their essential shape from the juxtaposition of contradictions and discordances.

If, indeed, I have provided a valid key to the thirteenth century, one that palpably departs from our "normal" view of what that century meant, then perhaps we are now in a position to formulate the central thesis of this paper. My position can be stated in two different but complementary ways.

The first relates to the fundamental configuration of medieval history: in its most mature form as realized in the thirteenth century, medieval Western European civilization was characterized by the incorporation into the total societal structure of fundamental dichotomies derived from a long struggle with cultural plurality. At maturation, the medieval political system, the social order, the economy, the religious system, thought, and expression all drew their basic configuration from an effort at coping with cultural plurality which sought resolution through the juxtaposition in the same system of contradictory components which bore little relationship to one another except that the medieval genius forced them into precariously constructed institutional and ideological containers. The medieval house was built of sticks and stones by craftsmen who could never decide which was superior and so used both to sustain each other; indeed, these builders so revered both sticks and stones that it never occurred to them to choose. The medieval mansion was a structure built like a Gothic cathedral by combining massive stones and empty space, although everyone knows that these are not compatible building materials–

everyone, that is, except the genius that combined them in precarious juxtaposition to create the cathedrals at Amiens or Rheims, structures which tell more about the essential character of the thirteenth century than does most other surviving evidence.

Having found the essential character of the medieval world symbolized in a thirteenth-century architectural form combining incompatible elements held together precariously by counterbalancing arches and buttresses, I am led to a second insight. If the thirteenth century as the culminating period in medieval history is indeed marked by the framing of a civilizational order that featured the juxtaposing of opposites into the total fabric of society, then a totally different relationship between the Middle Ages and subsequent Western European history suggests itself as a substitute for that directed by the long-reigning genetic approach. To put it more directly, a new paradigm concerning the place of the Middle Ages in the historical continuum emerges which resolves the troublesome anomalies surrounding the genetic paradigm and which invites a whole new approach to postmedieval history and its relationship to the Middle Ages.

The new paradigm provides a release from the conceptual limitations implicit in the genetic approach to Western European history. It allows the historian to cope with the entirety of the Middle Ages much more easily and effectively than does the genetic approach, which prevents the extending of his inquiries back beyond the tenth century. My paradigm legitimizes the experiences of the early Middle Ages— wherever one wishes to begin— as a period during which an amazingly rich but uncomfortable cultural plurality was imposed on Western Europe through processes that involved the intermingling of diverse "foreign" cultures and of superimposed indigenous institutions and ideas devised to bring order out of chaos.[24]

Beyond that, and even more challenging, the new paradigm provides a clue to the dynamism in the Western world: the driving force in that society derives from the tension of contradiction and opposition that was built into the very essence of Western institutions and ideas as they took shape in the thirteenth century after a troubled gestation. It has been the clash between revelation and reason, church and state, universalism and particularism, the sacred and the profane, individualism and communal responsibility, and innumerable other opposites that has repeatedly animated the Western world and stoked the vital energies of its participants since the High Middle Ages. From this perspective, the course of Western history is no longer the linear, one-dimensional evolution of what was in the Middle Ages to what is today, as the genetic approach would have it. Rather, Western European history has been an on-going struggle to find some definitive answer to the contradictions ingrained in the basic structure of society during the thirteenth century, a creatively challenging succession of confrontations in which the issue was making and validating an ultimate choice among contradictory alternatives already built into institutions, idea systems, and values as a consequence of the medieval experience.

And, finally, by providing some clue to development in Western society across several centuries other than simple movement toward the neutral ground of the present, the new paradigm offers me some intriguing possibilities concerning the nature of the present crisis in the Western world. Perhaps that world has lost its prime source of dynamism as a consequence of resolving the tensions of contradiction built into its fabric in the Middle Ages. It may be a society confused as to where to apply its creative energies now that it has opted for the predominance of one mode of acting or thinking already articulated in the Middle Ages over an opposite equally sanctioned in that seminal era. It is perhaps a culture that has tragically sacrificed its *élan vital* by definitively opting for such choices as reason over revelation, state over church, equality over hierarchy, and national and cultural ethnocentrism over universalism rather than continuing to tolerate the tensions caused by these and other dichotomies as co-existing parts of a civilizational order deriving from the medieval heritage.

But I have already exceeded the license allowed to a medievalist to meddle in postmedieval history; it remains for historians of modern Europe to judge whether the interpretation advanced in this paper concerning the place of the Middle Ages in a larger continuum has any utility in elucidating Western European development and in accounting for the unique features of Western European civilization. Besides, there are fresh tasks facing the medievalists if the new paradigm is worth considering. For that paradigm requires us to understand better the strange, dichotomous elements that found places in the cultural milieu of youthful and adolescent Western European society. It calls for a more careful scrutiny of mature medieval institutional and ideological patterns to clarify how contradictory were the elements that constituted each. It begs for a more precise elucidation of how truly Gothic the Middle Ages were, how much the ultimate forms of the medieval order involved a delicate balancing of things that should have collapsed but rather were sustained through the artful act of juxtaposing, of reenforcing one thing with its opposite, of combining discordant ingredients into a beautiful but fragile order. I take relish in this challenge as relief from reconstructing an increasingly illusionary medieval synthesis to serve as a point of departure leading to an increasingly inexplicable present through the working on an ineluctable evolutionary process that seems to explain badly or not at all the remarkable growth of the Western European world.

NOTES

A massive bibliography could be compiled to illustrate the many elements out of which the argument developed in this paper has been constructed; this is especially true with respect to those sections dealing with the historical events of the thirteenth century. No effort has been made to provide all the relevant references. Only a small selection of works particularly crucial in shaping my fundamental ideas is provided.

1. The basic ideas contained in this essay have served as the focal point for several graduate reading courses offered by me at Michigan State University. For some earlier reflections on the issue, see Richard E. Sullivan, "What Were the Middle Ages?" *Centennial Review* 2 (1958): 167–194.
2. Thomas S. Kuhn, *The Structure of Scientific Revolutions* (Chicago and London: University of Chicago Press, 1962).
3. Beryl Smalley, *Historians in the Middle Ages* (New York: Charles Scribner, 1974); Benoît Lacroix, *L'historien au Moyen Age* (Montreal: Institut d'Études Médiévales, 1971).
4. *Oeuvres complètes de Voltaire* (Paris, 1817), 4:510.
5. Useful in describing the intellectual traditions that shaped the "dark age" concept of the Middle Ages are Wallace K. Ferguson, *The*

Renaissance in Historical Thought: Five Centuries of Interpretation (Boston: Houghton Mifflin Co., 1948); Eduard Fueter, *Geschichte der neueren Historiographie*, 3rd ed. (Munich and Berlin: R. Oldenbourg, 1936); Peter Gay, *The Enlightenment: An Interpretation*, 2 vols. (New York: Alfred A. Knopf, 1966–69); and J. B. Black, *The Art of History: A Study of Four Great Historians of the Eighteenth Century* (New York: F. S. Crofts & Co., 1926).

6. Gottfried Salomon, *Das Mittelalter als Ideal in der Romantik* (Munich: Drei Masken Verlag, 1922); León Émery, *L'age romantique*, 2 vols. (Lyon: Les Cahiers Libres, 1957–58); Jacques Barzun, *Romanticism and the Modern Ego* (Boston: Little, Brown, and Co., 1924); and Georg G. Iggers, *The German Conception of History: The National Tradition of Historical Thought from Herder to the Present* (Middleton, Conn.: Wesleyan University Press, 1968).

7. Especially helpful on the emergence of scientific history are Fueter, *Geschichte der neueren Historiographie*; George P. Gooch, *History and Historians in the Nineteenth Century*, 2nd ed. rev. (London and New York: Longmans, Green, 1952); R. V. Sampson, *Progress in the Age of Reason: The Seventeenth Century to the Present Day* (Cambridge, Mass.: Harvard University Press, 1956); H. Stuart Hughes, *Consciousness and Society: The Reorientation of European Social Thought, 1890–1930* (New York: Alfred A. Knopf, 1958); Gertrude Himmelfarb, *Darwin and the Darwinian Revolution* (Garden City, N.Y.: Doubleday, 1962); and W. Stull Holt, "The Idea of Scientific History in America," *Journal of the History of Ideas* 1 (1940): 352–362.

8. Among the works particularly illustrative of this point are Charles Homer Haskins, *The Renaissance of the Twelfth Century* (Cambridge, Mass.: Harvard University Press, 1927); C. R. Beazley, *The Dawn of Modern Geography: A History of Exploration and Geographical Science*, 3 vols. (New York: Peter Smith, 1949); Robert L. Reynolds, *Europe Emerges: Transition Toward an Industrial World-Wide Society, 600–1750* (Madison: University of Wisconsin Press, 1961); Walter Prescott Webb, *The Great Frontier* (Boston: Houghton Mifflin Co.,

1952; new ed., Austin: University of Texas Press, 1964); Robert S. Lopez, *The Commercial Revolution of the Middle Ages, 950–1350* (Englewood Cliffs, N.J.: Prentice-Hall, 1971); Lewis Mumford, *Techniques and Civilization* (New York: Harcourt, Brace and Co., 1934); and Norman Cohn, *The Pursuit of the Millennium: Revolutionary Millennarians and Mystical Anarchists of the Middle Ages*, rev. ed. (New York: Oxford University Press, 1970). For a somewhat more emphatic statement, see Lynn White, Jr., "The Legacy of the Middle Ages in the American Wild West," *Speculum* 40 (1965): 191–202.

9. E. N. Johnson, "American Medievalists and Today," *Speculum* 28 (1953): 844–854.

10. For example, R. R. Palmer and Joel Colton, *A History of the Modern World*, 4th ed. (New York: Alfred A. Knopf, 1971), pp. 14–52.

11. The efforts of the medievalists who produced the *Monumenta Germaniae Historica* will forever epitomize thorough scholarship. All historians owe a debt for exciting new approaches to the past to the *Annales* school, which owed its genesis largely to a medievalist, Marc Bloch.

12. My thinking on this point has been influenced especially by Karl Popper, *The Poverty of Historicism* (Boston: Beacon Press, 1957); Carlo Antoni, *L'historicisme*, trans. Alain Dufour (Geneva: Librarie Droz, 1963); R. G. Collingwood, *The Idea of History* (Oxford: Clarendon Press, 1946); Karl Mannheim, *Ideology and Utopia: An Introduction to the Sociology of Knowledge*, trans. Louis Wirth and Edward Shils (New York: Harcourt Brace and Co., 1936); Raymond Aron, *Introduction to the Philosophy of History: An Essay on the Limits of Historical Objectivity*, trans. George J. Irwin (Boston: Beacon Press, 1961); and, above all, Arnold J. Toynbee, *A Study of History*, 12 vols. (London: Oxford University Press, 1934–61).

13. Examples of the search for origins of things modern in the tenth century are Joseph Calmette, *L'effondrement d'un empire et la naissance d'une Europe, IXe–Xe siècles* (Paris: Aubier, 1941); *L'Europe aux IXe–XIe siècles aux origines des états nationaux*, Actes du Colloque international sur les origines des États européens aux IXe–XIe siècles, tenus à Varsovie et Poznán du 7 au

13 septembre 1965, publiés sous la direction de Tadeusz Manteuffel et Alexander Gieysztor (Warsaw: Panstwowe Wydawn, Naukowe, 1968); Geoffrey Barraclough, *The Crucible of Europe: The Ninth and Tenth Centuries in European History* (Berkeley and Los Angeles: University of California Press, 1976); Eleanor Duckett, *Death and Life in the Tenth Century* (Ann Arbor: University of Michigan Press, 1967); and Robert S. Lopez, *The Tenth Century: How Dark the Dark Ages?* (New York: Rinehart, 1959).

14. Henri Pirenne, *Mohammed and Charlemagne*, trans. Bernard Miall (New York: W. W. Norton and Co., 1939). For a sampling of the criticism of the Pirenne thesis, see William C. Bark, *Origins of the Medieval World* (Stanford: Stanford University Press, 1958); and Alfred F. Havighurst, ed., *The Pirenne Thesis: Analysis, Criticism, and Revision* (Boston, D. C. Heath, 1958).

15. Richard E. Sullivan, "New Light on the Dark Ages," *Bucknell Review* 10 (1961): 28–45.

16. This mode of interpreting the thirteenth century is illustrated in simplest terms in the basic medieval history textbooks with their pivotal sections on the "High Middle Ages"; see, for example, Robert S. Lopez, *The Birth of Europe* (New York: M. Evans and Co., 1966); Robert S. Hoyt and Stanley Chodorow, *Europe in the Middle Ages*, 3rd ed. (New York: Harcourt Brace Jovanovich, 1976); and Brian Tierney and Sidney Painter, *Western Europe in the Middle Ages, 300–1475*, 2nd ed. (New York: Alfred A. Knopf, 1970). However, the period embracing the tenth through the thirteenth centuries is often given an integrated treatment as a self-contained period marking the culmination of medieval history; excellent examples are Jacques Le Goff, *La civilisation de l'Occident médiéval* (Paris: Arthaud, 1964); Karl Hampe, *Das Hochmittelalter: Geschichte des Abendlandes von 900 bis 1250*, 5th ed. (Cologne: Böhlau-Verlag, 1963); Louis Halphen, *L'essor de l'Europe (XIe–XIIIe siècles)*, 3rd ed. (Paris: Presses Universitaires de France, 1948); Joan Evans, ed., *The Flowering of the Middle Ages* (London: Thames and Hudson, 1966); and John W. Baldwin, *The Scholastic Culture of the Middle Ages, 1000–1300* (Lexington,

Mass.: D. C. Heath, 1971). For an interesting example of a less conventional treatment of the High Middle Ages centering in a topical approach which ends up focusing attention on the thirteenth century, see V. H. H. Green, *Medieval Civilization in Western Europe* (London: Edward Arnold, 1971). Two excellent recent studies have concentrated on the thirteenth century, but neither projects a strong interpretation of the era; see Léopold Genicot, *Le XIIIᵉ siècle européen* (Paris: Presses Universitaires de France: 1968); and John H. Mundy, *Europe in the High Middle Ages, 1150–1309* (London: Longman, 1973). The same cannot be said for another work centering on the thirteenth century; see Friedrich Heer, *The Medieval World: Europe, 1100–1350*, trans. Janet Sondheimer (Cleveland: World Publishing Co., 1962).

17. Classic statements on the organic character of thirteenth-century civilization are Henry Adams, *Mont-Saint-Michel and Chartres* (Boston and New York: Houghton Mifflin Co., 1913); and Erwin Panofsky, *Gothic Architecture and Scholasticism* (Latrobe, Pa.: Archabbey Press, 1951).

18. Both Genicot (*Le XIIIᵉ siécle européen*, pp. 139–193, 351–359) and Mundy (*Europe in the High Middle Ages, 1150–1309*, pp. 364–459) offer perceptive conclusions supporting this position, but without explicitly saying so.

19. R. W. Southern, *Western Society and the Church in the Middle Ages* (Harmondsworth, Engl.: Penguin Books, 1970), provides some extremely revealing suggestions challenging those interpretations of the medieval church that emphasize its monolithic character; this work has not been properly appreciated.

20. Halphen, *L'essor de l'Europe (XIᵉ–XIIIᵉ siècles)*, p. 329. It is difficult to find much support among intellectual historians of the Middle Ages for the thesis presented in this paper. One is tempted to think that intellectual historians are inclined by the nature of their métier to insist on celebrating synthesis and holism as the indices of a mature civilizational order. And it appears that other historians listen. Thus the potent influence exercised on medieval studies by Henry Adams, Henry Osborn Taylor, Jacob Burckhardt, Etienne Gilson, John Herman Randall, J. J. Walsh, Erwin Panofsky, Gustave Schnürer, and Chris-

topher Dawson, to mention only a select few "contemporary" historians of medieval intellectual development. Perhaps other "histories" can catalog a comparable tyranny of the intellectual historians, e.g., Perry Miller, Mao Tse-Tung, V. I. Lenin, Georg Hegel, Sigmund Freud, Friedrich Nietzsche, and Oswald Spengler.

21. See Genicot, *Le XIIIe siècle européen*, especially pp. 49–139, 335–350; Mundy, *Europe in the High Middle Ages, 1150–1309*, pp. 111–202; and Georges Duby, *Rural Economy and Country Life in the Medieval West*, trans. Cynthia Postan (Columbia: University of South Carolina Press, 1968).

22. Christopher Brooke, *The Structure of Medieval Society* (New York: McGraw-Hill Book Co., 1971); and Fredric L. Cheyette, ed., *Lordship and Community in Medieval Europe: Selected Readings* (New York: Holt, Rinehart, and Winston, 1968).

23. Some intriguing suggestions on this point can be found in Sidney R. Packard, *12th Century Europe: An Interpretive Essay* (Amherst: University of Massachusetts Press, 1973); R. W. Southern, *The Making of the Middle Ages* (London and New York: Hutchinson's University Library, 1953); and Colin Morris, *The Discovery of the Individual, 1050–1200* (London: SPCK, 1972).

24. Although innumerable medieval historians have given lip service to the idea that Western European civilization was an amalgam of diverse cultures (the conventional triad is Graeco-Roman, Judeo-Christian, and German), it seems amazing that an age so concerned with pluralism has seen no serious effort to treat the most obvious feature of early medieval history, that is, cultural plurality. Perhaps this is a consequence of the genetic paradigm.

Iter Sancti Sepulchri: The Piety of the First Crusaders

Bernard McGinn

THE FAILURE OF THE HOLY FIRE

On Easter Sunday, April 21, 1101, the city of Jerusalem was in turmoil. Morning had dawned, and the Holy Fire, the fire that for centuries had been miraculously sent down from heaven on Holy Saturday to enkindle the lamps in the tomb of the Lord, had still not appeared.[1]

On the previous day all the Christian sects in Jerusalem, swollen by bands of pilgrims, had gathered in the basilica built by Constantine to recite the customary prayers in expectation of the miracle. After antiphonal chanting by Latins and Greeks, at about three in the afternoon a Greek cleric led the congregation in chanting the Kyrie eleison in an ancient manner unfamiliar to the Westerners, the signal for the descent of the fire.[2] But a search within the Sepulchre revealed that nothing had happened. Prayer continued and Daimbert, the Latin Patriarch of Jerusalem, locked the doors of the tomb and prostrated himself in prayer for a long time. When he reopened the Sepulchre late in the day the Holy Fire had still not appeared. As one contemporary noted, "A sorrow lamentation and fear greater than any since the earliest days of the Christian religion seized all, so much so that some almost fell into despair . . . ."[3] Affected by this somber mood, the Patriarch sent everyone home and ordered the church closed for the night.

The Piety of the First Crusaders · 33

Two interpretations soon appeared in an attempt to explain the unheard-of event. The most popular explanation was that God was punishing his people for their sins. The accounts dependent on Fulcher of Chartres, chaplain to King Baldwin and one of the foremost historians of the early days of the crusading movement, and Ekkehard of Aura's *Hierosolymitana* stressed the degree to which the pilgrims' sinfulness had offended the Most High.[4] As the Pseudo-Fulcher claimed: "Although because of our sins we should have been hoping that something that had never happened in former years was about to take place, each of us still sought in his heart to amend for what he had done against God."[5]

A more optimistic party among the clergy offered another explanation. Perhaps the miracle, known to have existed for so long while Moslems dominated Jerusalem, no longer was needed now that the city had been restored to the Christians.[6] The Holy Fire, a sign of protection for the handful of faithful who in former years had been bold enough to be present for the Great Feast, had been succeeded by the protective presence of the Crusaders themselves.[7] One can imagine the sleepless households in Jerusalem that night as the Crusaders discussed the meaning of the portent.

The drama moved into its second phase early on Easter morning, when investigation of the Sepulchre still revealed no fire. The Patriarch Daimbert, in the presence of Cardinal Maurice of Porto, the recently arrived papal legate, attempted to allay the fears of the people by a public address. Later accounts claimed that he presented an extravagant confession of his sins and virtually surrendered the Patriarchate.[8] A more likely report found in the Genoese Caffaro indicated that he echoed the clerical argument that "God makes miracles for unbelievers, not for the faithful," while admitting that the miracle might be important for the sake of the weaker Christians in the congregation.[9] In any case, it is likely that it was Daimbert who reminded the crowd that Jerusalem was not a city of one miracle alone.[10] Texts in the Third Book of Kings promised an efficacious hearing to all who made devout petitions in the Temple of Solomon.[11] Christians identified this temple with the Dome of the Rock, that most splendid of Moslem monuments in the Holy City. It was then resolved to organize a penitential procession to Solomon's Temple to beg forgiveness for the sins that had impeded the appearance of the Holy Fire.

Easter Sunday morning was a rather unusual time for an act of public penance, but many of the city's inhabitants participated in the ritual. King Baldwin, who had received the crown of the precarious Kingdom of Jerusalem on the previous Christmas, marched barefoot to the temple in the company of his magnates, the clergy, and many of the people.[12] The procession was seen as a visible manifestation of the harmony of the kingdom. Pseudo-Fulcher and Guibert of Nogent both noted the reconciliation effected between bitterly opposed parties; even the Eastern Christians, who did not take part, continued to pray for the miracle.[13]

The united outpouring of penance achieved its aim. Immediately upon their return to the Church of the Holy Sepulchre the pilgrims were greeted by rumors that one of the lamps outside the tomb had been ignited. Only the official approbation of the Patriarch could confirm the miracle. Daimbert went into the tomb, bearing with him the keys that he had carried during the procession, probably to avoid any suspicion of fraud.[14] He saw the miraculous fire and immediately made his discovery known to the people. Pseudo-Fulcher reported: "When all of us who had gone forth tearfully crying out 'Kyrie eleison' saw this, we rejoiced with great joy. We then exulted in the miracle even more than we had been cast down in sorrow."[15] The Te Deum was intoned and all endeavored to have their candles lit from the Holy Fire. King Baldwin, wearing his crown, assisted at the Easter Mass. He then returned to the Temple of Solomon for a festive banquet.[16]

Later in the day came reports that God had been doubly pleased by the conversion of his people, and that a second outpouring of the Holy Fire had ignited a multitude of lamps in the great church. Like a new Pentecost, the sacred fire had been witnessed by all nations.[17] As the Russian pilgrim Abbot Daniel was to remark about a far less dramatic appearance of the same celestial miracle five years later, "He who has not taken part in the glory of that day will not believe the record of all that I have seen."[18]

This striking incident, which has been generally neglected by modern historians of the Crusaders, offers important insights into the piety of the first Crusaders.[19] King Baldwin, his chaplain Fulcher, and many of those present in Jerusalem on Easter 1101 were among the survivors of the epic that had begun at Clermont in November 1095, when Pope Urban II had proclaimed the Crusade. Less than two years before, many of them had been perishing of thirst before the hostile walls of Jerusalem. The incident of the Holy Fire serves as a prism that refracts key elements in the religious experience of those who had undergone this unusual rite of passage.

This sacral crisis can be best understood in the light of a complex of religious attitudes that had been achieved by the experience of the journey to Jerusalem. The *iter sancti Sepulchri*, the crusading pilgrimage to the Tomb of the Lord, forms the pattern for the reaction to the events at the tomb in 1101. A study of the elements of this reaction in turn illuminates the early accounts of the journey and allows us an insight into what one historian has aptly called the inner history of the Crusade.[20]

The Holy Fire was a miraculous sign of the unique character of the city of Jerusalem, an *inennarabile misterium*.[21] Like many early medieval miracles, it was a localized manifestation of divine power; unlike them, it possessed a universal significance from its association with Jerusalem, the center of the world, at the key moment of the liturgical year that reenacted the central even of the history of salvation. The miracle was an archetypal hierophany.[22] Its yearly repetition was a guarantee of the stability of the world or, to put it in Christian terms, a visible manifestation of divine providence. So potent was its appeal that, according to one account, Pope Urban himself used it at Clermont as a motive to fire the imagination of his listeners.[23] This is not very likely, but it does show the fame that the miracle acquired during the course of the twelfth century.[24]

No greater sacral disaster could be imagined than the failure of the Holy Fire. Fulcher noted that the new Kingdom of Jerusalem could ill afford any hesitation or doubt about its providential status. Hemmed in by enemies, isolated from Western Europe, the very existence of the kingdom seemed a miracle.[25] Nor could King Baldwin afford untoward omens. At the time of the conquest of the city in 1099, the clergy had unsuccessfully attempted to block the election of a king in order to establish a clerical theocracy under the Patriarch.[26] Godfrey of Bouillon, who was elected by the barons to head the state, had compromised by calling himself not king but "Advocate of the Holy Sepulchre." His younger brother Baldwin, summoned from Edessa at Godfrey's death in the summer of 1100, had no such hesitations. Despite the opposition of the ambitious and wily Patriarch Daimbert, he assumed the title of king and was anointed and crowned at Bethlehem on Christmas Day, 1100.[27] Both king and country required the confirmation of the miraculous fire.

The events surrounding the temporary failure of the Holy Fire may seem unimportant in light of the epic of the march to Jerusalem or the complex history of the building up of the crusader states in the Holy Land. But the reaction to the failure in 1101 deserves close study, for it can provide a key to early crusading piety. The steps taken to appease divine wrath in this case follow the pattern of a ritual that had been developed to deal with the crises experienced on the march to Jerusalem. While the elements in this ritual were not unique to the Crusaders, their fusion into a whole under the sign of Jerusalem and the association of this whole rite with the most miraculous moments of the *iter sancti Sepulchri* were the obvious reasons why they were called upon at this significant moment.

The basic elements of the ritual were three–*confessio, concordia,* and *processio.* When God's favor has been visibly withdrawn because of sin, man must first make a sincere confession, not the kind of perfunctory chanting of the Kyrie that had taken place on Easter Saturday. Profound recognition of individual sinfulness alone was sufficient basis for the petition of a devout heart that might appease God's anger.[28] Such petition, however, must be a communal and not merely an individual effort, the work of the whole Christian people united before God. But the crusading kingdom was seriously divided into rival factions. True penance made necessary a laying aside of all these differences in an attempt to achieve a visible concord that was the manifestation of what anthropologist Victor Turner has called *communitas,* a primitive egalitarian bond uniting society on a level different from but complementary to normal social structures.[29] Finally, *confessio* and *concordia* were to be made manifest in a penitential procession. With bared feet, chanting litanies of forgiveness, the whole Christian people were to recapitulate the pilgrimage to Jerusalem, to repeat in ritual form the great *iter* that in itself was a type of the pilgrimage of life.

The elements of *confessio, concordia,* and *processio,* clearly present in the events of Easter 1101, are basic to understanding the piety created by the First Crusade. To demonstrate this claim it will be necessary to look at the background of the crusading movement and to study the process of the First Crusade itself.

THE BACKGROUND TO THE CRUSADE

For over a generation it has been customary to speak of the Crusade as a fusion of holy war and pilgrimage to Jerusalem.[30] The fundamentals of this analysis still stand and provide an important starting point for our investigation. Both elements, however, must be viewed in the light of the activity of the Reform Papacy in order to grasp the full meaning of the origins of crusading piety.[31]

Christianity was not born militant, but from the time of the conversion of Constantine an explicit accommodation with warfare became evident. Roman law provided a background for theories of just war; a literal interpretation of some Old Testament themes could justify seeing the wars of the new people of God as divinely ordained. These two traditions, while theoretically distinguishable, were historically intermingled throughout the medieval period.[32]

After the collapse of the Carolingian empire, the heir to the claims of Rome, a new relationship between Christianity and warfare appeared in Western Europe. Without a powerful central ruler, warfare devolved into the hands of the *potentiores*, the armed nobility. The existence of a Christian emperor had been an a priori condition in earlier just-war traditions. What argument could legitimize warfare in a society where violence was endemic, no central authority existed, and force was exercised purely for selfish ends by a professional class of semibrigands? The Church's answer to this situation is best described under the rubric of the baptism of the knight.

In the early tenth century Odo, the reforming abbot of Cluny, had written an account of the life of a late-ninth-century lord, Gerald of Aurillac, trying to show that it was possible to conduct warfare from proper motives.[33] During the tenth and eleventh centuries, liturgical innovations, such as the growth of the cult of warrior saints, the use of blessed banners, and special consecrations of weapons, were signs of the attempt to sacralize the violence and gradually channel it in more acceptable directions. Starting in 989 local church councils sought to limit warfare. They used the "Peace of God" in an attempt to protect certain persons and property from violence and the "Truce of God" to prescribe the times when recourse to arms was allowed.[34] The Church had also begun to suggest to the military aristocracy that battle against the enemies of Christ was not only an exercise of war free from sin, but also one that could even be considered a special form of piety. While there are a few precedents for this idea in earlier periods, it appears that only in the eleventh century did this attitude become widespread.[35]

The second major theme in the background of the Crusade was pilgrimage, especially pilgrimage viewed in the light of the penitential system of the early middle ages.[36] In 335 the Emperor Constantine dedicated the great basilica built over the Sepulchre of the Lord to house the True Cross discovered by his mother. From the early fourth century on we have accounts of journeys to Jerusalem from as far away as Gaul and Spain. The religious motivation of these ancient pilgrimages was summed up by Paulinus of Nola, who wrote: "No other sentiment draws men to Jerusalem than the desire to see and touch the places where Christ was physically present, and to be able to say from our very own experience, 'We have gone into his tabernacle and adored in the very places where his feet have stood' (Ps. 131:7)."[37] The growth of the cult of the saints and devotion to their relics led to a proliferation of pilgrimage sites, such as those in Rome, the shrines of St. Martin at Tours and of Michael the Archangel at Monte Gargano, and many others.

The barbarian invasions and the collapse of the Empire in the West affected the practice of pilgrimage. In the late sixth century missionary monks from Ireland began the introduction of new methods of private penance based upon tariffs for classes of sins set out in handbooks of penance.[38] Pilgrimage was a penance enjoined by these handbooks for the most severe sins, especially in the case of the clerics, who by reason of their state were not subject to the ancient public penitential system of the Church. Although these penitential pilgrimages were first conceived of as a form of wandering exile, from the ninth century definite goals were prescribed, Rome and Jerusalem being the earliest mentioned.[39] Obviously, the two forms of pilgrimage, the religious and the penitential, did not exist in isolation from each other. Religious pilgrimages specified the goals for the penitential exercise, and the notion of penance for sins, either voluntarily undertaken or enjoined in sacramental confession, colored the great growth of pilgrimage in the following centuries.

The same centuries that saw the most fervent attempts to Christianize the activities of the military aristocracy also saw the flowering of pilgrimage to Jerusalem. Powerful rulers whose hands were deeply stained with blood did penance for their sins by taking the road to the East. Duke Robert of Normandy, who had murdered his brother, traveled to Jerusalem in 1035. Fulk Nerra, Count of Anjou, made at least three journeys to the Holy City. Not only important individuals, but also large groups of pilgrims set forth. Among the collective expeditions of the century, two deserve special mention. The Cluniac historian Raoul Glaber notes the movement of masses of people to Jerusalem in 1033 and records the apocalyptic interpretation given this outpouring by some contemporaries.[40] In the year 1064 at least seven thousand Germans set off for the Holy City under the leadership of a group of noble bishops.[41] A later *Life* of Bishop Altmann of Passau, who accompanied this expedition, notes apocalyptic overtones to the journey.[42] This intense enthusiasm for pilgrimages to the Holy City at a time when important political changes, especially the increased power of the warlike and militant Turks, had made access to Jerusalem more difficult suggests that the image of Jerusalem was especially important in eleventh-century piety.

It is impossible to recapture the full range of meaning that the name *Jerusalem* would have evoked in the eleventh or twelfth century. Our sources provide us with considerable information about the speculations of learned clerks; we are on more treacherous ground when we attempt to guess how far these interpretations were understood among the wider population. The meaning of Jerusalem was so closely tied to the Scriptures that a society which no longer uses holy writ as its essential textbook and daily spiritual bread is at an obvious disadvantage in trying to grasp the significance of the Holy City.

Biblical interpretation may, at least, provide us with a starting point.[43] St. Jerome, following the lead of Eusebius, gave the etymological meaning of Jerusalem as *visio pacis*, the vision of peace.[44] In the early fifth century, John Cassian, commenting on the passage in Galatians where Paul proferred the allegorical meaning of Jerusalem, laid down the classic division of ways in which the city was to be understood: ". . . according to history it is the city of the Jews; according to allegory, the Church of Christ; according to anagogy, that heavenly city of God which is the mother of us all; according to tropology, it is the soul of man."[45] Each of these meanings contributed to the associations surrounding Jerusalem that would have been available to an eleventh-century pilgrim or crusader.

We must note that the meanings of Jerusalem in the biblical text involved complex understandings. The Holy City of the Jews of the Old Testament was the center of God's providential care for his people. Its axial position in sacred history and cosmology, signified in the history of David, Solomon, and the Temple, reached fulfillment in the Life and Death of Christ. Since the key events of sacred time had taken place in Jerusalem, symmetry demanded that the same city must also be the cosmological center of the universe.[46] In this city one could engage in a physical *imitatio Christi* that was possible in no other place on earth. This sense of physical contact was heightened by Jerusalem's possession of the most famous of all relics, the True Cross. The cross not only had reference to the Passion and Death of Jesus, but also was a potent symbol of the transformation of death into life.

Allegorically, Jerusalem signified the Church. While this did indeed imply a spiritualization of the meaning of Jerusalem, this was not one of the cases where a spiritual meaning was necessary because no legitimate literal meaning existed. Rather, the relation between the letter and the spirit suggested that there was an intimate bond between the dogmatic Jerusalem, the central institutional object of faith, and the historical Jerusalem, the city of Palestine. Was not the literal, historical Jerusalem a part of the inheritance of the Church? Was the Church truly the Church without the possession of the earthly Holy City?

Both the literal and the allegorical meanings of Jerusalem were completed in the anagogical significance, Jerusalem as the *visio pacis*, the heavenly city whose prime characteristics were true freedom (Gal. 4) and perfect peace (Rev. 20–22). The intimate connection between the heavenly and the earthly Jerusalem affected medieval thought in many ways.[47] As H. de Lubac has pointed out, the anagogical sense could be used in two quite different ways in classic medieval exegesis– what might be termed horizontal anagogy connected with the last things conceived in some historical manner and the vertical anagogy that sought to achieve present realization of heaven on earth.[48] It was in the latter sense that the monastic cloister was described as Jerusalem, and this helps explain the hesitations that some monastic thinkers had about monks setting off for the physical Jerusalem.[49] Horizontal anagogy was never absent from the complex of notions evoked by Jerusalem. Its presence as apocalypticism in the mass pilgrimages of the eleventh century has already been noted; its significance for the earliest Crusaders will be discussed below.

The tropological sense is directly ordered to personal appropriation of the meaning of Jerusalem in the life of the believer. If the journey to the historical Jerusalem and worship at its holy places involved a physical *imitatio Christi*, the developing pilgrimage piety made it clear that external imitation was incomplete without internal imitation, the establishment of peace and freedom within the soul. While the full flowering of pilgrimage-crusade as personal reformation was not to be complete until the mid-twelfth century, its seeds were sown by Urban in his appeal of 1095.[50]

The Reform Papacy drew the diverse elements together.[51] The Crusade as a synthetic new form of lay piety cannot be understood apart from the activities of the popes from Leo IX (1049–1054) to Urban II (1088–1099). The reaction to the preaching of Urban at Clermont may have gone beyond his original intentions, and the march to Jerusalem did produce a distinctive religious experience and the rituals proper to it, but it was the pope who made the Crusade.

Both Leo IX and Alexander II (1061–1073) made extensive use of the ideology of holy war, but it was Gregory VII (1073–1085) who did the most to lay the foundations of the Crusades. Gregory went further than his predecessors in forging the alliance between the papacy and the warlike aristocracy of Europe. In his struggles against the German Emperor Henry IV, the pope turned to the faithful knights of Europe and sought to enlist them under the banner of papal primacy as the *militia sancti Petri*.[52] In Gregory's letters *militia* is less a warfare against vices in the context of monastic spirituality and more the wielding of the material sword against the enemies of the papacy. Even more, the pope extended the promise of absolution for sins to those who engaged in this holy work, a new type of commutation of penance that was roundly condemned by his opponents.[53] Wenrich of Trier wrote to him: "They declare that . . . you incite to bloodshed secular men seeking pardon for their sins; . . . that the property of St. Peter must be defended by force; and that to whomsoever dies in this defense you promise freedom from all his sins."[54] The Gregorian propagandists who sprang to the defense of this practice about 1085 were the first theorists of the crusade ideal.[55]

The disastrous defeat of the Byzantines by the Turks at Manzikert in 1071 had prompted the Eastern emperors to turn to the papacy for aid, thus offering an opportunity to undo the unfortunate split between Rome and Constantinople of 1054.[56] Gregory was doubtless anxious not only to defend Christianity against the heathen but also to vindicate the claims of the papacy over the Eastern churches. He even came to envisage Jerusalem as the goal of such an expedition, for in a letter of 1074 he wrote to his future foe, Henry IV, "This summons [to the East] has been readily accepted by the Italians and the northerners by divine inspiration as I believe–nay as I can absolutely assure you–and already fifty thousand men are preparing, if they can have me as their leader and prelate, to take up arms against the enemies of God and push forward to the Sepulchre of the Lord under his supreme leadership."[57] Thus it appears that most of the major components of the Crusade were already present in the mind of Gregory VII. But historical circumstances dictated that Urban II would initiate the Crusade.

THE RITE OF PASSAGE

We are now in a position to analyze the inner meaning of that great rite of passage, the First Crusade.[58] This meaning was not formed overnight.[59] As E. O. Blake puts it: "The picture of the 'crusade' as a coherent phenomenon, with the capture of Jerusalem as its centrepiece, seems to have emerged only after a much slower and gradual process of gathering and interpreting impressions. These are reflected in the letters and first-hand accounts of some of the participants themselves."[60] These limited and imperfect sources show a pattern of interpretation gradually emerging from the collective experience of the Crusade.[61] This attempt to understand the pattern will start with an investigation of the intentions of Pope Urban, survey the reaction produced by the summons, and concentrate on the meaning given to the march to Jerusalem by those who actually took part in it.

We possess five versions of the speech that Urban gave at Clermont on November 27, 1095.[62] None was written down until after the capture of Jerusalem. Nevertheless, three letters of the pope and other contemporary materials allow for some penetration into Urban's intentions.[63]

Despite the opposition of two German scholars, C. Erdmann and H. E. Mayer, it is difficult to believe that Urban did not give central attention to the liberation of Jerusalem.[64] Not only does the precedent of Gregory VII argue this, but also Urban's letters all give Jerusalem prominent mention.[65] Furthermore, the contemporary notices in chronicles and charters and the second canon of the Council of Clermont also feature the Holy City as the announced goal.[66] Urban, not the popular preachers of 1096, was responsible for proclaiming Jerusalem as the object of the new holy war, however much later events may have added elements that were not present in his original plans.

Jerusalem, as we have seen, immediately brought to mind both peace and freedom. The Council gave the first papal approbation to the peace movements that had been carried on for over a century largely under local auspices. The first canon of Clermont, which endorsed the "Truce of God," suggested that the knights of Europe were to abandon their sinful combat in favor of righteous warfare against the enemies of God.[67] The establishment of peace at home through the redirection of martial instincts toward a legitimate goal was a prominent motif in the pope's proclamation of the Crusade.[68]

Jerusalem, the "vision of peace," was also "she who is above, the free Jerusalem that is our mother" (Gal. 4:26). Under the aegis of freedom another important complex of themes becomes evident. Given the history of Byzantine appeals to the papacy since 1071, and all the evidence relating to Urban's speech, there can be no doubt that the pope intended the liberation of Eastern Christendom to be fundamental to his expedition.[69] Freedom for persecuted Eastern Christians and freedom of the Holy City suffering under the Moslem yoke were indissolubly linked, but the full implications of Jerusalem as the mother of freedom were not exhausted by these external hopes. As the letter of Scripture finds its true fulfillment in the spirit, so the literal freeing of the Holy Sepulchre was the means of spiritual liberation of Christian knights from the burden of sin. The pilgrimage motif and Urban's singular innovation, the crusading indulgence, were the key to the remarkable response that met the pope's summons.

As I. S. Robinson noted, the remission of sins was "the cardinal spiritual need of Christian society in the eleventh century."[70] In this disorganized and violent era even the most pious of knights found it difficult to avoid sins that weighed heavily on his soul. The case of King Baldwin of Jerusalem shows that self-interest and brutality could co-exist with excessive, and as far as it is given us to judge, sincere repentence.[71] It was an age of moral and emotional extremes, frequently combined in the same person. To meet this religious need the second canon of Clermont declared, "If anyone through devotion alone, and not for the sake of honor or gain, goes to Jerusalem to free the church of God, the journey itself shall take the place of all penance."[72]

This canon has frequently been seen as the first example of a plenary indulgence, or a full remission of the temporal punishment due to sin. H. E. Mayer has argued that the pope really intended only a full remission of the canonical penances prescribed for sins already forgiven, and that the notion of *remissio peccatorum*, understood as a remission of all temporal punishment both now and in the hereafter, was the result of the popular preaching of the Crusade.[73] Nevertheless, a month after Clermont, Urban wrote to the people of Flanders: "we visited areas of France and in great part incited the princes and subjects of that land to free the Eastern Churches. In the Council held in the Auvergne we frequently enjoined on them an expedition of this sort for the remission of all their sins."[74]

Although it is difficult to estimate how far Urban intended this formula to be understood, again it was the pope and not the popular preachers who introduced "remission of sins" as the great reward of the Crusade. His stroke of genius combined both the "new form of absolution" present in the letters of Gregory VII, that is, holy war waged under papal banner, with the most potent instrument of penance known to the age, pilgrimage to Jerusalem. Furthermore, Urban's canon implied not only sincere repentence for sins on the part of all who undertook the expedition (the *remissio peccatorum* was never a substitute for sacramental confession), but also adherence to the moral conduct expected of a pilgrim.[75] When the Crusaders failed to demonstrate this pilgrim morality in their conduct, they were abandoning their pledge and they knew it.

Since undertaking a pilgrimage commonly involved taking a vow to complete the journey, Urban recognized that this would provide an important element of cohesion for his expedition.[76] The power of the vow to worship in Jerusalem was certainly increasingly evident in the experience of the journey.[77] Pilgrims enjoyed important privileges in eleventh-century society, and while the list of advantages was not as lengthy as it was to become during the later development of the Crusade as an institution, the special status of the pilgrim provided the foundation for the crusader privileges.[78] Finally, it is certain that Urban envisaged that the march should be conducted under ecclesiastical leadership: his appointment of Adhémar of Le Puy, an experienced and when necessary warlike bishop, as *dux* of the expedition shows that.[79] It is less clear what plans the pope had for the Crusade after it had liberated Jerusalem and freed the Eastern Christians, although it is quite possible that he looked forward to the establishment of some form of theocratic state according to Gregorian principles.[80]

The reaction to Pope Urban's summons has provided a puzzle to historians of the Crusade. What one makes of the famous Peoples' Crusade is only the most obvious element. Did the pope preach one message, a holy war of Western knights to help Eastern Christians, and popular religious enthusiasm fanned by wandering preachers respond with another, an apocalyptic mass pilgrimage to Jerusalem? P. Alphandéry took the apocalyptic theme as the central theme of the inner history of the Crusade.[81] More recently, H. E. Mayer has seen the crusading movement almost immediately slipping out of the hands of the pope due to the emphasis on Jerusalem and the *remissio peccatorum* understood as plenary indulgence first advanced by the popular preachers.[82] But a radical split between Urban's intentions and the intentions of the popular preachers, mirrored in two separate crusades, seems an exaggeration of a complex process.[83] Our sources for the Peoples' Crusade, as well as for the "popular" elements in formal Crusade, are limited.[84] Only a naïve confidence in some of their most questionable elements can support the thesis of a radical break.

Urban had invoked the image of Jerusalem at Clermont; he had proclaimed a special form of absolution. These were the basic elements that initiated the *iter sancti Sepulchri*. The force of the reaction undoubtedly surprised the pope; his creation was far more powerful than he had anticipated.[85] Part of this reaction was due to the activity of the wandering preachers, such as the well-known Peter the Hermit, who preached the Crusade far and wide, usually without papal approbation. The *Wanderprediger* was a distinct religious type in eleventh- and twelfth-century Western Europe. Eremetical figures without ties to the formal religious establishment, they exerted power that centered on the notion of repentence shown in their own manner of life and in the message they preached. There is no evidence for special interest in Jerusalem among the *Wanderprediger* before the Council of Clermont; but once the pilgrimage to Jerusalem had been given special papal approbation, it is understandable how this unique new form of penance would have fit right in with their usual activities.[86]

Elements of the apocalyptic and messianic implications of the image of Jerusalem were probably present in their preaching and doubtless exercised some influence on the outpouring of enthusiasm in the year following the announcement at Clermont; but direct evidence regarding the content of the preaching during this period is lacking, and apocalyptic elements seem to have been at best a partial element.[87] The late eleventh century was not a time of widespread fear of the end of the world, and the association of Jerusalem with the final events of history was so closely involved with the imperial apocalyptic figure of the Last Emperor that it is difficult to conceive of a strong apocalyptic motif in a papal project, especially at a time when the pope and the emperor were at loggerheads.[88] Guibert of Nogent, writing a decade after the conquest of Jerusalem, introduced an apocalyptic element into Urban's speech, as well as his own apocalyptic interpretation of the fall of Jerusalem; but he revealed more about how events could be understood than about what had inspired them.[89] Ekkehard of Aura and Guibert both spoke of the portents accompanying the outset of the march; and Ekkehard and Albert of Aix related the amusing story of the Germans who decided to follow a goose to Jerusalem.[90] Thus the preaching of the Crusade tapped a rich well of enthusiasm containing, among other elements, both apocalypticism and superstition; but our information by no means suggests that messianic apocalypticism was the main religious motivation of the Crusaders.[91]

Among the most disturbing passions aroused by this preaching was the savage antisemitism of the disorganized bands of the Peoples' Crusade. It is important to note that the main crusading armies did not engage in systematic pogroms, though they were not above some crude extortion. Despite the massacre of Jews along with Moslems that followed the fall of Jerusalem, there is little in the sources to indicate that hatred of the Jews was a distinctive factor during the march to Jerusalem, though it cannot be denied that the crusading movement in general marks a sad new stage in the history of the relations of Judaism and Christianity.

A study of the actual experience of the Crusade confirms a basic continuity with papal intentions, despite the growth of distinctive cores of meaning and rituals that could not have been foreseen. The story of the march to Jerusalem has been told often and well.[92] Thus, it is not necessary to summarize the events, but we must analyze the pattern of religious meaning that the accounts of this collective experience convey to us.

As A. Dupront has shown, one way to approach the piety of the Crusade is through an analysis of the terms used to describe the expedition and its participants.[93] In contemporary letters neglected by Dupront, the formulae used to describe the Crusade are not as clearly defined as they become in the later narrative accounts, but there is no essential difference: the experience of the journey was already perceived in terms of the same key notions.[94] According to the letters, crusader piety centered on the image of Jerusalem. As the home of Christ, the site of the Sepulchre of the Lord, it offered fellowship with the heavenly Jerusalem.[95] In a letter written after the fall of Antioch, the leaders of the Crusade begged the Holy Father to come to help them complete the journey to Jerusalem.[96] Aid to the Eastern Church, on the other hand, plays only a minor role, and the beginning of an attitude hostile to the Eastern Christians becomes evident.[97]

Pilgrim piety is the most pervasive theme in the letters. The basic sacramental practices of any pilgrim appear; more noteworthy are the special accents of the Crusade.[98] The imitation of Christ that was required of the Crusader is seen as an imitation of his Passion in a concrete way in which death in battle is equated with martyrdom.[99] The Crusader is meant to be a penitent; but should he err and fall away from the state of true penance by committing further sin, he felt that God would not totally abandon him.[100] After the sinner confessed his fault, through vision and miracle God will show that he still fights on the side of his chosen army and guarantees its eventual success.[101] A visible manifestation of divine providence shows God's people that their warlike piety is acceptable to him.[102]

The picture broadly sketched in the letters was filled in by the authors of the three eyewitness narrative accounts. They are important because the presence of a similar pattern in these three indicates that it was the product of those who underwent the rite of passage and not just an interpretation foisted on it by subsequent reflection in peaceful European monasteries.[103]

The final and greatest miracle, the capture of the city of Jerusalem, assured the triumph of the teleological interpretation, the Crusade as the *iter sancti Sepulchri*.[104] Victory gave the elements of the struggle a definite shape. The terms used to describe the crusading host in the narratives are useful indicators of the fixation. The Crusaders are certainly spoken of as "soldiers of Christ," but they are increasingly also "pilgrims" (*peregrini*) or "those bound for Jerusalem" (*Hierosolymitani*).[105] In the telling phrase of the anonymous chronicler, they are the *Christi milites peregrini*, the "pilgrim knights of Christ"; in the words of Fulcher, *peregrini nostri*, "our pilgrims"; or, as Raymond of Aguilers put it, the *peregrina ecclesia Francorum*, "pilgrim church of the Franks."[106]

The *iter sancti Sepulchri*, the warlike pilgrimage to the Holy Sepulchre, demanded a morality specially suited to this most unusual of pilgrimages. Here again, reflection upon the events served to provide a more or less fixed interpretation. The asceticism unique to the Crusade was the asceticism of physical combat.[107] The general imitation of Christ implied in taking up one's cross, which had always played a part in pilgrimage to Jerusalem, was undoubtedly present at the time of the preaching of the Crusade.[108] But the warlike knight's imitation went a step further by offering his life in physical combat for the cause of the Lord. Those who died in battle were seen as martyrs.[109] They were cross-bearers, not just in the customary internal sense, but in a miraculous external way. The outward sign of their imitation of Christ was not just in the uniforms they wore as a sign of their commitment, but in the crosses supposedly found imprinted on the bodies of dead Crusaders.[110]

The course of the Crusade made it evident that engaging in combat with the enemies of Christ was not enough. Urban's intentions in invoking the internal transformation intended by pilgrim status continued as a potent force during the journey to Jerusalem. Neither the crusading leaders, the individuals about whom we have the fullest information, nor their followers were turned into saints by their assumption of the cross. Their pride, vanity, cruelty, and duplicity were revealed during the march. The rank-and-file was certainly no better. Like any large army on the move, it could scarcely be described as a training ground in sexual morality; avarice, lack of concern for religious duties, and other vices were also rife.[111] The *iter sancti Sepulchri* demanded authentic pilgrim piety on the part of the Crusaders; the army obviously failed to live up to these expectations. How then could the Crusade hope to achieve the goal that God had ordained for it? In finding an answer to this paradox the distinctive religious rituals of the Crusade were forged.

Again, we must remember that most of our accounts were written down after the Crusade ended. After the miraculous conquest of Jerusalem, events acquired a sense of purpose and articulation not available previously. Despite the disunity of Islam and the other factors that have been pointed out as facilitating the conquest, the remarkable conclusion of the expedition seems almost miraculous. No later Crusade achieved anything comparable. No greater confirmation of the providential status of the *iter* could have been demanded.[112] In the light of this crowning miracle the manner in which the Crusaders regained God's favor after their moral lapses was now understood as the central ritual of crusading piety.

The main lines of this ritual encapsulation of the meaning of the Crusade can be briefly portrayed, and with this sketch we will have come full circle, because the cycle of sin–repentence–providential confirmation that is discerned here is the same as that which served as the basis for the reaction to the failure of the Holy Fire in 1101. According to Raymond of Aguilers, from the beginning God had predestined the army to avenge the insults offered his name by the infidel.[113] Later authorities, such as Guibert and Ekkehard, provide the same interpretation by their accounts of the portents that accompanied the outset of the march.[114] The Crusaders experienced their first military confirmation of God's providential care in the difficult victory won at Dorylaeum of July 1, 1097. According to Fulcher, the initial onslaught of the Turks was so ferocious that the army seemed about to perish. The pilgrims then realized that this trial was a result of their sins. "Then we confessed that we were culprits and sinners, humbly begging mercy from God. . . . Many, fearing immediate death, ran to the priests and confessed their sins."[115] Pleased with this conversion of heart, God gave his army victory in miraculous fashion. Raymond noted that some participants saw two invulnerable heavenly warriors fighting on the side of the Crusaders.[116]

It was the crisis at Antioch between October 1097 and July 1098 that transformed this pattern into a definite ritual.[117] Pinned down for months outside the formidable walls of the city, reduced to misery by famine, disease, and the determined resistance of the Turkish garrison, and in despair over the approach of rumored relieving forces, the Crusaders seemed doomed. After an earthquake and other signs at the beginning of 1098, the papal legate Adhémar organized a public penitential service consisting of prayer, almsgiving, and processions.[118] This is the earliest example of the type of ritual that we have seen in its fully developed form at Easter of 1101. Adhémar's innovation seemed partially successful; God had not totally abandoned his people. Providential victories were won in skirmishes, and on June 3 the city was betrayed into the hands of the Christians by an Armenian official of the Turkish government.

But an even more serious crisis became evident: a few days later Kerbogha of Mosul and his large force arrived and the exhausted Crusaders were now caught between this fresh army and the strong garrison of Turks still holding out in the citadel of the city. The religious fervor of the Crusade now came to the rescue. A series of visions was announced proclaiming messages of repentence to the army. On June 10 a poor Provençal named Peter Bartholomew told Count Raymond of Toulouse and Bishop Adhémar that St. Andrew and a mysterious companion had appeared to him four times since the previous December revealing the secret burial place within Antioch of the Holy Lance that had pierced the side of the Lord.[119] The bishop was skeptical; but on June 14 the Lance was uncovered, and even critics had to note the encouragement that this talisman of the Passion gave to the crusading army that was now doubly conscious of its identification with the suffering Christ.[120]

At the same time, a priest named Stephen received a vision of Christ no less significant, especially for its stress on the Passion. After preparation by penance and confession of faith, Stephen recognized his divine visitor by the dazzling cross that appeared above his head. Christ announced himself as "mighty and powerful in battle" and, through the priest, commanded Adhémar to proclaim a general call to repentence.[121]

As a result of these visions and the discovery of the Holy Lance, the princes swore a new oath of loyalty to the Crusade, and a carefully orchestrated public rite of repentence was conducted.[122] Three days were spent in fasting, almsgiving, and processions. Then the Crusaders confessed their sins, received absolution, and partook of communion.[123] On June 28, against what seemed like overwhelming odds, the army advanced in the manner of a liturgical procession under the banner of the Holy Lance.[124] Aided by a refreshing miraculous shower, and another appearance of celestial warriors to help them, the Crusaders won an astounding victory, annihilating Kerbogha's superior force.[125] It was perhaps the most remarkable triumph of the "pilgrim Church of God."

As a result of the annealing experience undergone at Antioch, the host began to associate itself more and more with Old Testament examples of holy war waged under divine protection.[126] The pattern of recognition of sinfulness, penitential ritual, and miraculous intervention evident at Antioch was frequently repeated in the remaining year of the journey to Jerusalem. The pilgrims continued to be spurred on their way and reminded of their obligations by visions and miraculous events. In the fervid atmosphere of the final stages of this most arduous of pilgrimages, direct divine intervention was taken for granted in a manner unparalleled in any later expedition. To borrow a phrase from the anthropologists, it was the most "liminal" phase of the Crusade, the time when, freed from their normal social roles and obligations, the pilgrims experienced a more direct access to God.

Despite the limitations of our sources for this final period of the *iter*, the important moments stand out. The hesitations of a number of great leaders notwithstanding, the intense desire to push on to Jerusalem kept the major portion of the army true to its purpose.[127] Alphandéry and other historians claimed this represented the conquest of the official Crusade by the revived forces of the popular apocalyptic Crusade, but this explanation seems too simplistic.[128] Great lords, such as Tancred, supported the push to Jerusalem enthusiastically, and of the major leaders only Baldwin and Bohemund were not present at the siege of Jerusalem. The differences of opinion about the rate of march were as much due to strategic questions as to anything else. The death of Bishop Adhémar in August at Antioch also left the fractious barons with no central figure to adjudicate their disputes, and this too slowed down progress.

The visionary element remained strong during these last months. Peter Bartholomew's most recent messages must have become something of a bore to all but the most devout adherents of the Holy Lance, such as Raymond of Aguilers. On August 3, 1098, the recently deceased Adhémar appeared to him, confessing the minor punishments he was compelled to suffer due to his former doubts regarding the Lance and pleading for unity among the leaders.[129] In September came yet another vision which confirmed the authority of the Lance and enjoined penance on Count Raymond himself.[130] This was followed by further appearances in December of 1098 and April 1099.[131] Along with the repeated defense of the authenticity of the Lance, the main themes were the call to penance, the necessity of unity among the Crusaders, and the identification of the army with Christ in his Passion. In the final vision Christ says of the most heroic group of Crusaders: "They die for me as I died for them, and together we reside spiritually, one in the other."[132]

But Peter Bartholomew's repeated defenses of the Lance undoubtedly indicate that many were suspicious of the relic. On April 8, 1099, he underwent an ordeal by fire to defend its authenticity. Despite the tendentious account of Raymond, the trial was a failure and he died of his burns within a few days.[133] The Lance receded into the background, except for the Provençal party: it had served its great purpose at Antioch. As the Crusade drew near Jerusalem, new visions confirmed the expedition's providential status and conveyed important instructions. After the trial of the Lance, Bishop Adhémar appeared to the priest Stephen guaranteeing divine aid and discreetly giving his own processional cross precedence over the Holy Lance.[134]

The Piety of the First Crusaders · 53

On June 7, 1099, three years after the armies had set forth, the remnant of the Crusaders finally caught sight of the Holy City. It should not surprise us that our accounts of the siege fall into an easily discernible pattern, that of the piety of the *iter sancti Sepulchri*. Untrue to their pilgrim state, the Crusaders had failed to approach Jerusalem with bared feet.[135] Although a holy hermit told them if they attacked the city immediately God would deliver it into their hands, the assault was unsuccessful because the army had forgotten God.[136] In the midst of this final crisis, supernatural assistance once more came to the rescue. Bishop Adhémar appeared to the priest Peter Desiderius and again prescribed his sovereign remedy: a ceremony of penance including a confession of sins, establishment of harmony among the whole Christian brotherhood, and a barefoot procession around the walls of Jerusalem.[137] On July 8 the procession took place; from that time on, the Crusaders sensed they were once more on God's side.

July 14 saw the beginning of the final assault. On July 15, in the midst of the most perilous moments of the attack, God seemed to refresh his wearied people; indeed, an unknown celestial warrior signaling from the Mount of Olives played a key role when Godfrey of Bouillon finally gained a foothold on the walls, and some testified that they saw Adhémar himself leading the way.[138] The crusading host had entered into its providential inheritance. Worshipping at the Holy Sepulchre, they could repeat the words of the psalm: "Let us now adore in the place in which his feet have stood."[139] Like the chosen people of the Old Testament on whom they had come to model themselves, the Crusaders systematically destroyed every remnant of the unholy Moslems and Jews who had unjustly possessed the sacred city.

The expeditions that set off from Europe in 1096 were unique. However much the Crusade had been prepared for by earlier developments, the combination of holy war, pilgrimage to Jerusalem, and the new style of penance preached by the pope was strikingly original. The reaction to Urban's summons was equally remarkable. Earlier mass pilgrimages were dwarfed by the gigantic outpouring that went far beyond the pope's intentions—in terms of numbers we can be fairly sure that no later crusade ever approached it. But the most singular aspect of the Great Crusade was the experience itself.[140]

If the march to Jerusalem was at least analogous to the rites of passage described by the anthropologists and historians of religion, it was certainly a rite of passage with some very special characteristics. Having no real predecessors, it had to form its own meaning out of a combination of elements understood in the light of the events of the *iter* itself. This meaning was inchoate until the conquest of Jerusalem had been achieved. Only in the light of this miracle could the full dialectic of sin–repentence–special providential intervention become clear. For those who stayed on in the new Kingdom of Jerusalem, the sense of the sacred they had gained on the *iter sancti Sepulchri* was there to be called upon in other times of crisis, such as the failure of the Holy Fire in 1101. For those who went back to Europe, it provided a beginning for the theological interpretations of the Crusade.

NOTES

1. Three of the accounts of the events of Easter 1101 go back to eyewitness reports. The Genoese Caffaro, although he did not compose his *De liberatione civitatum orientis* until about 1155, was certainly present. His account may be found in the *Recueil des historiens des croisades: Historiens Occidentaux* (Paris: Publications Académie des Inscriptions et Belles Lettres, 1895), 5:61–62. (Hereafter abridged as RHC with appropriate volume and page. Other sections in the *Recueil* will be given standard designations, as below.) The German Ekkehard of Aura, who wrote his *Hierosolymitana* about 1115, bases his version on that of the eyewitness Hermann (RHC, 5:36). A complex question arises concerning the witness of Fulcher of Chartres, the chaplain of King Baldwin. Only one manuscript of Fulcher's *Historia Hierosolymitana* gives a detailed rendition of the events. In his edition of Fulcher (*Fulcheri Carnotensis Historia Hierosolymitana* [Heidelberg: Winter, 1913], pp. 395–396 n.), H. Hagenmeyer has argued convincingly that this account (hereafter referred to as the Pseudo-Fulcher) was not present in the editions of the text for which Fulcher was actually responsible, but that it did depend on his personal reminiscences. Two other accounts connected with Fulcher are found in Guibert of Nogent, *Gesta Dei per Francos* (RHC, 4:255–256), and

Bartolph of Nangis, *Gesta Francorum* (RHC, 3:524–526). In addition, William of Malmesbury made use of the Pseudo-Fulcher in his *De gestis regum Anglorum*, vol. 4 (Rolls Series, 52: 443–444). There is also a brief report in the *Chronicle* of Armenian historian Matthew of Edessa (RCH, Documents Arméniens, 1:54–55), and a legendary memory is found in the *Historia peregrinorum* of the Pseudo-Tudebord (RHC, 3:214–215).

2. The most complete information about the standard observances surrounding the miracle of the Holy Fire in the twelfth century comes from the account of the Russian Abbot Daniel, who visited the Holy Land in 1106–1107, and from a late-twelfth-century "Ritual of the Holy Sepulchre" preserved in Barletta. Both accounts suggest the hour of nones as the customary time for the miracle, a point confirmed by some of the reports of the incident of 1101. For these descriptions, see "The Pilgrimage of the Russian Abbot Daniel in the Holy Land," in *Palestine Pilgrim Texts Society* (London: Adelphi, 1888), 4:78; and C. Kohler, "Un rituel et un Bréviaire du Saint-Sepulchre de Jérusalem (XIIᵉ–XIIIᵉ siècle)," *Revue de l'orient latin* 8 (1900–01): 421.

3. Bartolph (RHC, 3:524).

4. This theme is also present in the account of Matthew of Edessa (RHC, Doc. Arm., 1:54–55), who blames it on the Latins for having introduced women into the services.

5. RHC, 3:386 (ed. Hagenmeyer, p. 832).

6. The earliest report of the miracle is found in the narrative of the Carolingian pilgrim Bernard the Wise (ca. 870); see *Palestine Pilgrim Texts Society*, 3:7. A supposed Byzantine text of the late tenth century referring to the miracle is highly suspect, as noted by P. Riant in *Archives de l'orient latin* 1 (1881): 375–376. The Arab references, critical in nature, are briefly discussed by A. S. Tritton, "The Easter Fire at Jerusalem," *Journal of the Royal Asiatic Society for 1963*, pp. 249–250, who mistakenly cites Fulcher's account as the earliest Western notice.

7. Also found in the Pseudo-Fulcher (RHC, 3:386; ed. Hagenmeyer, p. 832), which ascribes it to some of the clergy who were ignorant of what the Lord was soon to perform.

8. Found in Bartolph's account (RHC, 3:524). This version also mistakenly places the address on Saturday evening.

9. RHC, 5:61.
10. Caffaro explicitly mentions Daimbert's initiative.
11. 3 Kings 8:29 ff. and 9:2–3. Pseudo-Fulcher also mentions Matt. 7:7, a text not directly related to Jerusalem but arguing in a similar vein.
12. Baldwin's presence on the procession is mentioned in all reports. Bartolph (RHC, 3:525) contains the unlikely report that the king publicly confessed his sins and wished to lay aside the crown.
13. Guibert (RHC, 4:256); and Pseudo-Fulcher (RHC, 3:386; ed. Hagenmeyer, p. 832).
14. Pseudo-Fulcher (RHC, 3:387; ed. Hagenmeyer, p. 833; and Bartolph (RHC, 3:525).
15. Pseudo-Fulcher (RHC, 3:387; ed. Hagenmeyer, p. 833).
16. Pseudo-Fulcher notes the crown wearing "pro more regio coronatus." This seems more likely than Guibert's account that the crown was worn especially to honor the miracle.
17. The new Pentecost theme signalled by the witness of the nations is found in Ekkehard and in Bartolph.
18. *Palestine Pilgrim Texts Society*, 4:78–79.
19. It is not mentioned in K. M. Setton, ed., *A History of the Crusades*, vol. 1: *The First Hundred Years*, ed. M. W. Baldwin (Madison: University of Wisconsin Press, 1969); or in S. Runciman, *A History of the Crusades*, vol. 2 (Cambridge: At the University Press, 1954). Runciman even says under 1101 that "Maurice forbade Daimbert to take part in the Easter ceremonies, which he performed alone" (p. 81). This view depends upon the mistaken report of Albert of Aix (RHC, 4:538–541), who confuses the events of 1101 with those of 1102 when Daimbert was actually suspended by the papal legate.
20. The phrase is that of P. Alphandéry, *La chrétienté et l'idée de croisade*, ed. A. Dupront (Paris: Editions Albin Michel, 1954), 1: 81, 186, 189.
21. Bartolph (RHC, 3:525; ed. Hagenmeyer, p. 834).
22. To use the language of M. Eliade, whose *Patterns in Comparative Religion* (New York: Meridian Books, 1963), especially chapters 10 and 11, helps one to understand the intimate bond between the "center" and the sacred.

23. Balderic of Dol (RHC, 4:13).

24. Among other witnesses to its fame, see Peter the Venerable, *Sermo in laudem sancti Sepulchri (Patrologia Latina* [hereafter abridged as PL], 189:986–987). In the thirteenth century the miracle fell into disrepute among the Latins and its practice was forbidden by a bull of Gregory IX (March 9, 1238), probably because of financial abuses that had grown up about it. The descent of the Holy Fire remained important for Eastern Christians well into the present century.

25. *Historia*, 2:6 (ed. Hagenmeyer, p. 389).

26. Raymond of Aguilers, *Historia Francorum qui ceperunt Jerusalem*, chap. 20 (RHC, 3:296, 301).

27. Daimbert, Archbishop of Pisa, had been appointed legate to the Crusade in late 1098 by Pope Urban. His control over the Pisan fleet made him a valuable ally of Bohemund, who engineered his election as patriarch. The opposition of King Baldwin and Daimbert's own venality led to his deposition in 1102.

28. "Corde devoto," Ekkehard (RHC, 5:36); "mundo corde," Caffaro (RHC, 5:61).

29. Victor Turner, *Dramas, Fields and Metaphors* (Ithaca: Cornell University Press, 1974), pp. 45–52, 169–171, 202–203, 231–270.

30. Carl Erdmann, *Die Entstehung des Kreuzzugsgedankens* (Stuttgart: Kohlhammer, 1935), is the classic study of the development of the holy war. See also H. E. J. Cowdrey, "The Genesis of the Crusades: The Springs of Western Ideas of Holy War," in *The Holy War*, ed. T. P. Murphy, pp. 9–32 (Columbus: Ohio State University Press, 1976). No single work performs similar functions for the pilgrimage component of the Crusade.

31. For an expansion on what is given here, see also B. McGinn, *The Crusades* (Morristown, N.J.: General Learning Press, 1973), pp. 4–10, where these themes are treated under the rubric of the "Proto-Crusade."

32. See F. Russell, *The Just War in the Middle Ages* (Cambridge: At the University Press, 1975), p. 2.

33. See PL, 133:647. On Odo's views, see B. Rosenwein and L. K. Little, "Social Meaning in the Monastic and Mendicant Spiritualities," *Past and Present* 63 (1974): 8–16.

34. For an introduction, see H. E. J. Cowdrey, "The Peace of God and the Truce of God in the Eleventh Century," *Past and Present* 59 (1970): 42–67.
35. Examples of the Proto-Crusade in Spain are summarized in Setton, *History*, 1:31–39; Runciman, 1:89–91; and H. E. Mayer, *The Crusades* (New York and Oxford: Oxford University Press, 1972), pp. 19–20.
36. Of the extensive literature on pilgrimage, I mention only the following: H. Leclercq, "Pèlerinage aux lieux saints," *Dictionnaire d'archéologie chrétienne et de la liturgie* (Paris: Letouzey et Ane, 1939), 14:65–176; the papers in *Pellegrinaggi e Culto dei Santi in Europa fino alla Prima Crociata*, Convegni del Centro di Studi sulla Spiritualità Medievale IV (Todi: Accademia Tudertina, 1963); Runciman, *History*, 1:38–50; J. Sumption, *Pilgrimage* (Totowa, N.J.: Rowman and Littlefield, 1975); E. R. Labande, "Recherches sur les pèlerins dans l'Europe des XIᵉ et XIIᵉ siècles." *Cahiers de civilisation médiévale* 1 (1958): 159–169, 339–347; and A. Dupront, "Pèlerinage et lieux saints," *Mélanges Fernand Braudel* (Toulouse: Privat, 1973), 2:189–206.
37. *Epistola*, 48:14 (trans. of J. Sumption, *Pilgrimage*, p. 89).
38. See the study of C. Vogel, "Le pèlerinage penitentiel," in *Pellegrinaggi e Culto*, pp. 39–94.
39. Ibid., pp. 57–58, 76. The Penitential of the Pseudo-Egbert assigns a pilgrimage to Rome for the murder of a cleric or a near relative. In the mid-ninth-century, the Carolingian noble Fromond went to Jerusalem to do penance for an unintentional homicide; see *Peregrinatio Frotmondi* (*Acta Sanctorum*, Oct. Tom. X, Oct. 24, p. 847).
40. *Historiae*, 4:6 (PL, 142:680–682).
41. The best account is E. Joranson, "The Great German Pilgrimage of 1064–65," in *The Crusades and Other Historical Essays Presented to Dana C. Munro*, pp. 3–43 (New York: Crofts, 1928). This expedition has sometimes been viewed as a prototype of the Crusades, but Joranson's study does not support this view.
42. The *Vita Altmanni* (*Monumenta Germaniae Historica*, Scriptores, 12:230; hereafter abridged as MGH, SS), written two generations after the events, asserts that many believed the end of the

world would come on an Easter Sunday following a Good Friday that fell on March 25, the Feast of the Annunciation. The only year in the eleventh century on which this conjunction took place was 1065.

43. On the meaning of Jerusalem in the middle ages, see S. Mähl, "Jerusalem in mittelalterlicher Sicht," *Die Welt als Geschichte* 22 (1962): 11–26; R. Konrad, "Das himmlische und das irdische Jerusalem im mittelalterlichen Denken," in *Speculum historiale*, ed. C. Bauer, L. Boehm, and M. Müller, pp. 523–540 (Munich: Karl Alber, 1965); A. Bredero, "Jérusalem dans l'Occident médiévale," in *Mélanges Crozet*, pp. 259–271 (Poitiers: Société d'études médiévales, 1966); and H. de Lubac, *Exegèse médiévale* (Paris: Aubier, 1959), vol. 1, part 2, pp. 645–648.

44. Eusebius, *In Ps. 75* (*Patrologia Graeca*, 23:879); Jerome, *Liber de nominibus hebraicis* (PL, 23:873, 886, 892). The etymological definition was popularized by Augustine, *De civitate Dei*, 19:11; and Isidore of Seville, *Etymologiae*, 8:1, 6.

45. *Collationes*, 14, 8 (PL, 49:964). Another classic text for the various meanings of Jerusalem was *De civ. Dei*, 17:3. For a summary of Augustine's view of the Holy City, see Bredero, "Jerusalem," pp. 261–262.

46. Based on Ezek. 5:5 and Ps. 73:12, the claim that Jerusalem is the center of the earth is found in Christian literature as early as Jerome, *Commentarium in Ezechielem*, vol. 2 (PL, 25:52). For further references, cf. Mähl, "Jerusalem," pp. 17–20; Konrad, "Jerusalem," pp. 531–532; and Bredero, "Jerusalem," pp. 264–265.

47. See Mähl, "Jerusalem," pp. 24–25; and Konrad, "Jerusalem," p. 531. In his *Chronicle*, 7:7, Otto of Freising spoke of the crusading parties of 1100 as "ex omnibus mundi partibus ad Hierusalem terrestrem, caelestis typum gerentem, . . . confluerent" (MGH, SS, ed. A. Hofmeister [Hanover: Hahn, 1912], p. 316).

48. Lubac, *Exegèse médiévale*, vol. 1, part 2, pp. 624, 640–642.

49. About 1095, Anselm of Canterbury warned Bishop Osmund about monks going to Jerusalem (Letter 195 in F. Schmitt, ed., *Sancti Anselmi opera omnia*, 4:85). Bernard of Clairvaux, despite

his preaching of the Crusade, was against monks' taking part (Letter 399 in PL, 182:612).

50. On the flowering of the theological notion of the Crusade in the writings of St. Bernard, see E. O. Blake, "The Formation of the 'Crusade Idea,'" *Journal of Ecclesiastical History* 21 (1970): 27–30; B. Flood, "St. Bernard's View of the Crusade," *Cistercian Studies* 9 (1974): 22–35; and J. Leclercq, "L'attitude spirituelle de St. Bernard devant la guerre," *Collectanea cisterciensia* 36 (1974): 195–225.

51. For a broader sketch of the papal role, see McGinn, *The Crusades*, pp. 5–9.

52. For a good recent picture of this relation, see I. S. Robinson, "Gregory VII and the Soldiers of Christ," *History* 58 (1973): 169–192. Among older works, Erdmann, *Die Entstehung*, pp. 185–211, is still useful.

53. Not as clearly expressed as Gregory's enemies would have it, but certainly present in such letters as *Register*, 7:14a; 9:3, and by implication in 6:7 (E. Caspar, ed., MGH, Epistolae selectae, 2:486, 574, 423–424). On this question, see Robinson, "Gregory VII," pp. 180–183, 190–192.

54. MGH, Libelli de lite, 1:296 (trans. of Robinson, "Gregory VII," p. 180).

55. For example, John of Mantua, Anselm of Lucca, and Bonizo of Sutri; see Robinson, "Gregory VII," pp. 184–190.

56. For a survey of these overtures, see Setton, *History*, 1:223–230.

57. *Register*, 2:31 (Caspar, ed., p. 166; I am using the translation of E. Emerton, *The Correspondence of Pope Gregory VII* [New York: Norton, 1969], p. 57). See also W. Ullmann, *The Growth of Papal Government in the Middle Ages* (London: Methuen, 1955), pp. 306–307.

58. My use of the term "rite of passage" has been colored by the discussions of anthropologists and historians of religion, beginning with the classic work of A. van Gennep, *The Rites of Passage* (Chicago: University of Chicago Press, 1960; trans. of the French original of 1908). Van Gennep himself suggested the application of the term to the pilgrimages of the high religions (pp. 184–185), an application furthered by V. Turner, especially in his essay "Pilgrimages as Social Processes," in *Dramas,*

Fields, and Metaphors, pp. 166–230. Unfortunately, Turner sees the Crusade as a species of "failed pilgrimage" where "force" replaced "grace" (p. 206). This misconstrues the real, if admittedly paradoxical, religious values of the Crusade, especially the internal establishment of "communitas" at moments of crisis.

59. Among the many works on the religious meaning of the Crusade, besides those of C. Erdmann, P. Alphandéry, and E. O. Blake already mentioned, the following should be noted: M. Villey, *La croisade: Essai sur la formation d'une théorie juridique* (Paris: Vrin, 1942); P. Rousset, *Les origines et les caractères de la première croisade* (Neuchatel: A la Baconnière, 1945); the papers devoted to "L'Idée de croisade," in *The International Congress of Historical Sciences: Relations of the Tenth Congress* (Rome: Sansoni, 1955), 3:544–652; A. Dupront, "La spiritualité des croises et des pèlerins d'après les sources de la première croisade," in *Pellegrinaggi e Culto*, pp. 450–483; and G. Miccoli, "Dal Pellegrinaggio alla Conquista: Povertà e Richezza nelle Prime Crociate," in *Povertà e Richezza nella Spiritualità dei Secoli XI e XII*, Convegni del Centro de Studi sulla Spiritualità Medievale VIII, pp. 45–80 (Todi: Accademia Tudertina, 1969).

60. Blake, "Crusade Idea," p. 20. Among the sources for the Crusade in process, first rank belongs to the twenty-three letters written on the march or shortly after and edited by H. Hagenmeyer, *Die Kreuzzugsbriefe aus den Jahren 1088–1100 (Epistulae et Chartae ad historiam primi belli sacri spectantes)* (Innsbruck: Wagner, 1901), pp. 129–181. Among the narratives of the First Crusade, all of which were written down after the conquest of Jerusalem, by far the most important are the three eyewitness accounts. That of an anonymous Norman, the *Gesta Francorum et aliorum Hierosolimitanorum*, the earliest version of which was completed about 1101, was the source for many of the later reports. The author was a literate Norman knight originally in the service of Bohemund. The edition used here is that of R. Mynors and R. Hill, *Gesta Francorum* (London: Nelson, 1962). Raymond of Aguilers, the chaplain of Raymond of Toulouse and propagandist of the Holy Lance, finished his text

about 1102. It may be found in RHC, 3:235–305. Finally, the *Historia Hierosolymitana* of Fulcher of Chartres has already been frequently mentioned above. Unfortunately, Fulcher left the main Crusade to accompany his patron, Baldwin, to Edessa, before the dramatic events occurring between Antioch and Jerusalem, so his report is second-hand in this crucial area.

61. Blake ("Crusade Idea," pp. 12, 20–24) lays out the broad lines by which the process of the mature concept of the Crusade was formed.

62. The versions of the speech may be found in Fulcher (RHC, 3:322–324), Robert the Monk (RHC, 3:727–730), Balderic of Dol (RHC, 4:12–15), Guibert of Nogent (RHC, 4:137–140), and William of Malmesbury, *De gestis regum anglorum* (Rolls Series, 52:393–398). Robert and Balderic claim that they were present; Fulcher and Guibert may have been.

63. Letter to the Faithful of Flanders of December 1095 (Hagenmeyer, *Die Kreuzzugsbriefe*, pp. 136–137); Letter to the Citizens of Bologna of September 19, 1096 (Hagenmeyer, *Die Kreuzzugsbriefe*, pp. 137–138); and Letter to the Monks of Vallombrosa of October 7, 1096, discussed in H. E. J. Cowdrey, "Pope Urban's Preaching and the First Crusade," *History* 55 (1970): 177–188.

64. Erdmann distinguished between a primary *Kriegsziel*, aid to the Eastern Church, and a secondary *Marschziel*, the Holy City (e.g., *Die Entstehung*, pp. 363–377). H. E. Mayer (*The Crusades*, pp. 10–11, and the lengthy note on pp. 290–291), though disturbed by the evidence gathered by Cowdrey, takes refuge in a series of unconvincing arguments to minimize Urban's interest in Jerusalem.

65. The *Vita Urbani* in the *Liber pontificalis* notes that Urban followed Gregory's lead in preaching the liberation of Jerusalem.

66. That Jerusalem was the goal of the papal proclamation has been ably argued by Cowdrey, "Pope Urban's Preaching," as well as by Blake, "Crusade Idea," pp. 17–18; Rousset, *Les origines*, pp. 55–62; and F. Duncalf, "The Councils of Piacenza and Clermont," in Setton, *History*, 1:243–244. The position is also adopted in D. C. Munro, "The Speech of Pope Urban II at Clermont, 1095," *American Historical Review* 11 (1905): 231–242.

67. J. D. Mansi, *Sacrorum conciliorum nova et amplissima collectio*, 20:815–820. See also F. Duncalf in Setton, *History*, 1:237.

68. This theme reached a culmination in the crusading propaganda of Bernard of Clairvaux; see Leclercq, "Pèlerinage," pp. 202–205.

69. Munro ("Speech of Pope Urban II," p. 236) surveys the accounts. Both the diplomatic history and the witness of the letters shows the indubitible presence of this intention.

70. Robinson, "Gregory VII," p. 190.

71. Originally trained for the Church, Baldwin's ascent to the supreme position was a remarkable combination of good luck along with a political ability and duplicity unmatched by his rivals. According to William of Tyre (*History*, 10:2), he was privately given over to sins of the flesh; but he was also certainly capable of extravagant demonstrations of public piety, as in the case of his confesson of sins before the First Battle of Ramleh (Fulcher, *History*, 2:11).

72. Mansi, *Sacrorum conciliorum*, 20:816. A similar phrase is found in Letter to the Bolognese (Hagenmeyer, *Die Kreuzzugsbriefe*, p. 137).

73. Mayer, *The Crusades*, pp. 25–37, 39.

74. Hagenmeyer, *Die Kreuzzugsbriefe*, p. 136. Another early witness, the Chronicle of Bernold, notes under the year 1095: "Nam et in praeteritis sinodis studiosissime omnes de hac expeditione praemonuit, eamque eis in remissionem peccatorum faciendam firmissime commendavit" (MGH, SS, 5:464).

75. Bernold (MGH, SS, 5:464) explains the failure of the Peasants' Crusade in terms of its lack of true penitential pilgrim practice.

76. The Letter to the Faithful of Flanders explicitly mentions the vow (Hagenmeyer, *Die Kreuzzugsbriefe*, p. 137); the Letter of the Monks of Vallombrosa (Cowdrey, "Pope Urban's Preaching," p. 187) refers to the special dedication (*oblatio*) of the knights.

77. For example, the renewal of vows by the leaders during the crisis at Antioch (see *Gesta Francorum*, ed. Mynors and Hill, p. 59) and the fact that after the conquest of Jerusalem both Bohemund and Baldwin felt compelled to fulfill their vow, despite the extreme danger involved (Fulcher, 1:33–34; ed. Hagenmeyer, pp. 322–343).

78. See J. Brundage, *Medieval Canon Law and the Crusader* (Madison: University of Wisconsin Press, 1969), for the most complete treatment.
79. The Letter to the Faithful of Flanders mentions him as *dux* (Hagenmeyer, *Die Kreuzzugsbriefe*, p. 136). All accounts testify to his special position.
80. For a brief survey of the theocratic notions of some of the patriarchs of Jerusalem, see M. Spinka, "Latin Church of the Early Crusaders," *Church History* 8 (1939): 111–131.
81. Alphandéry's thesis may be summarized as follows: (1) preparatory large-scale pilgrimages were primarily apocalyptic in motivation (*La chrétienté*, pp. 24–26); (2) Urban's main interest was not Jerusalem but the deliverance of Eastern Christianity (pp. 33–35); (3) famine, disease, and other crises were at the basis of the messianic hopes that inspired the masses to undertake the Crusade (pp. 46–50); (4) the Peasants' or Peoples' Crusade can be characterized as "an immense movement of eschatological migration, perhaps inspired by the necessity of millenarian renewal" (p. 78); (5) the popular apocalyptic Crusade came to the rescue of the papal Crusade in the crisis at Antioch (pp. 90–107) and provided the power that saw the expedition through to its goal (pp. 127–135). This interpretation, seriously misleading as it is, has been almost totally accepted by N. Cohn in his *The Pursuit of the Millennium*, rev. ed. (New York: Oxford University Press, 1970).
82. Mayer, *The Crusades*, pp. 25–37.
83. A. Dupront, Alphandéry's student and subsequent editor, seems to have begun to recognize this. In his later article, "La spiritualité des croises . . . ," pp. 456–457, although he still emphasizes the existence of two groups of Crusaders, *milites* and *peregrini*, he sees them as more and more intermingled and complementary. Blake ("Crusade Idea," p. 14) rightly denies that the religious motivations of the Crusaders can be divided along class lines, with the aristocracy primarily following the holy-war motif and the *pauperes* acting from eschatological and pilgrimage motives.
84. All sources make some mention of the Peoples' Crusade. The most informative are those of Ekkehard and Albert of Aix, both of

whom used the reminiscences of participants. For a survey in English, see F. Duncalf, "The Peasants' Crusade," *American Historical Review* 26 (1920–21): 440–453. Another source is the *Chanson d'Antioche*, ed. L. Sumberg (Paris: A. and J. Picard, 1968), of some importance for the later appearance of "popular" elements.

85. Urban's Letters to the Bolognese and to the monks of Vallombrosa (Hagenmeyer, *Die Kreuzzugsbriefe*, p. 137; and Cowdrey, "Pope Urban's Preaching," p. 187) indicate that he was unhappy about the number of noncombatants, especially clergy, who had vowed to undertake the journey.

86. In this connection, see the evaluation of P. Classen, "Eschatologische Ideen und Armutsbewegungen im 11. und 12. Jahrhundert," *Povertà e Richezza nella Spiritualità dei Secoli XI e XII*, pp. 141–144. Classen notes the exaggeration of the Alphandéry-Cohn approach (pp. 144–148) and concludes that the poverty movement and eschatological ideas did not really join forces until the thirteenth century.

87. For the apocalyptic understanding of Jerusalem, cf. Bredero, "Jerusalem," pp. 267–270; Mähl, "Jerusalem," pp. 20–24; and Konrad, "Jerusalem," pp. 535–540.

88. See C. Erdmann, "Endkaiserglaube und Kreuzzugsgedanke im 11. Jahrhundert," *Zeitschrift für Kirchengeschichte* 51 (1932): 382–414; and the still classic study of F. Kampers, *Die Deutsche Kaiseridee in Prophetie und Sage* (Munich, 1896; repr., Aalen: Scientia Verlag, 1969).

89. *Gesta Dei*, iv and xxi (RHC, 4:138–139, 237–240).

90. For the portents, see Guibert (RHC, 4:149) and Ekkehard (RHC, 5:18–19). For the curious episode of the followers of the goose, Albert (RHC, 4:295) and Ekkehard (RHC, 5:19).

91. The apocalyptic thesis of Alphandéry and Cohn is heavily dependent upon a "crisis" theory of the origin of messianic movements, in this case the insistence that plague, famine, and other crises provided the breeding ground for the mass migration of the poor toward Jerusalem (Alphandéry, *La chrétienté*, pp. 44–50, 68; Cohn, *Pursuit of the Millennium*, p. 63). The crisis theory has been effectively criticized by F. Duncalf, who says, ". . . the movement . . . originated in favorable economic

conditions rather than in famine and distress" and "the *via sancta* was not for the *pauper* . . ." ("The Peasants' Crusade," pp. 452, 453). See also his remarks in Setton, *History*, 1: 255–256.

92. Notably by Runciman in the first volume of his *A History of the Crusades*.

93. Dupront, "La spiritualité des croises," pp. 453–465.

94. Among the terms used in the letters are (*a*) military terms, such as *exercitus christianus* (Hagenmeyer, *Die Kreuzzugsbriefe*, p. 141), *exercitus Hierosolymitanus* (p. 177), *exercitus Domini* (pp. 144, 149, 157), and *militia Domini* (pp. 146, 148); and (*b*) pilgrimage terms, such as *peregrini sancti Sepulchri* (p. 154) and *Hierosolymitani* (p. 161).

95. Jerusalem is the home of Christ (ibid., p. 149) and the place of the Holy Sepulchre (p. 164). It offers fellowship in the heavenly Jerusalem (p. 146). Letter 20 (pp. 175–176), written in December of 1099, is a hymn of praise to the Holy City as the *locus* of redemption. See also Letter 21 of the Patriarch Daimbert (p. 177).

96. Letter 16 (ibid., pp. 164–165).

97. Aid to Eastern Christians is mentioned only in Letter 8 (ibid., pp. 145–146), written in November 1097. The letters of Pope Paschal II after the fall of Jerusalem show that he had not abandoned Urban's hopes for a rapprochement with the Eastern Christians (pp. 175, 178). For hostile attitudes to the Easterners see Letters 16 and 20 (pp. 164, 176).

98. Basic sacramental practices, for example, penance, confession, and communion (Letter 8 in ibid., p. 144), and prayer and devotion in Letter 12 (p. 155).

99. Letters 9, 16, and 21 (ibid., pp. 147–148, 164, 171).

100. Letter 15 (ibid., p. 157).

101. God fights for his army (Letters 6 and 10 in ibid., pp. 142, 149–152). Miracles are a sign of divine providence (Letters 16, 17, and 18, pp. 163, 167, 169–170).

102. The providential understanding of the Crusade is clearly brought out in G. Miccoli, "Dal Pellegrinaggio alla Conquista," pp. 55–59.

103. Contrary to Dupront ("La spiritualité des croises," pp. 459–463),

who gives the later chroniclers too large a role in the triumph of the pilgrimage motif.

104. Blake ("Crusade Idea," p. 23) notes that for the anonymous Norman, "the momentum of the whole exercise is supplied by the *via Sancti Sepulchri*." There are many appearances of this theme in his text (e.g., pp. 7, 12, 40, 62, 72, 76, 80, 81 of the Mynors-Hill edition). The Holy Sepulchre appears in conjunction with God or Christ as motive for action on pp. 19–20, 26, 37, 41, 70, 77, 97. Worship at the Holy Sepulchre is the goal of the pilgrimage on pp. 89–90, 92.

105. *Milites Christi, miles veri Dei, militia Christi, athleta Christi* and *exercitus Dei* are all used by the chroniclers. Dupront ("La spiritualité des croises," pp. 453–459) surveys the relative weight of the terms, but his interpretation overstresses the distinction between two classes of participants, the *milites* and the *peregrini* whom they protected (pp. 456–457), and also mitigates the role of pilgrimage in the early accounts (p. 459). For the use of *peregrinus Christi* as the equivalent of *pauper Christi*, see Rousset, *Les origines*, pp. 40–41.

106. Anonymous Norman (*Gesta Francorum*, ed. Mynors and Hill, p. 73); Raymond (RHC, 3:261), and Fulcher (1:x; ed. Hagenmeyer, p. 185).

107. Dupront, "La spiritualité des croises," p. 475. Blake ("Crusade Idea," p. 24) speaks of it as "a distinctive morale, centered on the theme of the delivery of the Holy Places and of a piety peculiar to the warrior pilgrim."

108. See the use of New Testament texts on taking up one's cross (e.g., Matt. 16:24) at the outset of the anonymous Norman's account (*Gesta Francorum*, ed. Mynors and Hill, pp. 1–2).

109. Anonymous Norman (*Gesta Francorum*, ed. Mynors and Hill, pp. 4, 17, 40, 65, 85); Fulcher (Prologue and 1:xvi; ed. Hagenmeyer, pp. 117, 226–227).

110. Fulcher (1:viii; ed. Hagenmeyer, pp. 169–170) tells the story of the crosses found on the bodies of the Crusaders drowned off Apulia. Raymond speaks of crosses on the slain at Marra (RHC, 3:272), and Ekkehard notes the appearance of crosses on foreheads among the portents of the Crusade (RHC, 5:19). Guibert tells of an Abbot Baldwin who burned a cross on his forehead

in order to coax more money from the pious for the support of his journey (RHC, 4:182–183), and Bernold's *Chronicle* speaks of crosses on bodies without precise localization (MGH, SS, 5:464).

111. The sources stress this throughout. According to Fulcher (1:xv; ed. Hagenmeyer, p. 223), both unmarried and married women were driven from the camp at the time of the penance ritual before the conquest of Antioch. St. Peter warned Peter Bartholomew about adultery in the army, according to Raymond (RHC, 3:269). One of the most entertaining stories of Albert of Aix (RHC, 3:375–376) concerns a cleric who was surprised and killed by the Turks while playing dice with a lady friend in a hidden glade near Antioch.

112. Robinson ("Gregory VII," p. 184) notes the generally poor record of the fighting forces that supported Gregory VII in his struggles. After a series of disasters, it must have been a relief to the papacy to have achieved such signal vindication. Rousset (*Les origines*, pp. 180–186) has valuable remarks on the notion of "immanent justice" implicit in this view of divine intervention.

113. Raymond (RHC, 3:254).

114. Guibert (RHC, 4:149) and Ekkehard (RHC, 5:17–18).

115. Fulcher (1:xi; ed. Hagenmeyer, pp. 196–197).

116. Raymond (RHC, 3:240). The anonymous Norman does not dwell on the theme of repentence or mention heavenly warriors in his account of Doryleum, but he does see the victory as a result of God's aid (*Gesta Francorum*, Mynors and Hill, pp. 20–21).

117. This is especially evident in Raymond, whose central theme is the *magnalia Dei* (RHC, 3:235). Rousset (*Les origines*, pp. 145–147) notes the significance of these rituals, which he terms "la technique de guerre sainte."

118. Raymond (RHC, 3:245). Fulcher's second-hand report of this penance is also important (1:xv; ed. Hagenmeyer, pp. 222–224).

119. On the history of the Holy Lance, see S. Runciman, "The Holy Lance found at Antioch," *Analecta Bollandiana* 68 (1950): 197–209; and his *History*, 1:241–254, 273–274.

120. The most complete account of the Holy Lance is that in Raymond, who claims to have been present at its discovery. As the

apologist of Peter Bartholomew and the Lance, his descriptions of Peter's nine visions and subsequent ordeal must be treated with extreme caution in many details, but they are among the most important sources for the piety of the Crusade. The anonymous Norman gives a fairly sober account of the visions, the discovery, and the Battle of the Lance which does not disagree with Raymond in the main (*Gesta Francorum*, ed. Mynors and Hill, pp. 59–60, 65, 67–70). He does not mention the ordeal. Fulcher, who was not present at Antioch, considered the whole business a fraud and records that Peter Bartholomew died of the ordeal (1:xviii; ed. Hagenmeyer, pp. 235–241). A similar skeptical position is found in Raoul of Caen (RHC, 3:676–680, 682). On the Lance, also see Letters 16, 17, and 18 (Hagenmeyer, *Die Kreuzzugsbriefe*, pp. 163, 167, 170).

121. Raymond (RHC, 3:255–256); the anonymous Norman (*Gesta Francorum*, Mynors and Hill, pp. 57–58); and Fulcher (1:xx; ed. Hagenmeyer, pp. 244–247).

122. In Raymond the call to penance is tied to a fifth vision given to Peter, one which again stresses identification with the suffering Christ (RHC, 3:258).

123. The anonymous Norman recounts the full scenario (*Gesta Francorum*, ed. Mynors and Hill, pp. 67–68). Raymond speaks only of almsgiving, confession, and communion (RHC, 3:258). Fulcher notes the three-day fast in 1:xx (ed. Hagenmeyer, p. 247). Letter 16 speaks of confession of sins, Letter 17 mentions the three-day fast and the procession, and Letter 18 also speaks of the procession (*Die Kreuzzugsbriefe*, Hagenmeyer, pp. 163, 167, 170).

124. Raymond (RHC, 3:260). See RHC, 3:285, for another comparison of the line of battle to a liturgical procession.

125. Raymond (RHC, 3:261); anonymous Norman (*Gesta Francorum*, ed. Mynors and Hill, p. 69).

126. Whether or not the Crusaders actually made the association at the time, this is when our sources begin to stress it. At the outset of the siege, Raymond praises a Christian victory in a skirmish as a feat surpassing that of the Maccabees (RHC, 3:245). For the use of Old Testament texts in the crusading narratives, see Dupront, "La spiritualité des croises," pp. 468–471; and

P. Alphandéry, "Les citations bibliques chez les historiens de la première croisade," *Revue de l'histoire des religions* 99 (1929): 139–157, who notes on p. 156 that this form of biblical rhetoric was not applied to other holy wars of the eleventh century. See also Rousset, *Les origines*, pp. 189–192.

127. Raymond (RHC, 3:267, 286, 289, 291); anonymous Norman (*Gesta Francorum*, ed. Mynors and Hill, pp. 72, 76). Raymond paints a poignant picture of the desire for Jerusalem at this time: "Etenim licet ex longo tempore inceptum esset iter, tamen quotidie videbatur nobis incipere quum iter ageremus, quia nondum fuerat completum" (p. 270).

128. Alphandéry, *La chrétienté*, pp. 97–98, 107–119.

129. Raymond (RHC, 3:262–264).

130. Ibid., 3:265–266.

131. Ibid., 3:268–269, 279–281.

132. Ibid., 3:279: "Moriuntur pro me, egoque pro eis mortuus sum: et ego sum in eis, et ipsi sunt in me."

133. Ibid., 3:283–285.

134. Ibid., 3:286–287.

135. Raymond notes (ibid., 3:292) that St. Andrew had commanded this in one of Peter Bartholomew's visions.

136. The theme is strong in Raymond (ibid., 3:293–295).

137. Raymond gives the fullest account of the penance (ibid., 3:296–297). Both the anonymous Norman (*Gesta Francorum*, ed. Mynors and Hill, pp. 90–91) and the Letter of Daimbert (Hagenmeyer, *Die Kreuzzugsbriefe*, p. 171) mention the procession.

138. RHC, 3:299–300.

139. Ps. 131:7, a favorite text of Fulcher, though one not cited in his report of the entry of the pilgrims into the Holy Sepulchre (1: xxix; ed. Hagenmeyer, pp. 304–306). Both Fulcher and Raymond (RHC, 3:300) make heavy use of the imagery of the Psalms in their accounts of the entry; the anonymous Norman is more restrained (*Gesta Francorum*, ed. Mynors and Hill, p. 92).

140. My interpretation is opposed to that of J. Prawer, *The Latin Kingdom of Jerusalem* (London: Weidenfeld and Nicolson, 1972), pp. 471–475, who has valuable remarks on the uniqueness of the First Crusade, but who mistakenly sees a decline in religious fervor as the march proceeded.

Hans Böhm:
Shepherd, Piper, Prophet

Bede Karl Lackner

Hans Böhm attracted public attention for but a few weeks during the summer of 1476, and history books devote only a handful of lines, if any, to his activities. Even reference works restrict themselves to summaries that characterize Böhm as either a social reformer, a millenarian, or an advocate of communistic ideas. Böhm's dialectically rich personality, with its manifold medieval and modern components, obviously deserves a fuller treatment. It was Böhm, an unlettered and ignorant layman in the scholastic sense, who stood up and created the first nationwide movement in the German Empire that championed the cause of the little man and challenged the established feudal order, which had outlived its usefulness.

To understand Böhm's importance in its wider ramifications, it is necessary to review the chronic tensions that prevailed in Germany throughout the fifteenth century. Political instability victimized both the nobility and the common man. This was hardly surprising, given the defects in the structure of the state, with its weak emperor, the jumble of centrifugal principalities, and the power structure of a wealthy Church. Well entrenched since the days of Otto the Great, the Church firmly controlled the laity through its political power and ecclesiastical jurisdiction. The princes, ecclesiastical as well as secular, jealously guarded their privileges, always at the expense of the common man, whom they oppressed with excessive taxes and burdens and whose freedom they endeavored to restrict in the cities as well as in the countryside.

Brighter prospects appeared briefly during the so-called Neuss War (1474–75), when the poorer classes enthusiastically rallied behind the emperor and princes to repel the invasion of Charles the Bold, Duke of Burgundy, whose scheming seemed to threaten the very foundations of the existing Christian order. But this hope was utterly shattered when the emperor, Frederick III, and the princes settled the whole affair on the basis of class and family interest.

The emperor's "treason" and his collusion with the princes, the forces of oppression, were bitterly resented, especially in southwestern Germany. Hence the admiration of the little man for the Swiss, who had twice defeated Charles the Bold in their support of the Empire and, more importantly, had been quite successful in eliminating the economic and political restrictions of the feudal past in their homeland.[1]

The general distress of the common man also inspired intermittent local uprisings. The riots in the episcopal cities of Worms and Speyer during the winter months of 1431–32 roused some four thousand commoners against the Jews, the clergy, and the nobility. When many authorities responded by expelling the Jews from their territory, popular discontent came to focus on the hierarchy and the clergy. Clerical hatred throve particularly in Franconia, whose princes, the bishops of Würzburg, had for a long time been guilty of extravagance and utter mismanagement of their territory. But the little man also lost his respect for the lower clergy, which enjoyed fiscal and judicial immunity and had in countless instances fallen victim to selfishness and sensuality, as innumerable episcopal reform decrees testify.[2] Other factors which contributed to the general unrest included the repeated outbreaks of the Black Death and the constant Turkish threat; they added an element of fear and anxiety to an already troubled world.

Religion offered a welcome escape from this plight. Penitential preachers held their audiences spellbound. Flagellants scourged themselves publicly, and fanatics shed their clothes in honor of the Madonna. Sectarians embraced "voluntary poverty" to attain the state of certain perfection. A Franciscan friar predicted the disappearance of the papacy, to be followed by the destruction of Rome in 1524, while a Bohemian peasant demanded the abolition of all ecclesiastical and secular authorities because they had supposedly falsified the gospel of love. Children roamed about for years (1455–1459) or flocked, as in

1475, to the sanctuary of Mont-Saint-Michel, while their elders undertook incessant pilgrimages to shrines and sanctuaries throughout the century.

These pilgrimages let the little man forget his troubles and his oppressors. They enabled him to enter a better world than his own and to secure much-desired indulgences. Indulgences merely released Church penalties attached to personal sins upon the performance of a good act or payments made for a worthy cause, but the simple man, misled by clumsy preachers, easily confused the finer theological distinctions and convinced himself that the payment of a sum of money sufficed to secure him the remission of his sins. Jubilee years, or holy years, proclaimed by the popes at regular intervals, even promised plenary indulgences. In 1475 such a jubilee year was celebrated. It mobilized the already excited crowds and created a favorable climate for Hans Böhm's pilgrimage to Niklashausen in the following year.[3]

Hans Böhm, a country shepherd and Sunday musician, appeared in front of the village church of Niklashausen on Laetare Sunday, March 29, 1476, to embark on a new mission. Niklashausen was a rich and picturesque village on the Tauber River in Franconia, a short distance southeast of Wertheim, the seat of the local lord. Its church, which boasted of a wonder-working image of the Virgin Mary, had "in times of old attained great fame on account of remarkable miracles." Pope Innocent VI therefore granted a special indulgence of forty days to all pilgrims who visited the shrine on specified feasts, performed pious exercises, donated vessels to the church, or gave money for the support of its chaplain.[4]

In front of this church Böhm told the crowds that he had had a vision of the Virgin Mary who had appeared to him on a Saturday in a white robe. She asked him to burn his drum, give up his sinful ways, and serve, instead, the common man with his public preaching. Above all, he was to reveal God's anger, for "the whole country was mired in sin and wantonness, and, unless our people were ready to do penance and change their wicked ways, God would let all Germany go to destruction."[5] The Lady particularly wished that all persons should turn away from sin; discard long hair, fancy clothes, and jewels; and visit her shrine at Niklashausen to obtain indulgence and grace.[6]

Archives, chronicles, and even folk songs report more about Hans Böhm than about any other peasant reformer in pre-Reformation

Germany. Johannes Trithemius (1462–1516), abbot of Sponheim, recorded in his *Annales* what he "had heard from those who had been present." Lorenz Fries (1491–1550), the historian of the bishops of Würzburg and of the Peasant War in Franconia, described the Böhm affair on the basis of the official acts to which he had ready access. Siegfried von Bacharach wrote down, very ably, events for the *Rats-Chronik*, the city chronicle of Würzburg between 1475 and 1505. Far from the scene but equally well informed was Konrad Stolle, vicar in the city of Erfurt, the author of a *Memoriale* in which he set down "what priests, clerics and lay students, merchants, burghers, peasants, pilgrims, knights and other people" had told him, in order to preserve an accurate mosaic of the time. Among the near-contemporary witnesses, one must mention Georg Widmann, of Schwäbisch-Hall, whose *Chronika* (1544–1550) supplies vital information not offered by other sources, including the seamier side of the pilgrimage.

In 1850, Friedrich Reuss edited a lengthy German poem in glorification of Böhm's enemies, written by an eyewitness of the pilgrimage. Eight years later Karl Barack published a collection of twenty-nine contemporary documents, mostly letters and decisions–some of them in dialects of the time–issued by the authorities involved in the Böhm matter. This collection includes elements of a sermon Böhm preached on July 2, 1476, recorded by agents of the ecclesiastical authorities.[7] Unfortunately, this source material has not yet been subjected to a systematic analysis; hence the need for additional pioneering before a definitive study about Böhm can be attempted.

Hans Böhm–the sources refer to him as Beheme, Behaim, Beha, der Böhme (the Bohemian)–did not hail from Bohemia, as some historians claimed in order to explain his teachings on the basis of Hussite origins. He was actually born at Helmstadt, a town between Wertheim and Würzburg, in the Tauber Valley, around the year 1450. Dieter von Isenburg, the Archbishop of Mainz to whose diocese Niklashausen belonged, referred to him as "the peasant whom they call the youngster," thus indicating that Böhm belonged to the unpropertied country populace, the common people. According to Trithemius, Böhm was a swineherd. Widmann called him a shepherd. Woodcuts also portray Böhm as a shepherd, a very likely occupation since sheep farming was widespread in this area. Hans Böhm's vocation would be quite consonant with his new mission, particularly if one recalls that, ever since antiquity, shepherds were thought to be in communication with a more spiritual world.

Böhm was also a musician and, in the popular belief, music established contacts with the other world. Böhm played the drum and the bagpipe–hence his nicknames, "the Drummer" or "the Piper." Moving about in the Tauber Valley, he made music to the country people, especially the womenfolk, on Sundays, church feasts, and popular festivals, summoning his listeners to drink, dance, and merriment.

To the Archbishop of Mainz, Böhm was an unskilled and worthless rustic whose disgraceful life, devoted to suggestive dances, feminine diversions, and license since his adolescent years, earned him nothing but disgrace and scorn. Stolle called him a "half-wit, as one could see from his infancy," a poor fellow, a rather ignorant and wicked layman. Others portrayed him as an illiterate and unmannered peasant who lacked all formal education and, to quote Trithemius, was totally incapable of speaking or thinking coherently about one subject. The religious education of this simple young man proved just as defective. Dieter von Isenburg claimed that "he was ignorant of the basic precepts of the Catholic faith," and he gave no evidence whatever of being a Christian. The Bishop of Würzburg added, "he did not even know the Apostles' Creed or the Lord's Prayer."[8]

Thus characterized by his contemporaries and hostile chroniclers, it is difficult to ascertain Böhm's true personality and character. Nevertheless, he remains the most attractive and at the same time the most mysterious of all fifteenth-century German popular leaders. A careful study reveals that Böhm was an introspective young man endowed with an alert mind and a rich imagination. He loved music, "composed songs and cantilenas," and sang even at the very end of his tragic life. His personality and speech must have been rather attractive to draw masses by the thousands from such distant regions. They called him by the endearing name of "Hanselin," or "Johnny." Free of the restrictive thinking of the sectarians, he was able to address himself to diverse social groups. He retained an unwavering and childlike belief in the rectitude of his cause, even if it meant martyrdom. He preached "with vehemence," proclaiming in time such a radical program that recent historians have no hesitation to characterize him as a peasant Savonarola.

The masses believed in him; he was their prophet, "Our Lady's Messenger," or, simply, their "holy adolescent." The Piper, who had no formal education, inspired a popular movement whose waves reached far into southern and central Germany. Had he been a deceiver, as his opponents charged, he would hardly have drawn large crowds for weeks. Nor did he act as the puppet of others; his teachings indicted the very people who could have pulled the strings from the background.[9]

It was an altogether unique situation to see a layman stand up at the shrine of Niklashausen to preach to the people, because lay preaching had been prohibited since the days of Peter Waldo by Pope Lucius III. Böhm called on the masses to turn away from sin and to proceed as pilgrims to Niklashausen where the Virgin Mary had told him she wanted to be venerated more than anywhere else in the world. Accordingly, one could obtain greater and more perfect graces in the Tauber Valley than even in Rome or any other sanctuary. At Niklashausen all would find forgiveness of sin and a plenary indulgence. People who died there would go directly to heaven; and if they should be consigned to hell, then Böhm would lead them out with his own hands, for the Lady had promised to fulfill all his wishes.[10]

Little is known about Böhm's preaching even though, on July 2, 1476, notaries and other witnesses commissioned by the ecclesiastical authorities hastily recorded some twenty random statements in a language almost too sketchy to gauge their full implication. The Archbishop of Mainz singled out nine specific errors of a more or less theological nature, while Fries restricted himself to a brief enumeration of an equal number of Böhm's social teachings. Trithemius specified six aberrations which, in his belief, necessitated the prohibition of the pilgrimage and caused Hans Böhm's violent death. The Bishop of Würzburg also gave brief summaries of the latter's teachings in a series of letters addressed to a number of authorities in order to solicit their cooperation in stopping the pilgrimage.[11]

Trithemius succinctly summarized Böhm's teachings: "He dogmatized novelties against the clergy and the princes." Böhm preached on Sundays and at feasts before the crowds who had come to Niklashausen.[12] The greatest portion of his recorded utterances dealt with the clergy, which, he claimed, had been chiefly responsible for God's anger and the troubles of the world. He announced that God was no longer willing to tolerate the avarice, pride, and luxury of the clerics and priests. Unless they reformed their lives quickly, the whole world would be in danger on account of their crimes.

Böhm saw the root cause of these evils in clerical wealth. "The priests have too many benefices," he declared. He also demanded that they should stop exacting tithes and yearly rents from the common people. Instead, the people should give free alms to clerics or institutions of their choice, not by obligation but for the love of God. Böhm insisted that clerics must do without fixed incomes–benefices, altar revenues, and other emoluments–and have no more provisions than what they needed from one meal to another. Finally, "ecclesiastical lords should have as much as the common people." The people should have an equal share in the wealth of the clerics and princes; then all would have enough.[13]

Böhm's message was clearly understood by his clerical opponents. "What could be sweeter to a rustic," Trithemius noted, "than to be freed from every obligation to pay rent and service, and have all things in common with the clerics and the princes? And what could be more desirable to a layman, than to see the clergy and the priests deprived of every privilege, liberty, and revenue?"[14]

The Piper condemned with equal vehemence the other source of clerical power, ecclesiastical jurisdiction. He denied the validity of the ban of excommunication, denounced censures and ecclesiastical penalties as outright abuses, and assailed the clergy for using canon law to thwart the laws of God. Therefore, he called on his listeners to disregard clerical and episcopal ordinances altogether.[15]

Böhm held out no hope for the clergy. According to the bishop's informer, he would rather work on the salvation of the Jews than labor for the betterment of the priests. Joining the ranks of earlier fifteenth-century prophets, he predicted "the time is approaching when all the priests will be slain and anyone who killed thirty of their number will be entitled to great rewards." Böhm foretold that priests would cover their shaven heads with their hands in order to avoid recognition, but in vain. He believed that the clergy could no longer claim special powers from God: "It is all over." Indeed, soon no more priests, monks, or religious orders would exist on the earth.[16]

Böhm's anticlerical utterances fell on understanding ears. In Widmann's testimony, "this Drummer preached with such persistence against the clergy that, among their other *Kreuzlieder* [crusading songs], the pilgrims publicly chanted

> To God in heaven we complain
> *Kyrie eleison*
> That the priests cannot be slain
> *Kyrie eleison.*

Understandably, the authorities promptly outlawed this 'as well as the other songs fabricated by this heresy.'"[17]

Not confining his criticism to local ecclesiastics, Böhm had the temerity, the Bishop of Würzburg charged, to preach against the two supreme heads of Christendom, the pope and the Roman emperor. According to the bishop's informer, Böhm proclaimed that "the pope is nothing," or, to quote Dieter von Isenburg, "he perversely rejected the most eminent see of Peter and denied its sacred authority." One is reminded here of Pope Pius II's lament voiced just a few years before: "Pope and emperor are considered as empty titles and ornate figureheads." Böhm's assertion, "if the pope is godly at the hour of his death, he will go directly to heaven, else he will find himself in hell," alludes to the pope's shameful trafficking in ecclesiastical offices and benefices. It was clearly a linking of office and virtue which accepted no middle ground between right and wrong.[18]

Strictly speaking, Böhm's anticlericalism did not aim at Church doctrine, even though he denied the legitimacy of the priestly class in its contemporary form; instead, Böhm condemned Church politics, ecclesiastical privileges, and practices which had been responsible for numerous social inequalities. By challenging the power base of the pope and all ecclesiastics, he put an ax to the very roots of the feudal Church which, he implied, had betrayed the ideals of the early Church as exemplified by the Jerusalem community.

Böhm also rejected the secular authorities, including the temporal head of Christendom, the Roman emperor. "He holds little of the emperor," the bishop's informer advised his master. To Böhm the emperor was a man of evil, a *Bösewicht*, since it was he who granted to the lords the right to tax the common people and to exact all kinds of dues from the little man. The Archbishop of Mainz branded it a blasphemy to revile and undermine the majesty of the emperor, whom the Lord had placed over his people to reward the good and punish the wicked and whose decrees must be obeyed because they were prescribed by the law of God.[19]

Here, too, as in the case of the pope, hostility to the emperor was based on Böhm's conviction that only personal moral excellence could justify the holding of an office or the exercise of authority. Furthermore, the attack on pope and emperor implied a repudiation of the established social order.

Böhm not only repudiated the pope and emperor; he also condemned all ecclesiastical and secular lordships. He told his listeners, "The princes–ecclesiastical and secular–as well as the counts and knights have too much"; yet they demanded unjust dues and taxes from the little man. Therefore, pope, emperor, princes, counts, viscounts, knights, burghers, and the common people must become equals. "If the common people had what the lords have, then all of us would have enough." Böhm prophesied that the time would come when all people would secure their livelihood from the labor of their hands, "when princes and lords will have to work for their daily wages." The Virgin Mary had told him, "Henceforth there will be no more princes, emperor, or any spiritual or temporal lordships; they will be done away with, and everyone will be the brother of his fellow man."[20]

The Piper next proceeded to reject the exploitation of the common man by the authorities, both secular and ecclesiastical. He insisted "that hunting, fishing, the use of water and forest must be free for the use of every Christian: the poor as well as the rich, the peasant as well as the bishop or the prince." This also meant that "pastures and ponds should be free everywhere." Protesting against the expropriation of the village common and the ongoing exploitation of the peasant by the nobility, Böhm simply called for the restoration of the ancient–natural and "divine"–peasant rights, the so-called *Markrechte*.[21]

To attain such objectives, Böhm demanded that all ecclesiastical and secular lords–princes, counts, and squires–give up not only tithes and annual rents, but also all other customary payments and burdens exacted from the common people–"the poor devils," as he called them. He insisted that "all road moneys, tolls, boon-service, levies and aids given to prelates, princes, and nobles as well as all other burdens imposed on the poor must be completely abolished." The poor people must no longer pay rents, taxes, animals, and labor to the local lord or duties and tolls to the territorial lord.[22]

Böhm's teachings display a unique combination of religious, political, and social elements. Seeking to determine their provenance, historians have expressed the belief that Böhm stood on traditional Catholic grounds. According to Günther Franz, Böhm made no innovations and, had it not been for the stagnation of the Church, men like Böhm would have been canonized rather than declared heretics. Bernd Moeller pointed out that loyalty to the Church in the decades preceding the Reformation had reached a level unknown since the eleventh century, so that there were hardly any active sectarians in Germany. Wilhelm Zimmermann insisted that Böhm's religious fervor must not be associated with the Protestant Reformation. In Siegfried Hoyer's judgment, Böhm adhered to traditional ways; otherwise he would have alienated the predominantly orthodox masses. Even his social criticism remained free of restrictions common among sectarians.[23]

A closer look at Böhm's teachings, however, reveals definitely heterodox elements clearly opposed to standard Church doctrine and discipline. Dieter von Isenburg and Trithemius accused him of spreading numerous heretical teachings, and Böhm himself stated, "The priests say that I am a heretic." His disbelief in lesser sins meant a rejection of purgatory, just as his promise to rescue souls from hell and his insistence that an office depended on the personal merits of the office holder were contrary to traditional teaching. Such, also, was his rejection of the ministerial priesthood. His claim that a visit to Niklashausen would bring indulgence and forgiveness of sin was theologically untenable, while the attribution of apocalyptic expectations to the Virgin Mary was obviously heretical though not altogether uncommon, causing the Church to issue repeated prohibitions against excessive Marian devotions.[24]

Besides, Böhm, a layman, actually did perform clerical functions: he preached, absolved a number of persons from sin, and took it upon himself to act as a censor of human conduct. The Archbishop of Mainz charged that Böhm arrogated divine honors to himself when even the apostle Peter rebuffed Cornelius the centurion with the words, "I am only a man" (Acts 10:26). He also condemned Böhm's gift of prophecy as a presumptuous claim; no such grace had been given to the Virgin Mary and the saints.[25]

Böhm's teachings make him appear as an exponent of the Waldensian movement, since lay preaching had been a basic demand of Peter Waldo. The Waldensians denied the spiritual authority of the Church and its right to own property. They denounced the chasm that existed between the spiritual vocation of the clergy and its secular wealth and demanded a return to the poverty ideal of the early Church. They preached that tithes must be given to the poor and clerics must possess no more than what they needed from one meal to another. These Waldensian demands were prominent in Böhm's teaching; however, the Piper was not a Waldensian, for Marian devotion, pilgrimage, singing, and celebrating the mass had been anathema to the disciples of Peter Waldo.[26]

Trithemius claimed there were Hussite influences in the Piper's teachings. He warned that Böhm embraced the poisonous heresy of the Hussites by proclaiming that the clergy had no right to obligatory tithes and annual rents from the common people. John Huss had indeed written a treatise which called for the abolition of tithes in favor of pure alms. He also denied alternatives between virtue and vice and insisted that an office depended on merit. Therefore, no sinner could claim lordship, jurisdiction, or power over Christian people. Huss also rejected the papal office as a creation of imperial favor. He claimed that papal bulls and writings were unnecessary since the Bible sufficed in every respect, that obedience to ecclesiastics was an invention of the hierarchy, and that ecclesiastical jurisdiction was the product of clerical greed.[27]

The Hussites and the more radical Taborites advocated lay preaching and demanded freedom of water, pasture, and forest for the common man. They had nothing but hatred for the pope and emperor. The Taborite articles of 1430, exported to southern and southwestern Germany, sharply attacked the clergy for its avarice, pride, luxury, and idle living, again denying its right to compulsory tithes and the maintenance of an ecclesiastical jurisdiction. Priests were to do without temporal possessions and live according to the precepts of the Scriptures, following the example of Christ and the apostles.[28]

Even more radical were the demands of the Bohemian peasant Peter Chelčićky, who around 1440 called for a complete transformation of the existing social order. He criticized a society based on the rule of the estates–the clergy, the nobility, and the burghers–as a falsification of Christian ideals. He rejected every authority as the work of the anti-Christ and proposed radical changes: the old order, with emperor and pope, nobility, burghers, monks, universities, pastors, and all their institutional establishments, had to disappear and give way to a new society based exclusively on love–the love of God and Christ and of one's neighbor and enemy.[29]

In spite of these parallels between the Piper's teaching and the Bohemian articles, there is no documentary evidence of a direct Hussite influence on Hans Böhm, and the core and unifying element of Hussite teaching, the role of divine justice which gave the Hussite movement its supraregional significance, is totally absent in Böhm's utterances. Also, as in the case of the Waldensians, the Piper's Marianism and his retention of the mass, sacraments, and indulgences have no place in the Hussite movement, just as the Taborite call for total communism was far more radical than the Piper's social demands.

Nor was the Taborite demand for freedom of water, pasture, and forest a Hussite import to Germany, for complaints against the appropriation of the village common by the lords had been voiced in the law books of the thirteenth century, and protests against the nobility's attempt to further curtail the peasants' rights had been reiterated during the periodic peasant riots of the fifteenth century.[30] The exploitation of the peasants and their scandalous lack of freedom was similarly criticized by the *Reformatio Sigismundi*, a comprehensive reform program composed by an anonymous author of the late 1430's, probably associated with the council of Basel, which called for the restoration of commonage and the abolition of feudal burdens. This work was first published in 1476, the very year of Böhm's preaching, and reissued many times in later decades. Böhm, who envisioned a classless society, was seemingly unfamiliar with and therefore not influenced by this conservative document which strove to build on the existing social order.[31]

Finally, Böhm's vision of brotherhood and equality–the ideal of having all things in common and the demand that one must earn his living through personal labor–was inspired by none of the above sources, but by the desire to return to the ideal world of the early Christians as epitomized in the Acts of the Apostles. Of course, the Piper as an illiterate could not draw directly from the Scriptures. His "biblicism" was a simplified and uncomplicated understanding of the Bible which underscored his practical demands as they related to the situation of the little man, particularly those involving the overriding questions of poverty.[32]

If Böhm's teachings have not yet been properly classified, this must not be attributed to their diverse components but to historians who tended to follow and repeat the narratives of chroniclers on a rather selective basis. Historians often failed to see that there is a certain logic in Böhm's utterances: his religious, economic, social, and political concerns are singularly and consistently antifeudal in their condemnation of the temporal and spiritual establishment.

It is hardly surprising that the greater part of Böhm's recorded words dealt with his anticlericalism if one realizes that the persons who wrote down his teachings were without exception ecclesiastics. The "political" authorities attacked by Böhm were likewise ecclesiastics: for instance, the Bishop of Würzburg was also prince of Franconia, Dieter von Isenburg was the elector of Mainz, and the bishops of Speyer, Bamberg, and Eichstätt in the immediate neighborhood of Niklashausen were territorial lords. The social and political criticism that Böhm leveled against these rulers was not simply an expression of his anticlericalism but a direct attack on the feudal establishment.

Böhm's anticlerical utterances were aimed at the clergy as a privileged class maintaining itself by means of its spiritual and temporal power. Clerical prejudice, estate consciousness, and the exclusion or restriction of the layman and of the layman's freedom caused him to issue a general condemnation of the clergy. Böhm justified his actions from his divine mission, though anticlericalism had been nothing new in Germany given the long history of oppressive taxation which generated a growing resentment, especially when these payments landed in the pockets of a territorial lord who was also a hierarch of the Church.

A case in point was the diocese of Würzburg where, as a result of long mismanagement, taxes remained so high that in 1476, the year of Böhm's preaching, an episcopal official compared the peasants' lot to a heavily loaded wagon drawn by four horses. "Put a single egg on top of it, and the horses will no longer be able to pull the wagon."[33]

Intimately connected with Böhm's anticlericalism was his exaltation of the layman's role in a world dominated by the clergy. Böhm claimed to have been favored with visions and given a public mission. While calling for the abolition of all clerical privileges, he himself had no hesitation to preach, give orders to pilgrims, and perform priestly functions. As John Huss had proclaimed several decades before, God had "hidden the way of truth from the wise and prudent and revealed it to the layman." In Böhm the distinction between layman and priest yielded to the distinction between the saved and the damned; he preferred the dictates of the individual's conscience to the decisions of the clergy and the court of Rome.[34]

The economic and social demands of the Piper called for the restoration of peasant rights and liberties: the re-establishment of the village commons and freedom from all burdensome payments owed to Church and secular authorities. Serfdom, of course, hardly existed at this time in southern Germany–Böhm never mentioned it in his sermons–and the gifts left at the shrine of Niklashausen were actually indications of peasant wealth. But, as Henri Pirenne observed, the medieval peasants became more demanding precisely after they succeeded in making some initial gains in the improvement of their situation. In the second half of the fifteenth century, when the nobility felt strong enough to mount an offensive against the peasants in southern and southwestern Germany, the peasants protested more than they had done before. But while earlier protests–always local affairs–listed only particular grievances, Böhm launched a general attack against the ruling classes and the economic and social foundations of their power and rule. He echoed what John Ball had said in 1381, "Things cannot go well . . . nor will they, until all goods shall be in common."[35]

In its political implications, Böhm's teaching would have done away with the traditional division of medieval society–the nobility, the clergy, and the peasantry–and made equals of the three. The clergy he would have exterminated; the nobility he sought to reduce to the level of the working man. Thus there was to be no distinction between cleric, nobleman, and peasant, nor even between cleric and layman, but all were to become brothers and sisters. Again, as John Ball had announced before, things will go well only "when there shall be neither villeins nor gentles, but we shall all be one."[36]

Böhm's personality and the contents of his preaching drew crowds of very diverse social backgrounds. Most numerous were, of course, the peasants whose cause he espoused.[37] A second group included city dwellers, as can be gathered from the fact that the authorities of Nuremberg, Heidingsfeld, and Würzburg found it necessary to prohibit the pilgrimage.[38] Stolle also mentions that "ehrbare Leute," or members of the nobility, were among Böhm's supporters. In this category belong Kuntz von Thunfeld and his son Michael, who led the pilgrims' march to Würzburg; two lords of the von Stetten family and one of the Vestenbergs; and the Count of Wertheim, who allowed the Niklashausen pilgrimage to continue long after Böhm's death.[39]

The clergy viewed Böhm as a heretic and understandably stayed aloof from him. According to the informer, Böhm charged that even if a priest would come to hear him and give credence to his words, two or three others will fall upon him before he got home and so fill his ears that he would be worse than before. The only exception, at least at the beginning, was the local pastor and a certain Beghard who lived in a nearby cave and preached at Niklashausen repeating the errors of Böhm.[40]

Looking for other possible partisans not mentioned by the sources, Will-Erich Peuckert investigated the relationship between the Piper and the Humanists. He concluded that the older generation of Humanists, typified by the *doctores* of the University of Ingolstadt and consulted by Ludwig the Rich, Duke of Bavaria, before he prohibited the pilgrimage, remained in opposition to Böhm because they cherished different ideals. Nevertheless, Peuckert suggested that Böhm was related to the reform advocates who followed the *Reformatio Sigismundi*, for both envisioned a *reformatio Germaniae*, a rebirth willed by God, that was to proceed from the lower classes.[41]

Recently Carlheinz Gräter proposed, though did not prove, that Böhm attracted enthusiasts and wandering scholars. Today they would be called anarchists or disgruntled intellectuals who were acquainted with the revolutionary literature, pamphlets, and slogans of the time. As soon as Böhm finished his sermons, these extremist elements engaged in lively discussions in the local tavern. In Gräter's view, they infected the Piper, originally a visionary and penitential preacher, with the radical views that became so pronounced in Böhm's later preaching.[42]

Böhm was the first person to express, in a language clearly understandable to the little man, what ailed the contemporary world. He went beyond local issues which, as a rule, had prevailed in all previous protest movements and attacked the entire feudal system. This explains why the Niklashausen pilgrimage was the most radical and widespread of all popular movements in Germany prior to the great Peasant War during the Reformation.[43]

The pilgrimage, "the like of which has never been seen or heard of or survived in the memory of men, began eight days before Walburga's Day [May 1] and went on for a total of twelve weeks."[44] First came the peasants of the area; then the radius widened to include pilgrims from Franconia, Bavaria, Swabia, the Alsace and the Rhineland, the Wetterau, Hesse, Fulda, Saxony, and Meissen. "And the astonishing thing was,"–Fries remarked,–"that apprentices ran away from their workshops, farmhands from the plow, the hay-makers from their sickles and scythes, always without the permission of their masters. They left tools, plows, baskets, and all else behind and proceeded to Niklashausen in the clothes in which this madness had seized them. Many of them had nothing to eat, but the people who gave them shelter on the way provided them also with food and drink. And they greeted one another as *brother* and *sister*."[45]

The pilgrims–men, women, and children of every age–arrived by the thousands, usually on weekends. Trithemius estimated their number as ranging between ten thousand and thirty thousand people, while Stolle recalled that approximately seventy thousand pilgrims had gathered on a certain weekend–not an altogether exaggerated number since Böhm ordinarily concluded his sermons by calling on his listeners to return twice as numerously on the following weekend.[46]

To accommodate the great crowds, tents and stations were set up around the village where the pilgrims were offered food and drink. Some of the pilgrims soon felt the effects of the Tauber wine, because the grape harvest had been excellent in the previous year. Those who had come from a distance stayed overnight, sleeping in barns, tents, or open fields and wooded areas. Given the proximity of the sexes, "things were not entirely up to par," Widmann recalled or, as Trithemius put it, "there was a great deal of license."[47]

Böhm wore rough clothes and a cheap cap with tufts and held a staff in his hand, possibly in imitation of the Old Testament prophets. The crowds always followed him; to them he was a saint, a prophet, and a teacher of the truth whom God and the Virgin Mary had so manifestly preferred over all other mortals. They sought to meet, hear, or touch him and kiss his outstretched arm or his staff. They fell on their knees before Böhm, imploring his prayer and mercy with folded hands, and if he made a sign of the cross in their direction they felt themselves truly blessed and absolved from their sins.

Everyone who came close to Böhm sought to secure a piece of his clothing, and whoever obtained the smallest shred felt to be in the possession of a sacred relic. Pregnant women kept such shreds to have a safe delivery. Soon miracles were reported by individuals who managed to touch the Piper. People believed that pieces of his clothing had the power to cure ills and ease pain. Some pilgrims were convinced that they had been miraculously cured from illness at Niklashausen. Others reported cures and miracles in the neighborhood which they attributed to the power of the prophet.

Externally, the pilgrimage differed little from other contemporary pilgrimages both before and after 1476. The pilgrims carried flags, banners, and candles and sang their pilgrim songs. Every village brought a large candle carried by three or four men, while individual pilgrims left coins from as far as Innsbruck, clothing, gold, silver, jewels, candles, and other offerings at the shrine. Filled with a penitential zeal, the pilgrims cut off their pigtails; and they discarded shoes, embroidered handkerchiefs, robes, doublets, and similar male or female vanities. It seemed as though a multitude of carts would not suffice to haul away and burn these superfluities in a bonfire. Some men and women even took off all their clothes and walked away naked except for their shifts.[48]

At first the authorities voiced no objection to the pilgrimage because it began in honor of the Virgin Mary, and they themselves benefited from it in more than one way. Unconcerned about the pilgrimage's theological aspects, the Count of Wertheim, for instance, allowed it even in late September, long after the ecclesiastical authorities had decided otherwise.[49]

Things changed after a few weeks. Alerted by the Bishop of Würzburg, the Archbishop of Mainz found it necessary to take corrective measures as early as June 13. "Detained by various labors," he delegated the Bishop of Würzburg to take the appropriate steps to stop Böhm's unauthorized preaching, determine the source of his errors, and suppress them in Böhm as well as in his followers. The bishop was to make sure that "nothing contrary to canonical discipline or unworthy of the Christian religion and the clerical order was preached, stated, or allowed to take place" at Niklashausen.[50]

Even more stringent measures were taken by the secular authorities. After June 12, the cities of Nuremberg, Heidingsfeld, and Würzburg proscribed the pilgrimage under penalty, and within a few weeks the rulers of Franconia, Bavaria, the Palatinate, and, in all likelihood, Saxony issued similar prohibitions in their respective territories.[51]

The prime mover in the prohibition, the Bishop of Würzburg, addressed a number of letters to the authorities affected by the pilgrimage in order to solicit their cooperation. He argued that Böhm spread heresy, challenged the established Christian order, and attracted and deceived the always ignorant and credulous simple people, instilling in them nefarious designs. Furthermore, it was harvest time and people had to provide for their families. He warned that all these evils must be stopped before they caused considerable harm.[52]

The Duke of Bavaria consulted the *doctores* of sacred scripture and the two laws at the University of Ingolstadt before he prohibited the pilgrimage. He explained that "the Piper teaches and preaches items and articles that are contrary to the teachings of the holy Church, the sacred scriptures, and canon law." Frederick, Count of the Palatinate, proscribed the pilgrimage after it had become clear to him "that it is a deception and the people were not to be misled and allowed to flock there." Typical was the prohibition issued for the city of Würzburg: "No one shall journey or march to Niklashausen either alone or in a group, speak or chant the contemptible songs of this pilgrimage, or offer entry, passage, shelter, food, or drink to the pilgrims under penalty of *Leib und Gut* [imprisonment and confiscation of goods]."[53]

At the end of June the authorities decided in Aschaffenburg that Böhm must be seized and duly examined, and his teachings condemned. If he escaped capture, the two bishops involved would inform their clergy that no one was to associate with Böhm, eat or drink with him, listen to or give credence to his teachings, or chant the songs and cantilenas composed by him, under pain of excommunication. Furthermore, on July 2, the feast of the Visitation, notaries and witnesses were to be dispatched to Niklashausen to secretly record Böhm's teaching and have it notarized with due care.[54]

Evidently in response to the Aschaffenburg meeting, Böhm told his audience on Sunday, July 7, "let all the men return with their arms on the following Saturday, St. Margaret's Day, toward evening, – the women and the children were to stay at home – for he would reveal to them three words on the Virgin's command." Upon their arrival he would tell them "what Our Lady had in mind for them to do." Since Saturday, July 13, was also a feast day, many more pilgrims could be expected on account of the double holiday.[55]

The Bishop of Würzburg realized "that considerable harm could result from the matter if it is tolerated any longer and all those people are allowed to assemble with their arms." He concluded, "It will be much better to take preventive measures in time." He became apprehensive "that his fears could become a reality before his very eyes." Concerned about "the restless peasants and their Gospel," he decided not to wait until the following Saturday. With the concurrence of his counselors he dispatched a squadron of thirty-four horsemen to Niklashausen. They arrested the surprised preacher and took him to the Frauenberg, the bishop's castle at Würzburg, during the night of July 12.[56]

In Fries' version the knights captured the sleeping Piper and brought him to Würzburg on the same night. According to Stolle, however, "when Hans Böhm was taken prisoner, he was sitting naked in the tavern, preaching strange things to the people." This caused Norman Cohn, a foremost student of medieval millenarianism, to comment, "Was *that* not the very way in which the Bohemian Adamites had represented, symbolically, the return of the State of Nature to a corrupted world?"[57]

On the next day, some 34,000 men had assembled in answer to Böhm's request made on the preceding weekend, but many decided to return home after learning of their prophet's arrest. The others, approximately 16,000, were told by a peasant who claimed to have had a vision of the Holy Trinity that they "must proceed with their arms and candles to the Castle in Würzburg and free the holy youth, for its doors will simply open to them" as, one could add, the walls of Jericho had tumbled down in Old Testament days.

They set out for Würzburg on Saturday evening "with four hundred burning candles and their primitive weapons." Eventually Kuntz von

Thunfeld, his son Michael, and "several peasants" took over the leadership. Arriving at the castle in the morning, they tried to reclaim their prophet; but their negotiations with the episcopal marshal failed. The bishop's second envoy, the popular Konrad von Hutten, then reminded them that they were in no position to take the castle by force since they had no explosives or siege machinery. He indicated that the bishop would not release the Piper but would "punish him for his deeds, as was right." A few warning shots from the castle sufficed to sober and disperse the largely unarmed crowd and thereby break the spell of the expected miracle. The peasants' attempt to free the Piper collapsed when the Virgin failed to intervene on his behalf.[58]

While in prison Hans Böhm was tortured, as had been allowed by Pope Innocent IV. He made a full confession which repudiated his prophecies and the miracles associated with the pilgrimage. Böhm also described the devices used to revive the pilgrimage and named his accomplices, who included the local parish priest and the Beghard. His judges found "that the whole affair, devoid of true signs, was a deception, an empty scheme to mislead the people and procure money." They condemned Böhm after a few days and charged him with heresy, "because he attempted to stain and pervert the sacred orthodox and catholic faith of the Christians with his errors and because he exerted himself to spread these errors." The charge mandated death by burning, as a warning to others.

The sentence was carried out on Friday, July 19, on the Schottenanger, an open field behind the monastery of St. James. It was watched by nearly all the citizens of Würzburg, some of them sympathizers. Böhm loudly chanted German Marian songs until the smoke choked his voice. The executioner immediately threw his ashes into the Main River, "lest the frivolous devotion of the foolish populace make the place into a martyr's shrine."[59]

Böhm certainly hoped that his teaching would be implemented, for he repeatedly stated that this "will actually happen." Moreover, as Trithemius reported, "a multitude of simple and ignorant people gathered each day and discussed but one thing: how to carry out the injunctions of the often-mentioned Johnny." Yet the Piper did not offer any details. In spite of this, Alfred Meusel suggested that Böhm actually planned an armed uprising. He told his listeners to return with their arms, promised to tell them three words—"auf nach Würzburg," according to Meusel–and allied himself with Kuntz von Thunfeld and others who were to become the military leaders of his movement.[60]

Most historians, however, reject this interpretation for a number of compelling reasons. First of all, the informer who recorded Böhm's words on July 2 made no mention of such a call, nor did the knowledgeable *Rats-Chronik* of Würzburg state anything of the kind. And the march to Würzburg on the night of July 13 was by all accounts a spontaneous act which began only after a peasant claimed a vision of the Trinity, an indication that the nobles did not have charge of the masses at the outset. Also, if the peasants had been summoned for an armed uprising, they would have left the four hundred candles at the shrine and proceeded with more powerful weapons to the Frauenberg. "Madness overcame them all," Trithemius explained, "from the first to the last, for they firmly believed that the walls of the castle would immediately collapse once, approaching it, they invoked the name of their adolescent."[61]

Because the bishop's horsemen silenced Böhm before he could reveal the meaning of the three words, it is difficult to prove the existence of a conspiracy or to surmise the plan of an armed insurrection. But the significant thing is that the Piper's arrest caused no uprising or unrest anywhere else in the German lands.

The discrepancy between the Drummer's attested illiteracy and his ability to draw great crowds raises the additional question of whether he had allies or was manipulated by people who remained in the background. In the account of the Archbishop of Mainz, the pilgrimage was started "by the adolescent and some associates." According to Fries, "at his– Böhm's– side stood usually the parish priest who whispered things in his ear."[62] The local pastor was certainly a Böhm supporter, if only to revive the stagnant pilgrimage which netted him considerable material advantages. After his arrest, the pastor confessed that "he had lights set up in the rectory and in the church of Niklashausen during the night, in the hope that this would be seen in the darkness and bring about the pilgrimage to that place." He also admitted that "he publicly proclaimed the signs and miracles [attributed to Böhm] as if they had been true and had actually happened."[63]

Trithemius claimed there was another accomplice: "It is reported that a few times a certain friar, a fugitive monk, whispered to him what to preach; therefore, he often addressed the people from a window so as to have his instructor nearby, close to his ear, without being discovered." The ordinance of Aschaffenburg which decreed Böhm's arrest also spoke of a "preacher, a Beghard friar, who was preaching at Niklashausen, repeating the errors of Hans Böhm." This Beghard is certainly identical with the mendicant mentioned by Trithemius. The latter also reported, "When interrogated and put to the torture, he–Böhm–admitted that all his utterances were fictions, falsehoods, and lies, and then freely confessed in a loud voice that the already mentioned fugitive mendicant and turncoat had concocted the whole thing."[64]

Stolle explained that Böhm "had been taught and prompted by three noblemen, surely bad Christians and heretics, and by the local priest, for the sake of money and other advantages of the kind." These individuals launched Böhm on his preaching career, told him what to preach and later prevailed on him to disregard the ecclesiastical prohibition, "for they kept the money and the gifts left by the pilgrims." When they learned about the Drummer's arrest, "they became angry, bound themselves by an oath and attracted many people to their side." Kilian von Bibra, an official of the cathedral chapter in Würzburg, actually named four noblemen who joined the expedition that tried to free the imprisoned prophet. On the basis of this evidence, Will-Erich Peuckert characterized the Piper as a mere tool, manipulated by several noblemen for the sake of money.[65]

Yet the question of possible mentors cannot be resolved that easily. In his captivity the pastor confessed only that he promoted the pilgrimage and exploited the purported miracles even though he had no certainty about their authenticity. And all the investigators were able to extract from the friar was that things had been done which tended "to divide and confuse the common people." The noblemen and the pastor could hardly have been the men who pulled the strings, for they could not benefit from Böhm's invectives against the clergy or his call for the abolition of all feudal privileges.[66]

Moreover, if things happened for the sake of money, or if the Piper had been a mere tool in the hands of shrewder men, the peasants of the neighborhood who knew their Johnny and their pastor would not have allowed themselves to be deceived and misled for twelve weeks. They would have recognized the deception. Also, when the noblemen managed to escape after the futile attempt to rescue the Piper, the authorities showed no immediate interest in them at first, while they quickly burned Böhm as a heretic. Finally, one could argue that his teachings, drawn from greatly diverse sources, provide the best proof that he was not beholden to others.

There is no proof in support of the claim that the Piper was the tool of a special interest group. Böhm had no manipulators, only ideological friends standing at his side. The exclusive claim of the higher estates to education notwithstanding, the shepherd was quite capable of drawing his own conclusions about the necessary remedies to the oppressive feudal system. A member of the country proletariat and a shepherd on the village common which was no longer common property, he had been only too familiar with the needs of the peasants and the plight of the little man.[67]

Though Böhm had been silenced by the authorities, ideas voiced by him resurfaced in later popular and peasant movements, especially the great Peasant War of 1525. This, however, does not prove the existence of a direct link between the Piper and the Peasant War. Böhm relied on visions; rejected the pope, the emperor, and every lordship; and called for equal possessions. The leaders of the Peasant War, on the other hand, relied on the Bible and political justice, recognized the imperial and other authorities, and called for equal rights. Thus it is not surprising that the Franconian peasant leaders and the radicals of the Tauber Valley made no attempt in 1525 to recall the memory of Hans Böhm or that the intervening protest literature had kept total silence about the youthful peasant leader of 1476.[68] Therefore, all one can say about the latter is that, in a world which increasingly reached crisis proportions for the common man in Germany, Hans Böhm, the popular leader, effectively proclaimed the multitudinous concerns of his age and offered a simply stated but comprehensive reform program. Since all the expressions of discontent had religious overtones, religion served as an important vehicle for Böhm's movement.[69]

Böhm's death and the destruction of the church of Niklashausen on January 2, 1477, ended the first great popular movement in Germany.[70] No one took up Böhm's cause. The reason for all this was simple: the whole Böhm affair was basically a one-man crusade. Böhm had no organization, and his followers retained their diverse motivations, unable to form a united front against Böhm's chief target, the feudal establishment. Also, while Böhm proposed actions and remedies, he did not or could not implement them, for he lacked the means and resources.[71] And he allowed himself to be maneuvered into a web of contradictions and conflicting interests from which he was unable to disengage himself.[72]

Yet Böhm must not be dismissed as a failure, and the historians' verdict which saw him as a fraud or a simpleton deceived by others is no longer tenable. Leaving all the heterogeneous elements of the Böhm case aside, one must still admit that the Piper was a genuine champion of the little man: he talked to him, revealed his grievances, pinpointed the source of contemporary evils, and offered comprehensive and credible, if not altogether realistic, remedies.

Compared with other popular movements of the fifteenth century, Böhm's significance was that he overcame local particularism and was able to bring about an antifeudal mass movement. In this respect he outdid all the *Bundschuh* movements of the following decades. He proved that the *sermon*, which was the only instrument available to enlighten the simple man and which the clergy had wisely reserved to itself in spite of numerous protests by religious dissenters, could be successfully employed to organize a mass movement. Of course, a well-entrenched establishment could not be overturned by a single onslaught; that would be the task of future popular leaders and reformers. In 1476 the path to reform was not to be won by social insurrection, but Böhm took a positive step by bringing issues into the open. It would be simplistic to say that he was merely a dreamer.[73]

NOTES

1. Günter Franz, *Der deutsche Bauernkrieg* (Darmstadt: Hermann Gentner Verlag, 1956), pp. 46 ff. Johannes von Walter, *Die Geschichte des Christentums*, 2 vols.; vol 2: *Die Reformation* (Gütersloh: C. Bertelsmann Verlag, 1949), part 2, p. 71. See also Norman Cohn, *The Pursuit of the Millennium*, rev. ed. (New York: Oxford University Press, 1972), pp. 225–226; Siegfried Hoyer, "Hans Böhm– der revolutionäre Prediger von Niklashausen," *Zeitschrift für Geschichtswissenschaft* 18 (1975): 185–186; and Bernd Moeller, *Bauernkriegstudien*,

Schriften des Vereins fur Reformationsgeschichte, 189 (Gütersloh: Gerd Mohr, 1975), pp. 11–25.

2. Heinrich W. Bensen, *Geschichte des Bauernkrieges in Ostfranken* (Erlangen: Palm Verlag, 1840), pp. 192–193; Sigmund von Pölnitz, "Rudolf von Scherenberg: Ein Bischöflicher Reformer von der Reformation," *Zeitschrift für Bayerische Kirchengeschicte* 15 (1940): 42 ff. See also Franz, *Der deutsche Bauernkrieg*, p. 46; Cohn, *Pursuit of the Millennium*, pp. 225–226; Carlheinz Gräter, *Der Bauernkrieg in Franken* (Würzburg: Sturz, 1975), p. 19; Moeller, *Bauernkriegstudien*, pp. 11, 19, 21, 25; and Wilhelm Zimmermann, *Allgemeine Geschichte des grossen Bauernkrieges* (Stuttgart: Franz H. Kohler, 1841–1843), 1:117–118. For information on Jews and clergy in medieval cities, see Edith Ennen, *Die europäische Stadt des Mittelalters* (Göttingen: Vandenhoeck & Ruprecht, 1972), pp. 212 ff.

3. Franz, *Der deutsche Bauernkrieg*, p. 46. See also Margaret Aston, *The Fifteenth Century: The Prospect of Europe* (New York: Harcourt, Brace & World, 1968), p. 145; Cohn, *Pursuit of the Millennium*, pp. 212–213, 225; and Josef Lortz, *Die Reformation in Deutschland* (Freiburg i. B.: Herder, 1949), 1:100, 103–104. On pilgrimages, see Eberhard Gothein, *Reformation und Gegenreformation: Politische und religiöse Volksbewegungen von der Reformation* (München: Duncker & Humblot, 1924), pp. 11, 21; Hoyer, "Hans Böheim," p. 186; and Will-Erich Peuckert, *Die grosse Wende* (Darmstadt: Wissenschaftliche Buchgemeinschaft, 1966), 1:273–274. Peuckert also explains the complexities of the question of indulgences (pp. 275–276).

4. Karl A. Barack, *Hans Böhm und die Wallfahrt nach Niklashausen im Jahre 1476: Ein Vorspiel des grossen Bauernkrieges*, Archiv des Historischen Vereins von Unterfranken, 14, no. 3 (Würzburg: Friedrich Ernst von Thein, 1858), pp. 50, 107; Gothein, *Reformation*, pp. 10–11; Peuckert, *Die grosse Wende*, p. 263. The pilgrimage had greatly declined by the 1470's (Barack, *Hans Böhm*, pp. 55–56). On Niklashausen's history after 1476, see Gräter, *Der Bauernkrieg*, pp. 9, 14.

5. Georg Widmann, *Chronika*, Württembergische Geschichtsquellen, 6 (Stuttgart, 1904), p. 216; English translation in Gerald Strauss, ed., "Religious and Social Upheaval: The Drummer of

Niklashausen (1476)," in *Manifestations of Discontent in Germany on the Eve of the Reformation* (Bloomington: Indiana University Press, 1971), pp. 218–222. See also Barack, *Hans Böhm*, p. 59; Lorenz Fries, *Historie der Bischöfe zu Würzburg (1544)*, ed. Johann Peter Ludewig, Geschichtsschreiber von dem Bischofftum Wirzburg (Frankfurt: bey Thomas Fritschen, 1713), p. 852; Konrad Stolle, *Memoriale thüringisch-erfurtische Chronik*, ed. Richard Thiele, Geschichtsquellen der Provinz Sachsen, 39 (Halle, 1900), p. 380; Joannes Trithemius, *Annales Hirsaugienses* (St. Gallen, 1690), 2:486, and *Chronicon Spanheimense* (Frankfurt, 1601), p. 389. On Böhm's "conversion," see Cohn, *Pursuit of the Millennium*, pp. 226–227; Franz, *Der deutsche Bauernkrieg*, pp. 46, 49; Gothein, *Reformation*, pp. 12–13; Hoyer, "Hans Böheim," p. 190; and Peuckert, *Die grosse Wende*, pp. 263–264.

6. Above, n. 5, and Barack, *Hans Böhm*, pp. 97–98. See also Willy Andreas, *Deutschland von der Reformation: Eine Zeitwende* (Stuttgart: Deutsche Verlag-Anstalt, 1959), p. 174; Ernest B. Bax, *German Society at the Close of the Middle Ages* (London: Swan Sonnenschein & Co., 1894), p. 44; Franz, *Der deutsche Bauernkrieg*, p. 49; Gordon Leff, *Heresy in the Later Middle Ages* (New York: Barnes & Noble, 1967), 2:474; Alfred Meusel, *Thomas Müntzer und seine Zeit* (Berlin: Aufbau-Verlag, 1952), p. 185; Peuckert, *Die grosse Wende*, pp. 264, 275–276; and Zimmermann, *Allgemeine Geschichte*, p. 119.

7. Barack, *Hans Böhm*, pp. 50–108; Trithemius, *Annales*, p. 486; Fries, *Historie*, pp. 852 ff.; *Die Rats-Chronik der Stadt Würzburg*, ed. Wilhelm Engel (Würzburg: Ferdinand Schöningh, 1950), pp. 7 ff.; Stolle, *Memoriale*, pp. 379 ff.; Widmann, *Chronika*, p. 216; and Friedrich A. Reuss, "Die Wallfahrt nach Niklashausen im Jahre 1476," *Archiv des Historischen Vereins von Unterfranken* 10, no. 2 (1850): 305–318. See also Gustav A. Benrath, *Wegbereiter der Reformation*, Klassiker des Protestantismus, 1 (Bremen: Carl Schünemann Verlag, 1967), p. 236; Gothein, *Reformation*, p. 6; Gräter, *Der Bauernkrieg*, pp. 11, 14; Hoyer, "Hans Böheim," p. 185; Josef Kartels, *Lorenz Fries der fränkische Geschichtsschreiber und seine Chronik* (Würzburg: Bonitas Bauer, 1899), p. 17; Peuckert, *Die grosse*

Wende, pp. 271–272; and Carl Ullmann, *Reformatoren von der Reformation* (Hamburg: Friedrich Perthes, 1866), p. 424.

8. Barack, *Hans Böhm*, pp. 71, 98; *Rats-Chronik*, p. 38; Reuss, "Die Wallfahrt," p. 301; Stolle, *Memoriale*, pp. 380–381; Trithemius, *Annales*, pp. 485–489; and Widmann, *Chronika*, p. 216. See also Franz, *Der deutsche Bauernkrieg*, p. 48; Gothein, *Reformation*, pp. 10, 15; Hoyer, "Hans Böheim," pp. 186–187, 190; and Peuckert, *Die grosse Wende*, pp. 263, 267, 291.

9. Böhm, portrayed by most of the sources as a tool of certain ecclesiastics or noblemen, actually preached against the clergy and the nobility; see below, n. 67, and Hoyer, "Hans Böheim," pp. 186–187. See also Barack, *Hans Böhm*, p. 62; Trithemius, *Annales*, pp. 486–487; and Widmann, *Chronika*, p. 219.

10. Barack, *Hans Böhm*, p. 53; Fries, *Historie*, p. 852; Stolle, *Memoriale*, p. 381. See also Andreas Bigelmair, "Böhm, Hans," *Lexikon für Theologie und Kirche* 2 (1958): 559.

11. Barack, *Hans Böhm*, pp. 53–54, 66–72, 77–79, 85–87, 97–100; Fries, *Historie*, p. 852; Trithemius, *Annales*, pp. 487–488.

12. Reuss, "Die Wallfahrt," p. 301; Trithemius, *Annales*, p. 487.

13. Barack, *Hans Böhm*, pp. 53–54, 75, 98–99; Fries, *Historie*, p. 853; Stolle, *Memoriale*, p. 380; Trithemius, *Annales*, pp. 487–488, and *Chronicon*, p. 390; Widmann, *Chronika*, pp. 216–217. See also Cohn, *Pursuit of the Millennium*, p. 228; and Hoyer, "Hans Böheim," p. 190.

14. Trithemius, *Annales*, p. 488, and *Chronicon*, p. 390; and Cohn, *Pursuit of the Millennium*, p. 228.

15. Barack, *Hans Böhm*, pp. 53–54, 98–99; Trithemius, *Annales*, p. 488, and *Chronicon*, p. 390. Luther held similar views on the subject; see *Martin Luther: Selections from His Writings*, ed. John Dillenberger (Garden City, N.Y.: Doubleday, 1961), pp. 436, 453. Böhm's condemnation was certainly affected by the fact that churchmen enforcing their rights as territorial lords threatened the peasants with spiritual weapons to ensure prompt payments (see von Walter, *Die Reformation*, p. 71).

16. Stolle, *Memoriale*, pp. 380–381. See also Barack, *Hans Böhm*, pp. 53–54; Cohn, *Pursuit of the Millennium*, pp. 227–228; and Franz, *Der deutsche Bauernkrieg*, pp. 45–46.

17. Barack, *Hans Böhm*, pp. 62, 72; Widmann, *Chronika*, p. 219. For

other anticlerical songs, see Trithemius, *Annales*, pp. 589 ff.; and Franz, *Der deutsche Bauernkrieg*, pp. 46. See also Andreas, *Deutschland vor der Reformation*, p. 175.

18. Barack, *Hans Böhm*, pp. 53, 98, and 67, 69, 71, 81. See also Aston, *The Fifteenth Century*, p. 142; Hoyer, "Hans Böheim," p. 190; and Peuckert, *Die grosse Wende*, p. 282.

19. Barack, *Hans Böhm*, pp. 99, 53–54 (informer), and 81 (Rudolf von Scherenberg). See also Cohn, *Pursuit of the Millennium*, p. 228; Franz, *Der deutsche Bauernkrieg*, p. 50; and Peuckert, *Die grosse Wende*, pp. 282–285.

20. Fries, *Historie*, p. 852. See also Barack, *Hans Böhm*, pp. 53–54, 66–67, 81; Stolle, *Memoriale*, p. 380; Trithemius, *Annales*, pp. 487–488, and *Chronicon*, p. 390.

21. Barack, *Hans Böhm*, p. 53; Fries, *Historie*, p. 853; Trithemius, *Annales*, p. 488, and *Chronicon*, p. 390; and Widmann, *Chronika*, p. 216. See also Andreas, *Deutschland von der Reformation*, pp. 399 ff.; Bax, *German Society*, p. 46; Cohn, *Pursuit of the Millennium*, p. 228; Franz, *Der deutsche Bauernkrieg*, pp. 48, 51; Gothein, *Reformation*, pp. 10–11; Gräter, *Der Bauernkrieg*, p. 9; Hoyer, "Hans Böheim," pp. 185, 192, 195; Albert Mirgeler, *Geschichte Europas* (Freiberg, i. B.: Herder, 1958), pp. 148–149; Adolf Waas, *Bauern im Kampf um Gerechtigkeit, 1300–1525* (München: Verlag D. W. Callwey, 1964), pp. 5 ff.; and von Walter, *Die Reformation*, pp. 69–72.

22. Fries, *Historie*, p. 852; Trithemius, *Annales*, pp. 487–488, and *Chronicon*, p. 390; and Widmann, *Chronika*, p. 216. See also Andreas, *Deutschland vor der Reformation*, pp. 414–415; Franz, *Der deutsche Bauernkrieg*, p. 50; and Peuckert, *Die grosse Wende*, pp. 282–283.

23. Franz, *Der deutsche Bauernkrieg*, pp. 48, 50; Hoyer, "Hans Böheim," p. 190; Moeller, *Bauernkriegstudien*, pp. 21–22; and Zimmermann, *Allgemeine Geschichte*, p. 118. According to von Walter, it would be totally wrong to speak of a relaxation or disintegration of the traditional–sacramental and moralizing–piety during the late-medieval period (*Die Reformation*, p. 72). And Friedrich Engels insisted that Böhm's "plebeian and proletarian asceticism differs . . . from the bourgeois asceticism of the Lutheran burgher morality and of the English Puritans"

(*The Peasant War in Germany* [Moscow: Foreign Languages Publishing House, 1956], p. 79).

24. Barack, *Hans Böhm*, pp. 53, 56, 97–99; Stolle, *Memoriale*, p. 380; Trithemius, *Annales*, pp. 486–487, and *Chronicon*, p. 390. See also Hoyer, "Hans Böheim," p. 190. In a breve issued on February 7, 1478, Pope Sixtus IV praised the Bishop of Würzburg for his fight against seditious heresy (Barack, *Hans Böhm*, p. 106).

25. Barack, *Hans Böhm*, pp. 98–99, and 56, 76. Gothein, who believed Dieter von Isenburg made only *pro forma* charges against Böhm (*Reformation*, p. 19). He was obviously unfamiliar with the finer theological points.

26. Franz, *Der deutsche Bauernkrieg*, pp. 46, 48, 50–51; and Hoyer, "Hans Böheim," pp. 190–193. On the Waldensians, see Benrath, *Wegbereiter der Reformation*, pp. 1–24; and Leff, *Heresy*, pp. 452 ff.

27. Trithemius, *Annales*, pp. 487–488; Benrath, *Wegbereiter der Reformation*, p. 354n.12. See also Aston, *The Fifteenth Century*, pp. 126 ff.; and Josef Hergenröther, *Handbuch der allgemeinen Kirchengeschichte* (Freiburg, i. B.: Herder, 1915), 3:187.

28. Andreas, *Deutschland vor der Reformation*, p. 175; Cohn, *Pursuit of the Millennium*, pp. 205 ff., 226–227, 232; Franz, *Der deutsche Bauernkrieg*, pp. 46, 50–51; Hoyer, "Hans Böheim," pp. 190–191; and Leff, *Heresy*, pp. 474, 606 ff. On Hussite propaganda in Germany, see Friedrich Baethgen, *Schisma und Konzilszeit* (München: Deutscher Taschenbuch-Verlag, 1976), pp. 79–91; Benrath, *Wegbereiter der Reformation*, pp. 237, 368, 380 ff.; Gräter, *Der Bauernkrieg*, p. 20; Hoyer, "Hans Böheim," p. 192; and Peuckert, *Die grosse Wende*, p. 294.

29. Aston, *The Fifteenth Century*, p. 145; Benrath, *Wegbereiter der Reformation*, pp. 389–403; Cohn, *Pursuit of the Millennium*, pp. 212 ff.; and Lortz, *Die Reformation*, p. 103. For bibliographical information, see A. Schubert, "Chelčický, Peter," *Lexikon für Theologie und Kirche* 2 (1958): 1042.

30. Moeller, *Bauernkriegstudien*, p. 12. See also Franz, *Der deutsche Bauernkrieg*, pp. 46, 50–51; Gräter, *Der Bauernkrieg*, p. 20; and Hoyer, "Hans Böheim," pp. 185, 191–192. Gordon Leff correctly observes, "Even if we ascribe Böhm's outlook to influ-

ences other than Waldensian and Hussite reforming ideals, it took on significance through the ferment they had created" (*Heresy*, p. 475).

31. "The Reformation of the Emperor Sigismund," in *Manifestations of Discontent*, ed. Strauss, pp. 3–34. See also Baethgen, *Schisma und Konzilszeit*, pp. 97 ff.; Franz, *Der deutsche Bauernkrieg*, p. 51; Gräter, *Der Bauernkrieg*, p. 20; Hoyer, "Hans Böheim," p. 192; Moeller, *Bauernkriegstudien*, pp. 11–14; and Peuckert, *Die grosse Wende*, pp. 294–295.

32. Acts 2:42–47, 4:32; also Hoyer, "Hans Böheim," pp. 192–193.

33. Franz, *Der deutsche Bauernkrieg*, p. 48. See also Bensen, *Geschichte des Bauernkrieges*, pp. 192–193; Engels, *The Peasant War*, p. 49; *Rats-Chronik*, p. 49; and Zimmerman, *Allgemeine Geschichte*, 1:117 ff. and 3:662.

34. Barack, *Hans Böhm*, pp. 59, 66–67, 69, 71, 79, 81, 85, 87, 91; Trithemius, *Annales*, p. 488. See also Aston, *The Fifteenth Century*, pp. 117–147; and Hoyer, "Hans Böheim," p. 186. It is interesting to note that John Balbi, the Genoese friar and author of an etymological dictionary, still wrote at the end of the thirteenth century, "A layman is totally unversed in the science of letters." His was one of the first works printed in Mainz in 1460. See Erwin Iserloh, *Luther und die Reformation* (Aschaffenburg: Pattloch Verlag, 1974), p. 10.

35. Sir John Froissart, *The Chronicles of England, France, and Spain* (New York: E. P. Dutton, 1961), pp. 207–208. See also Aston, *The Fifteenth Century*, pp. 140 ff.; and Widmann, *Chronika*, p. 216.

36. Froissart, *The Chronicles*, pp. 207–208. See also Aston, *The Fifteenth Century*, p. 144; and Hoyer, "Hans Böheim," p. 185.

37. Barack, *Hans Böhm*, pp. 53, 56; Fries, *Historie*, pp. 853–854; Trithemius, *Annales*, p. 488. See also Franz, *Der deutsche Bauernkrieg*, p. 51; Gothein, *Reformation*, pp. 10–12; Gräter, *Der Bauernkrieg*, p. 9; Hoyer, "Hans Böheim," pp. 186, 192, 195; and Peuckert, *Die grosse Wende*, pp. 264–265, 270, 274, 280, 283, 287. The "peasant" class was far from homogeneous: it included freeholders, renters, and serfs. See Joel Hurstfield, ed., *The Reformation Crisis* (New York: Harper & Row, 1965), p. 85.

38. Barack, *Hans Böhm*, pp. 59, 63, 65, 69, 71, 73, 75, 80; Cohn, *Pursuit of the Millennium*, p. 228; Gräter, *Der Bauernkrieg*, p. 10; Hoyer, "Hans Böheim," p. 189; and Peuckert, *Die grosse Wende*, pp. 268, 270, 284, 290.
39. Barack, *Hans Böhm*, pp. 66, 74, 101, and 57, 66, 85, 87, 89; and Stolle, *Memoriale*, pp. 380–381, 383. See also Gothein, *Reformation*, p. 14; Hoyer, "Hans Böheim," p. 187; and Peuckert, *Die grosse Wende*, pp. 272, 284–288. The peasant proletariat was relegated to the status of "unehrliche Leute" (Gothein, *Reformation*, p. 10).
40. Barack, *Hans Böhm*, pp. 54–56, 62; Stolle, *Memoriale*, p. 381. See also Gothein, *Reformation*, pp. 12, 19; Hoyer, "Hans Böheim," p. 186; Peuckert, *Die grosse Wende*, pp. 264, 290; and Zimmermann, *Allgemeine Geschichte*, p. 121.
41. Peuckert, *Die grosse Wende*, pp. 291–294.
42. Gräter, *Der Bauernkrieg*, p. 21.
43. Franz, *Der deutsche Bauernkrieg*, pp. 48, 51; Gräter, *Der Bauernkrieg*, p. 9; Hoyer, "Hans Böheim," pp. 192, 195; and Peuckert, *Die grosse Wende*, p. 263.
44. *Rats-Chronik*, p. 38.
45. Fries, *Historie*, p. 853. See also Barack, *Hans Böhm*, pp. 63–64, 73 ff.; *Rats-Chronik*, p. 38; Stolle, *Memoriale*, pp. 381–382; Trithemius, *Annales*, pp. 486 ff., and *Chronicon*, p. 390; Widmann, *Chronika*, pp. 217, 219–220. Brief modern descriptions are found in Bax, *German Society*, p. 45; Franz, *Der deutsche Bauernkrieg*, p. 51; Gräter, *Der Bauernkrieg*, p. 11; Hoyer, "Hans Böheim," p. 189; Johannes Janssen, *History of the German People at the Close of the Middle Ages*, trans. A. M. Christie (St. Louis: B. Herder, 1900), 4:131; Meusel, *Thomas Müntzer*, p. 186; Peuckert, *Die grosse Wende*, p. 226. According to Cohn, the movement "could almost be called a new People's Crusade" (*Pursuit of the Millennium*, p. 226).
46. Fries, *Historie*, p. 853; Stolle, *Memoriale*, p. 381; Trithemius, *Annales*, p. 486. See also Peuckert, *Die grosse Wende*, p. 268.
47. Trithemius, *Chronicon*, p. 390; Widmann, *Chronika*, p. 217.
48. Widmann, *Chronika*, pp. 217–218; also Fries, *Historie*, p. 853; Stolle, *Memoriale*, pp. 381–382; Trithemius, *Annales*, pp. 486–487, and *Chronicon*, p. 390. See also Andreas, *Deutschland vor*

der Reformation, p. 175; Franz, *Der deutsche Bauernkrieg*, pp. 51–52; and Gothein, *Reformation*, pp. 12–13.

49. Barack, *Hans Böhm*, pp. 58, 85 ff.; and Gräter, *Der Bauernkrieg*, p. 11.

50. Barack, *Hans Böhm*, pp. 59–61. According to Stolle (*Memoriale*, p. 381), the Archbishop of Mainz took action after the Bishop of Würzburg had alerted him about "the foolishness of the people." It should also be noted that Würzburg was much closer to Niklashausen than to Mainz.

51. Barack, *Hans Böhm*, pp. 59 ff.; Fries, *Historie*, p. 854; Reuss, "Die Wallfahrt," p. 301; Stolle, *Memoriale*, p. 381. See also Cohn, *Pursuit of the Millennium*, p. 230; Hoyer, "Hans Böheim," pp. 188–189; Peuckert, *Die grosse Wende*, p. 268; and von Pölnitz, "Rudolf von Scherenberg," p. 60.

52. Barack, *Hans Böhm*, pp. 66 ff.

53. Ibid., pp. 72, 77–79.

54. Barack, *Hans Böhm*, pp. 61–62; *Rats-Chronik*, p. 38. See also Cohn, *Pursuit of the Millennium*, p. 230; and Hoyer, "Hans Böheim," p. 189. The Aschaffenburg meeting also decided that "a certain friar, preaching at Niklashausen and repeating the errors of Johann Beham, be arrested" (Barack, *Hans Böhm*, p. 62).

55. Fries, *Historie*, p. 853. Also Barack, *Hans Böhm*, p. 82; and Widmann, *Chronika*, p. 219. In spite of this testimony, Hoyer remains unconvinced that Böhm called on his audience to return with their arms ("Hans Böheim," pp. 193, 195).

56. Fries, *Historie*, p. 853; *Rats-Chronik*, p. 38; Stolle, *Memoriale*, p. 381; Trithemius, *Annales*, p. 488; and Widmann, *Chronika*, p. 219. See also Andreas, *Deutschland vor der Reformation*, p. 175; Cohn, *Pursuit of the Millennium*, p. 230; Franz, *Der deutsche Bauernkrieg*, p. 52; Hoyer, "Hans Böheim," p. 194; Meusel, *Thomas Müntzer*, p. 8; von Pölnitz, "Rudolf von Scherenberg," p. 60; and Sebastian Zeissner, *Rudolf II von Scherenberg, Fürstbischof von Würzburg, 1466–1495* (Würzburg: Nikolaus Schneider, 1952), p. 58. The Bishop of Würzburg may also have taken into account the rumor that "the Swiss are coming" (see Barack, *Hans Böhm*, p. 75; and Franz, *Der deutsche Bauernkrieg*, p. 47). The pastor of Niklashausen and the friar

were seemingly taken to Aschaffenburg (Barack, *Hans Böhm*, pp. 55–56, 62).

57. Cohn, *Pursuit of the Millennium*, p. 233; Stolle, *Memoriale*, p. 381; Trithemius, *Annales*, p. 488. See also Peuckert, *Die grosse Wende*, p. 267.

58. Trithemius, *Annales*, p. 489; Barack, *Hans Böhm*, pp. 65–66, 101–102; Fries, *Historie*, p. 854; *Rats-Chronik*, p. 38; and Stolle, *Memoriale*, pp. 381–383. The figures about the size of the crowd are given by Fries (pp. 853–854), who is a reliable witness. See also Andreas, *Deutschland vor der Reformation*, p. 175; Bax, *German Society*, pp. 47–49; Franz, *Der deutsche Bauernkrieg*, p. 52; Leff, *Heresy*, p. 475; Meusel, *Thomas Müntzer*, p. 8; Peuckert, *Die grosse Wende*, p. 268; and Zeissner, *Rudolf II von Scherenberg*, p. 89.

59. Trithemius, *Annales*, pp. 490–491; and Barack, *Hans Böhm*, p. 100; Fries, *Historie*, p. 854; *Rats-Chronik*, p. 38; Stolle, *Memoriale*, p. 383. See also Gräter, *Der Bauernkrieg*, p. 15; Henry C. Lea, *A History of the Inquisition of the Middle Ages* (New York: Russell & Russell, 1958), 2:420; Meusel, *Thomas Müntzer*, p. 8; and Peuckert, *Die grosse Wende*, pp. 268–269.

60. Meusel, *Thomas Müntzer*, p. 7; and Hoyer, "Hans Böheim," p. 188. Meusel's view is shared by Bax, *German Society*, p. 47; Cohn, *Pursuit of the Millennium*, p. 230; Gothein, *Reformation*, p. 14; and Hermann Haput, "Boehm, Hans," *The New Schaff-Herzog Encyclopedia of Religious Knowledge* 2 (1908): 209.

61. Trithemius, *Annales*, p. 488; and Hoyer, "Hans Böheim," pp. 188, 193–195. See also Barack, *Hans Böhm*, pp. 53–54, 65, 67, 69 ff., 73; Fries, *Historie*, p. 854; and *Rats-Chronik*, p. 38.

62. Fries, *Historie*, p. 853. See also Barack, *Hans Böhm*, p. 85.

63. Barack, *Hans Böhm*, pp. 55–56 and 54; Fries, *Historie*, p. 854; Stolle, *Memoriale*, p. 380. See also Andreas, *Deutschland vor der Reformation*, p. 174; Cohn, *Pursuit of the Millennium*, p. 232; Gräter, *Der Bauernkrieg*, p. 18; Hoyer, "Hans Böheim," p. 187; Peuckert, *Die grosse Wende*, pp. 265–266, 272–273; and Otto zu Stolberg-Wernigerode, "Böhm, Hans," *Neue Deutsche Biographie* 2 (1971): 382.

64. Trithemius, *Annales*, pp. 490 and 486. See also Barack, *Hans*

Böhm, p. 62; Stolle, *Memoriale*, p. 382; and Cohn, *Pursuit of the Millennium*, pp. 232–233; Hoyer, "Hans Böheim," p. 187; and Peuckert, *Die grosse Wende*, p. 264.

65. Peuckert, *Die grosse Wende*, pp. 284–289, esp. 288; and Barack, *Hans Böhm*, pp. 66, 85–97, 101; Fries, *Historie*, p. 854; Stolle, *Memoriale*, pp. 380–382. See also Cohn, *Pursuit of the Millennium*, p. 232; Gothein, *Reformation*, pp. 13–14; and Peuckert, *Die grosse Wende*, pp. 284 ff.

66. Barack, *Hans Böhm*, p. 37; Hoyer, "Hans Böheim," p. 187. Gothein implies that the nobles supported Böhm because he spoke of the future, not the present (*Reformation*, p. 14).

67. Stolle, *Memoriale*, p. 382. See also Andreas, *Deutschland vor der Reformation*, p. 174; Gräter, *Der Bauernkrieg*, p. 18; Hoyer, "Hans Böheim," p. 187; and Peuckert, *Die grosse Wende*, p. 288.

68. Gräter, *Der Bauernkrieg*, pp. 21 and 9–10. See also Barack, *Hans Böhm*, pp. 44–49; Benrath, *Wegbereiter der Reformation*, pp. 236–237; Günther Franz, *Quellen zur Geschichte des Bauernkrieges* (München: R. Oldenbourg, 1963), pp. 51–52, 174–179; Hoyer, "Hans Böheim," pp. 189, 192; Meusel, *Thomas Müntzer*, pp. 9, 17; Moeller, *Bauernkriegstudien*, pp. 19–24; Peuckert, *Die grosse Wende*, p. 296; and Ullmann, *Reformatoren*, pp. 392–393.

69. *Neue Deutsche Biographie*, 2:382. See also Hoyer, "Hans Böheim," p. 192; Peuckert, *Die grosse Wende*, p. 281; von Pölnitz, "Rudolf von Scherenberg," p. 60; and von Walter, *Die Reformation*, p. 72.

70. The Archbishop of Mainz resorted to this action because the interdict pronounced on October 10, 1476 (Barack, *Hans Böhm*, pp. 97–100) failed to stop the pilgrimage (pp. 104–105); permission to rebuild the church was given only in 1518 (see pp. 107–108 and 85, 87, 89). See also Cohn, *Pursuit of the Millennium*, p. 231; Franz, *Der deutsche Bauernkrieg*, p. 52; Gräter, *Der Bauernkrieg*, pp. 9, 15; and Peuckert, *Die grosse Wende*, p. 270.

71. Hoyer, "Hans Böheim," p. 195; Meusel, *Thomas Müntzer*, pp. 18, 25; Moeller, *Bauernkriegstudien*, p. 21; and *Rats-Chronik*, p. 38.

72. Ullmann pointed out a number of contradictions in the Piper's behavior: Böhm condemned ecclesiastical privileges, yet he did not hesitate to claim special prerogatives for himself as a prophet; he also allowed the talk about cures and miracles, which he must have known to be untrue; and, while he demanded a conversion of morals, he undertook nothing to stop the licence and the moral excesses of the pilgrims (*Reformatoren*, p. 433). See also Peuckert, *Die grosse Wende*, pp. 267, 296.
73. Hoyer, "Hans Böheim," pp. 186–189, 196; Moeller, *Bauernkriegstudien*, p. 22; and Peuckert, *Die grosse Wende*, p. 263.

Medieval Children

David Herlihy

In a fourteenth-century French poem, one of numerous surviving depictions of the danse macabre, the grim choreographer invites a baby to join his somber revels. "Ah, ah, ah," protests the infant, "I do not know how to speak; I am a baby, and my tongue is mute. Yesterday I was born, and today I must depart. I do no more than come and go."[1]

Many, perhaps most, children in most traditional societies did no more than come and go. And most never acquired, or were given, a voice which might have recorded and preserved their impressions concerning themselves, their parents, and the world they had recently discovered. Of all social groups which formed the societies of the past, children, seldom seen and rarely heard in the documents, remain for historians the most elusive, the most obscure.

The difficulties of interviewing the mute have doubtlessly obstructed and delayed a systematic investigation of the history of childhood. But today, at least, historians are aware of the commonplace assumption of psychologists, that childhood plays a critical role in the formation of the adult personality. Perhaps they are awakening to an even older wisdom, the recognition that society, in the way it rears its children, shapes itself. "Childhood is the foundation of life," wrote Philippe of Navarre, the thirteenth-century lawyer and chronicler, "and on good foundations one can raise great and good buildings."[2] This medieval man already sensed that the foundations of childhood help shape and support the structures of civilization.

Today, the literature devoted to the history of children in various places and epochs may be described, rather like children themselves, as small but growing daily. It remains, however, difficult to discern within that literature a clear consensus, an acceptable hypothesis, concerning the broad trends of children's history, even within Western societies. To be sure, there is frequent allusion within these recent publications to a particular interpretation which, for want of a better name, we shall call the "theory of discovered childhood." The principal formulator of this interpretation, at least in its most recent form, has been the French social historian Philippe Ariès. In a book published in 1960, called in its English translation *Centuries of Childhood*, Ariès entitled the second chapter "the discovery of childhood."[3] In it he affirmed that the Middle Ages of Western history did not recognize childhood as a distinct phase in life. Medieval people allegedly viewed and treated their children as imperfectly formed adults. Once the infant was weaned, medieval parents supposedly made no concessions to its special and changing psychological needs and took little satisfaction in the distinctive traits of the young personality. The corollary to this assumption is that, at some point in the development of Western society and civilization, the young years of life were at last discovered: childhood needed a Columbus.

Proclamations of the alleged discovery of childhood have become commonplace in the growing literature, but wide differences in interpretation still separate the authors. When, for example, was childhood first recognized? On this important question, Ariès himself is indefinite, even evasive, and seems to place the discovery over three or four hundred years, from the fifteenth to the eighteenth centuries.[4] A recent collection of essays, edited by Lloyd de Mause and published in 1974 under the title *The History of Childhood*, proposes several candidates, in several periods, for the honor of having first explored childhood in the Western world. M. J. Tucker, writing on English children between the years 1399 and 1603, begins his chapter with the now orthodox affirmation: "the medieval idea that children were not terribly important persists into the fifteenth century."[5] In the conclusion of the chapter, adopting the interpretation of Ivy Pinchbek and Margaret Hewitt, he declares: "a new consciousness of childhood was beginning."[6] Later in the same volume, Priscilla Robertson selects Jean Jacques Rousseau as the first advertiser of childhood: "special credit must go to Rousseau for calling attention to the needs of children. For the first time in history, he made a large group of people believe that childhood was worth the attention of adults, encouraging an interest in the process of growing up rather than just the product."[7]

The editor of this collection of studies, Lloyd de Mause, presents still another view of the emerging consciousness of childhood.[8] A devout believer in the idea of continuous and irreversible progress, De Mause traces the evolution in child-parent or child-mother relations through six styles of behavior, or psychogenic modes as he calls them: the infanticidal in the ancient world; abandonment in the Middle Ages; the ambivalent, intrusive, and socialization modes across the succeeding centuries; and now, at the term of this evolution, the helping mode. The helping mode "involves the proposition that the child knows better than the parent what it needs at each stage of its life."[9] Parents who help the child attain what he wants will render him "gentle, sincere, never depressed, never imitative or group-oriented, strong-willed, and unintimidated by authority."[10] According to De Mause, the full discovery of childhood and the full recognition across society of its special nature and distinctive needs are only now occurring.

If historians of the modern world do not agree concerning the date of childhood's discovery, their colleagues, working in more remote periods, show signs of restiveness with Ariès' postulate, that medieval people did not distinguish children from adults. A number of scholars– Christian Bec, Christiane Klapisch, Richard Goldthwaite, among others– have noted among the pedagogues, humanists, and even artists of fifteenth-century Italy a new orientation toward children, a new awareness of their problems, and an appreciation of their qualities.[11] The fat and frolicksome babies, the *putti*, who cavort through many solemn paintings of the Italian Renaissance, leave little doubt that the artists of the epoch knew how to depict, and they or their patrons liked to contemplate, children. A still more radical departure from Ariès' views was proposed, in 1968, by the French medievalist Pierre Riché. Riché accepted Ariès' phrase, the "discovery of childhood," but radically changed his chronology.[12] The initial explorers of childhood were, for Riché, the monastic pedagogues active in Western Europe between the sixth and eighth centuries. Their sensitivity toward the psychology of children allegedly transformed the harsh educational methods of classical antiquity and developed a new pedagogy which was finely attuned to the personality of the child-monk. Thus, over an extended period of time, from the early Middle Ages until the present, one or another author would have us believe that a consciousness of childhood was at last emerging.

The lessons that I would draw from this confusion of learned opinions are the following. Historians would be well advised to avoid such categoric and dubious claims, that people in certain periods failed to distinguish children from adults, that childhood really did lie beyond the pale of collective consciousness. Attitudes toward children have certainly shifted, as has the willingness on the part of society to invest substantially in their welfare or education. But to describe these changes, we need terms more refined than metaphors of ignorance and discovery. I would propose that we seek to evaluate, and on occasion even to measure, the psychological and economic investment which families and societies in the past were willing to make in their children. However, we ought also to recognize that alternative and even competitive sets of child-related values can coexist in the same society, perhaps even in the same household. Different social groups and classes expect different things from their children; so do different epochs, in accordance with prevailing economic, social, and demographic conditions. In examining the ways in which children were regarded and reared in the past, we should not expect either rigorous consistency across society or lineal progress over time.

In the current, lively efforts to reconstruct the history of children in Western civilization, the long period of the Middle Ages has a special importance. The medieval child represents a kind of primordial form, an "eo-pais," a "dawn child" as it were, against whom Western children of subsequent epochs must be measured if we are to appreciate the changes they have experienced. To be sure, the difficulties of observing medieval children cannot be discounted. Medieval documentation is usually sparse, often inconsistent, and always difficult. The halls of medieval history, running across one thousand years, are filled with lights and shadows. The shadows are particularly murky when they enclose those who "do no more than come and go." We can hope to catch only fleeting glimpses of medieval children in their rush through, or out of, life. On the other hand, even glimpses may be enough to dispel some large misconceptions concerning medieval children and to aid us toward a sound reconstruction of the history of children in the Western world.

In surveying medieval children, it is first necessary to consider the two prior traditions which largely shaped the medieval appraisal of the very young–the classical and the barbarian. It is important also to reflect upon the influence exerted upon child rearing by a special component of the ancient Mediterranean heritage: the Christian church.

Classical society, or at least the elites within it, cultivated an impressive array of intellectual traditions, which were founded upon literacy and preserved over time through intensive, and expensive, educational methods. Classical civilization would be inconceivable in the absence of professional teachers, formal instruction, and numerous schools and academies. But as social historians of antiquity now emphasize, the resources that supported ancient society were in truth scant. "The classical Mediterranean has always been a world on the edge of starvation," one historian has recently written, with much justice if perhaps some exaggeration."[13] Scarce resources and the high costs of rearing children helped form certain distinctive policies regarding the young. The nations which comprised the Roman Empire, with the exception only of the Jews, refused to support deformed, unpromising, or supernumerary babies.[14] In Roman practice, for example, the newborn baby was at once laid before the feet of him who held the *patria potestas* over it, usually the natural father. Through a ritual gesture called *susceptio*, the holder of paternal authority might raise up the infant and receive it into his family and household. But he could also reject the baby and order its exposure. Infanticide, or the exposure of infants, was a common and accepted social practice in classical society, shocking perhaps to modern sensibilities but rational for these ancient peoples who were seeking to achieve goals with limited means.

Here however is a paradox. Widespread infanticide in ancient society does not imply disinterest in or neglect of those children elected for survival. On the contrary, to assure a good return on the precious means invested in them, they were subject to close and often cruel attention and to frequent beatings. St. Augustine in his *Confessions* tells how his father, Patricius, and even his pious mother, Monica, urged him to high performance at school, "that I might get on in the world and excel in the handling of words, to gain honor among men and deceitful riches."[15] "If I proved idle in learning," he says of his teachers, "I was soundly beaten. For this procedure seemed wise to our ancestors; and many, passing the same way in the days past, had built a sorrowful road, by which we too must go, with multiplication of grief and toil upon the sons of Adam."[16] The memories which the men of antiquity preserved of their childhood were understandably bleak. "Who would not shudder," Augustine exclaims in the *City of God*, "if he were given the choice of eternal death or life again as a child? Who would not choose to die?"[17]

The barbarian child grew up under quite different circumstances. Moreover, barbarian practices of child rearing seem to have been particularly influential in the society of early medieval Europe, between the fifth and eleventh centuries. This is not surprising. Early in the Middle Ages, the cities which had dominated society and culture in antiquity lost importance, the literate social elites of classical society all but disappeared, and their educational institutions and ideals went down amid the debacle of the Western empire. On the other hand, barbarian practices were easily preserved within, and congenial to, the semibarbarized society of the early medieval West.

In a tract called *Germania*, written in A.D. 98, the Roman historian Tacitus has described for us the customs of the barbarian Germans, including their treatment of children. Tacitus, to be sure, likes to contrast barbarian virtues with Roman vices and doubtlessly exaggerates in his depictions of both, but his words are nonetheless worth our attention. The Germans, he claims, did not, like the Romans, kill their supernumerary children.[18] Rather, the barbarians rejoiced in a numerous progeny. Moreover, the barbarian mother, unlike her Roman counterpart, nursed her own baby and did not hand it over for feeding to servants or a hired nurse. On the other hand, Tacitus notes, the barbarian parents paid little attention to their growing children. "In every household," he writes, "the children grow up naked and unkempt . . ."[19] "The lord and slave," he continues, "are in no way to be distinguished by the delicacy of their bringing up. They live among the same flocks, they lie on the same ground . . ." Barbarian culture did not depend for its survival on the costly instruction of the young in complex skills and learned traditions; barbarian parents had no need to invest heavily in their children, either psychologically or materially. The cheap costs of child rearing precluded the adoption of infanticide as standard social policy but also reduced the attention which the growing child received from its parents. Only on the threshold of adulthood did the free German male re-establish close contacts with adult society. He typically joined the following of a mature warrior, accompanied him into battle, observed him, and gained some instruction in the arts of war, which, like the arts of rhetoric in the classical world, were the key to his social advance.

A casual attitude toward children seems embodied in the laws of the barbarian peoples–Franks, Lombards, Visigoths, Anglo-Saxons, and others–which were redacted into Latin largely between the sixth and the ninth centuries. The barbarian laws typically assigned to each member of society a sum of money–a fine, or wergeld–which would have to be paid to the relatives if he or she was injured or killed. The size of the wergeld thus provides a crude measure of social status or importance. One of the barbarian codes, the Visigothic, dating from the middle seventh century, gives a particularly detailed and instructive table of values which shows how the worth of a person varied according to age, sex, and status.[20] A free male baby, in the first year of life, was assigned a wergeld of 60 solidi. Between age 1 and age 9, his social worth increased at an average rate of only 3.75 solidi per year, thus attaining the value of 90 solidi in the tenth year of life. Between ages 10 and 15, the rate of increase accelerated to 10 solidi per year; and between ages 15 and 20 it grew still more, to 30 solidi per year. In other words, the social worth of the free Visigothic male increased very slowly in the early years of childhood, accelerated in early adolescence, and grew most substantially in the years preceding full maturity. Considered mature at age 20, he enjoyed a wergeld of 300 solidi–five times the worth of the newborn male infant–and this he retained until age 50. In old age, his social worth declined, to 200 solidi between ages 50 and 65 and to 100 solidi from age 65 to death. The old man, beyond age 65, was worth the same as a child of ten years.

The contrast between the worth of the child and the worth of the adult is particularly striking in regard to women. Among the Visigoths, a female under age 15 was assigned only one-half the wergeld enjoyed by males–only 30 solidi during her first year of life. Her social worth, however, increased enormously when she entered the years of childbearing, between ages 15 and 40 in the Visigothic codes. Her wergeld then leaped to 250 solidi, nearly equal to the 300 solidi assigned to the male and eight times the value of the newborn baby girl. The sterile years of old age brought a reduction of the fine, first to 200 solidi, which she retained to age 60, and then to 100 solidi. In old age, she was assigned the same worth as the male.

The contrasts in the social worth of the female child and the female adult are also sharp in the laws of the Salian and Ripuarian Franks. The wergeld of the free woman was tripled during her years of child-bearing, when she was also considered worth three times the free male.[21]

The low values assigned to children in these barbarian codes is puzzling. Did the lawgivers not realize that the supply of adults, including the especially valued childbearing women, was critically dependent on the protection of children? This obvious truth seemingly escaped the notice of the barbarian lawgivers; children, and their relation to society, did not loom large in their consciousness.

Apart from laws, one other source offers some insight into the treatment of children in the early Middle Ages: surveys of the population settled on particular estates and manors. These sporadic surveys have survived from the Carolingian period of medieval history, the late eighth and ninth centuries. The largest of them, redacted in the first quarter of the ninth century, lists nearly 2,000 families settled on the lands of the abbey of Saint-Germain-des-Prés near Paris.[22] The survey gives no exact ages, but of 8,457 persons included in it, 3,327 are explicitly identified as *infantes*, or children. Another 3,924 may be certainly regarded as adults, as they appear in the survey with a spouse or with offspring. Some 1,206 other persons cannot be classified by age; they are offspring not expressly called *infantes* or persons of uncertain age or status within the households.

The proportion of known children within the population is very low – only 85 children for every 100 adults. Even if all those of uncertain age are considered *infantes*, the ratio then becomes 116 children for every 100 adults. This peasant population was either singularly barren or it was not bothering to report all its children. Moreover, the sexual composition of the population across these age categories is perplexing. Among the known adults, men and women appear in nearly equal numbers.[23] But among the known children, there are 143 boys for every 100 girls – a male-to-female ratio of nearly three to two. Among those of uncertain age, the sex ratio is even higher. The high sex ratio among the known children may indicate widespread female infanticide, but if this were so, we should expect to find a similarly skewed ratio among the known adults.[24] The death of numerous baby girls inevitably would affect over time the proportions of adult women in this presumably closed population. But the proportions of males and females among the known adults are reasonably balanced. The more likely explanation is that the monastic surveyors, or the peasants who reported to them, were negligent in counting children and were particularly deficient in reporting the presence of little girls in the households. As the barbarian legal codes suggest, children, and especially girls, became of substantial interest to society, and presumably to their families, only as they aged.

The low monetary worth assigned to the very young, and the shadowy presence of children in the statistical documents of the early Middle Ages, should not, however, imply that parents did not love their children. Tacitus notes that the barbarian mother usually nursed her own babies. Kinship ties were strongly emphasized in barbarian society, and these were surely cemented by affection. The German epic fragment the *Song of Hildebrand* takes as its principal theme the love which should unite father and son.[25] The warrior Hildebrand flees into exile to live among the Huns, leaving "a babe at the breast in the bower of the bride." Then, after sixty years of wandering, he confronts his son as his enemy on the field of battle. He recognizes his offspring and tries to avoid combat; he offers the young warrior gold and, as the poet tells us, his love besides. But Hadubrand refuses to believe that the old warrior he faces is truly his father. The conclusion of the poem is lost, but the mood portends tragedy. The poet plays upon the irony that Hildebrand dearly loves his son but has been absent from his life for sixty years. The German warrior might have had difficulty recognizing his children, but he still felt affection for them. If classical methods of child rearing can be called cruel but closely attentive, the barbarian child grew up within an atmosphere of affectionate neglect.

The Christian church also powerfully influenced the treatment of children in many complex ways. Christianity, like Judaism before it, unequivocally condemned infanticide or the exposure of infants. To be sure, infanticide and exposure remained common social practices in Western Europe across the entire length of the Middle Ages. Church councils, penitentials, sermons, and secular legal codes yield abundant and repeated references to those crimes.[26] As late as the fifteenth century, if we are to believe the great popular preachers of the period, the streams and cesspools of Europe echoed with the cries of abandoned babies.[27] But medieval infanticide still shows one great difference from the comparable practice in the ancient world. Our sources consistently attribute the practice to two motivations: the shame of seduced and abandoned women, who wished to conceal illegitimate births, and poverty–the inability of the mother, and often of both parents, to support an additional mouth.[28] The killing or abandonment of babies in medieval society was the characteristic resort of the fallen, the poor, the desperate. In the ancient world, infanticide had been accepted practice, even among the social elites.

Christian teachings also informed and softened attitudes toward children. Christian scriptures held out several examples of children who enjoyed or earned God's special favor: in the Old Testament, the young Samuel and the young Daniel; in the New, the Holy Innocents and the Christ child himself. According to the evangelists, Jesus himself welcomed the company of children, and he instructed his disciples in the famous words: "Unless you become as little children, you will never enter the Kingdom of Heaven."[29]

This partiality toward children evoked many echoes among patristic and medieval writers. In a poem attributed to St. Clement of Alexandria, Christ is called the "king of children."[30] Pope Leo the Great writes in the fourth century: "Christ loves childhood, for it is the teacher of humility, the rule of innocence, the model of sweetness."[31] Christ's love for children seems to have given them occasional, unexpected prominence even in the religious wars of the epoch. Already in the Merovingian period, an account of a saint's life tells the story of Lupus, Bishop of Troyes in northern France, and his efforts to defend his community against Attila the Hun.[32] An angel instructs the bishop in a dream to recruit twelve little boys, baptize them, and march forth from the city, singing psalms, to confront the dread chieftain. The bishop and his youthful companions are martyred, but their sacrifice saves the city. It is easy to see, in this curious incident, the same sentiments which, later in the Middle Ages, at times made Crusaders out of children.[33]

A favorable appraisal of childhood is also apparent in the monastic culture of the early Middle Ages.[34] Western monasteries, from the sixth century, accepted as oblates to the monastic life children who were hardly more than toddlers, and the leaders of the monastic movement gave much attention to the proper methods of rearing and instructing these miniature monks. In his famous rule, St. Benedict of Nursia insisted that the advice of the children be sought in important matters, "for often the Lord reveals to the young what should be done."[35] St. Columban in the seventh century, and the Venerable Bede in the eighth, praised four qualities of the monastic child: he does not persist in anger; he does not bear a grudge; he takes no delight in the beauty of women; and he expresses what he truly believes.[36]

But alongside this positive assessment of the very young, Christian tradition supported a much harsher appraisal of the nature of the child. In Christian belief, the dire results of Adam's fall were visited upon all his descendants. All persons, when they entered the world, bore the stain of original sin and with it concupiscence, an irrepressible appetite for evil. Moreover, if God had predestined some persons to salvation and some to damnation, his judgments touched even the very young, even those who died before they knew their eternal options. The father of the Church who most forcefully and effectively explored the implications of predestination for children was again St. Augustine. Voluminous in his writings, clear in his logic, and ruthless in his conclusions, Augustine finally decided, after some early doubts, that the baby who died without baptism was damned to eternal fires.[37] There were heaven and hell and no place in-between. If you admit that the little one cannot enter heaven," he argued, "then you concede that he will be in everlasting fire."[38]

This cruel judgment of the great African theologian contrasts with the milder views of the Eastern fathers, who affirmed that unbaptized children suffer only the loss of the vision of God. The behavior of Augustine's God seems to mimic the posture of the Roman paterfamilias, who was similarly arbitrary and ruthless in the judgment of his own babies, who elected some for life and cast out others into the exterior darkness. And no one in his family dared question his decisions. Perhaps here as elsewhere, Augustine remains quintessentially the Roman.

Augustine was, moreover, impressed by the early dominion which evil establishes over the growing child. The suckling infant cries unreasonably for nourishment, wails and throws tantrums, and strikes with feeble but malicious blows those who care for him. "The innocence of children," Augustine concludes, "is in the helplessness of their bodies, rather than any quality of soul."[39] "Who does not know," he elsewhere asks, "with what ignorance of the truth (already manifest in babies), with what plenitude of vain desire (initially apparent in children) man enters this life? If he is allowed to live as he wishes . . . he will fall into all or many kinds of crimes and atrocities."[40]

The suppression of concupiscence thus becomes a central goal of Augustine's educational philosophy and justifies hard and frequent punishments inflicted on the child. While rejecting the values of pagan antiquity, he adheres to the classical methods of education. Augustine prepared the way for retaining under Christian auspices that "sorrowful road" of schooling which he, as a child at school, had so much hated.

Medieval society thus inherited and sustained a mix of sometimes inconsistent attitudes toward children. The social historian, by playing upon one or another of these attitudes, by judiciously screening his sources, could easily color as he pleases the history of medieval children. He could compile a list of the atrocities committed against them, dwell upon their neglect, or celebrate medieval views of the child's innocence and holiness. One must, however, strive to paint a more balanced picture, and for this we obviously need some means of testing the experiences of the medieval child. The tests we shall use here are two: the social investment, the wealth and resources which medieval society was apparently willing to invest in children; and the psychological investment, the attention they claimed and received from their elders. The thesis of this essay, simply stated, is that both the social and psychological investments in children were growing substantially from approximately the eleventh and twelfth centuries, through to the end of the Middle Ages, and doubtlessly beyond.

The basic economic and social changes which affected medieval society during this period seem to have required a heightened investment in children. From about the year 1000, the medieval community was growing in numbers and complexity. Commercial exchange intensified, and a vigorous urban life was reborn in the West. Even the shocking reduction in population size, coming with the plagues, famines, and wars of the fourteenth century, did not undo the importance of the commercial economy or of the towns and the urban classes dependent upon it. Medieval society, once a simple association of warriors, priests, and peasants, came to include such numerous and varied social types as merchants, lawyers, notaries, accountants, clerks, and artisans. A new world was born, based on the cultivation and preservation of specialized, sophisticated skills.

The emergence of specialized roles within society required in turn a social commitment to the training of children in the corresponding skills. Earlier educational reforms–notably those achieved under Charlemagne–had largely affected monks and, in less measure, clerics; they had little impact on the lay world. One novelty of the new medieval pedagogy, as it is developed from the twelfth century, is the attention now given to the training of laymen. Many writers now comment on the need and value of mastering a trade from early youth. Boys, notes Philippe of Navarre, should be taught a trade "as soon as possible." "Those who early become and long remain apprentices ought to be the best masters."[41] "Men from childhood," Thomas Aquinas observes, "apply themselves to those offices and skills in which they will spend their lives. . . . This is altogether necessary. To the extent that something is difficult, so much the more must a man grow accustomed to it from childhood."[42]

Later in the thirteenth century, Raymond Lull, one of the most learned men of the epoch, compares society to a wheel upon which men ride ceaselessly, up and down, gaining and losing status; the force which drives the wheel is education, in particular the mastery of a marketable skill. Through the exercise of a trade, a man earns money, gains status, and ultimately enters the ranks of the rich. Frequently, however, he becomes arrogant in his new status, and he neglects to train his children in a trade. His unskilled offspring inevitably ride the wheel on its downward swing. And so the world turns. A marketable skill offers the only certain riches and the only security, and "there is no skill," Lull affirms, "which is not good."[43]

One hundred and fifty years later, the Florentine Dominican Giovanni Dominici voices exactly the same sentiments. Neither wealth nor inherited status offers security. Only a marketable skill can assure that children "will not be forced, as are many, to beg, to steal, to enter household service, or to do demeaning things."[44] Addressing a woman who belonged to one of Florence's patrician families, he still urged her to make sure that her child learned a useful trade.

Although statistics largely elude us, there can be little doubt that medieval society was making substantial investments in education from the twelfth century. Guibert of Nogent, a monk who recounted his personal memoirs in the middle twelfth century, observed that the number of professional teachers had multiplied in the course of his own lifetime.[45] The chronicler Giovanni Villani gives us some rare figures on the schools functioning at Florence in the 1330's.[46] The children, both boys and girls, who were attending the grammar schools of the city, presumably between 6 and 12 years of age, numbered between eight and ten thousand. From what we know of the population of the city, better than one out of two school-aged children were receiving formal instruction in reading. Florentine girls received no more formal instruction after grammar school, but of the boys, between 1,000 and 1,200 went on to six secondary schools, where they learned how to calculate on the abacus, in evident preparation for a business career. Another 550 to 600 attended four "large schools" where they studied "Latin and logic," the necessary preparation for entry into the universities and, eventually, for a career in law, medicine, or the Church. Florence, it might be argued, was hardly a typical medieval community. Still, the social investment that Florentines were making in the training of their children was substantial.

Another indicator of social investment in children is the number of orphanages or hospitals devoted to their care, and here the change across the Middle Ages is particularly impressive. The care of the abandoned or orphaned child was a traditional obligation of Christian charity, but it did not lead to the foundation and support of specialized orphanages until late in the Middle Ages. The oldest European orphanage of which we have notice was founded at Milan in 787, but we know nothing at all concerning its subsequent history or that of other orphanages sporadically mentioned in the early sources.[47] The great hospital orders of the medieval Church, which sprang up from the twelfth century, cared for orphans and foundlings, but none initially chose that charity as its special mission.[48]

The history of hospitals in the city of Florence gives striking illustration of a new concern for abandoned babies which emerged in Europe during the last two centuries of the Middle Ages. In his detailed description of his native city, written in the 1330's, Villani boasts that Florence contained thirty hospitals with more than a thousand beds.[49] But the beds were intended for the "poor and infirm," and he mentions no special hospital for foundlings. A century later, probably in the 1420's, another chronicler, Gregorio Dati, in clear imitation of Villani, composed another description of the marvels of Florence. By then the city contained no fewer than three hospitals which received foundlings and supported them until an age when the girls could marry and the boys could be instructed in a trade.[50] This charity was, in Dati's phrase, "an estimable thing," and the moneys expended by the hospitals were, he claims, worth a city.

At Rome, the history of the hospital of Santo Spirito in Sassia shows a comparable, growing sensitivity to the needs of foundlings in the late Middle Ages. The hospital, administered by the Order of the Holy Spirit, had been founded at Rome in 1201, with the blessing and support of Pope Innocent III. From its thirteenth-century rule, Santo Spirito indiscriminantly accepted pilgrims, the poor, the sick and crippled, and foundlings.[51] After a period of disruption and decadence in the fourteenth and early fifteenth centuries, the hospital was re-formed, and, from about 1450, it devoted its principal resources to the care of foundlings.[52] At the same time, a legend grew up concerning the hospital's early benefactor, Pope Innocent III: Instructed by a dream, Innocent one day ordered fishermen to cast their nets into the Tiber. The men hauled in from the waters the bodies of 87 drowned babies and, after a second effort, 340 more. The shocked pope thereupon endowed the hospital of Santo Spirito and commissioned it to receive the unwanted babies of Rome. The legend is today celebrated in fifteenth-century frescoes which adorn the still-standing hospital of Santo Spirito. The story is without historical foundation, but it illuminates the novel sentiments toward foundlings which came to prevail at Rome, not in the thirteenth but in the fifteenth century.

Even a rapid survey of the foundling hospitals of Europe shows a similar pattern. Bologna seems not to have had an orphanage until 1459, and Pavia not until 1449.[53] At Paris, the first specialized hospital for children, Saint-Esprit en Grèves, was founded in 1363, but according to its charter it was supposed to receive only orphans of legitimate birth. Care of foundlings, it was feared, might encourage sexual license among adults.[54] But the hospital in practice seems to have accepted abandoned babies, and several similar institutions were established in French cities in the fifteenth century.[55]

This new concern for the survival of children, even foundlings, seems readily explicable. Amid the ravages of epidemics, the sheer numbers of orphans must have multiplied in society. Moreover, the plagues carried off the very young in disproportionate numbers.[56] Parents feared for the survival of their lineages and their communities. About 1400, the French philosopher Jean Gerson denounced the inordinate concern for the survival of children which he detected among his contemporaries.[57] The frequent creation of foundling hospitals and orphanages indicates that society as a whole shared this concern and was willing to invest in the survival of its young, even orphans and foundlings.

The medieval social investment in children thus seems to have grown from the twelfth century and to have passed through two phases: the first one, beginning from the twelfth century, largely involved a commitment, on the part of the urban communities, to the child's education and training; the second, from the late fourteenth century, reflected a concern for the child's survival and health under difficult hygienic conditions.

This social investment also presumes an equivalent psychological investment, as well as a heightened attention paid to the child and his development. This is evident, for example, in the rich tradition of pedagogical literature intended for a lay audience, which again dates from the twelfth century. One of the earliest authors to provide a comprehensive regimen of child care was Vincent of Beauvais, who died in 1264.[58] Drawing on the learning of the Muslim physician Avicenna, he gives advice on the delivery of the baby; its care in the first hours, days, and months of life; nursing and weaning; the care of older children; and their formal education. Later in the century, Raymond Lull, in his *Doctrina pueril*, written in Catalan but soon translated into French and Latin, is similarly comprehensive, including passages not only on formal schooling but also on the care and nourishment of the child. "For every man," he explains, "must hold his child dear."[59] In the following century, a Tuscan poet, Francesco da Barberino, who evidently had read Vincent of Beauvais, incorporated his advice on the care of infants in a long, vernacular poem intended for nurses.[60] The learning of the scholars seems to have spread widely, even among the humble social classes.

These medieval pedagogues also developed a rudimentary but real psychology of children. Vincent of Beauvais recommends that the child who does not readily learn must be beaten, but he warns against the psychological damage which excessive severity may cause. "Children's minds," he explains, "break down under excessive severity of correction; they despair, and worry, and finally they hate. And this is the most injurious; where everything is feared, nothing is attempted."[61] A few teachers, such as the Italian humanists Matteo Palmieri and Maffeo Vegio, wanted to prohibit all corporal punishment at school. For them, physical discipline was "contrary to nature"; it "induced servility and sowed resentment, which in later years might make the student hate the teacher and forget his lesson."[62]

The teacher – and on this all writers agree – should be temperate in the use of force, and he should also observe the child, in order to identify his talents and capacities. For not all children are alike, and natural differences must be recognized and developed. Raymond Lull affirms that nature is more capable of rearing the child than the child's mother.[63] The Florentine Giovanni Dominici stresses the necessity of choosing the proper profession for the child. Society, he notes, requires all sorts of occupations and skills, ranging from farmers to carpenters, to bankers, merchants, priests, and "a thousand others."[64] The aptitudes and inclinations of the young had to be acutely observed, "since nature aids art, and a skill chosen against nature will not be learned well." The young man who wishes to become a wool merchant will make a poor barber. God in his infinite wisdom has distributed all needed talents among all the members of the body social. If all young persons developed and exercised the particular talent which they possess, then, in Dominici's view, "lands would be well governed, commerce would be justly conducted, and the arts would progress in orderly fashion; the commonwealth would rejoice in peace and fat abundance, happy in all its affairs."[65]

To read these writers is inevitably to form the impression that medieval people, or some of them at least, were deeply concerned about children. Indeed, Jean Gerson expressly condemns his contemporaries, who, in his opinion, were excessively involved with their children's survival and success. In order to gain for them "the honors and pomp of this world," parents, he alleges, were expending "all their care and attention; they sleep neither day nor night and often become very miserly."[66] In investing in their children, they neglected charitable works and the good of their own souls. Gerson tells of a rich married couple who wished for offspring and performed many good works, so that God would grant them a baby. God rewarded them with the birth of a beautiful infant. But the new parents began at once to consider how their baby might achieve success in this world. They gave up their pious thoughts and deeds and turned all their attention and wealth to the upbringing of their child. God, angered at their neglect of the Church and of the poor, took back what he had given; the splendid child died. God does this often, Gerson instructs us, in order to rescue parents from inordinate dedication to the welfare of their offspring. Gerson, one suspects, would be surprised to learn of the opinion of recent historians, that medieval parents cared little for their offspring.

Medieval society, increasingly dependent upon the cultivation of sophisticated skills, had to invest in a supporting pedagogy; when later threatened by child-killing plagues, it had to show concern for the survival of the very young. But the medieval involvement with children cannot be totally described in these functional terms. Even as they were developing an effective pedagogy, medieval people were re-evaluating the place of childhood among the periods of life.

One indication of a new sympathy toward childhood is the revision in theological opinion concerning the salvation of the babies who died without baptism. Up until the twelfth century, the leading theologians of the Western church–Fulgentius of Ruspe, Pope Gregory the Great, Isidore of Seville, Anselm of Canterbury–reiterated the weighty opinion of St. Augustine, that such infants were surely damned.[67] In the twelfth century, Peter Abelard and Peter Lombard, perhaps the two most influential theologians of the epoch, reversed the condemnation of unbaptized babies to eternal fires. A thorough examination of the question, however, awaited the work of Thomas Aquinas, the first to use in a technical theological sense the term *limbus puerorum*, the "limbo of children." The unbaptized baby, he taught, suffered only the deprivation of the Beatific Vision. As the poet Dante described their plight in a famous passage from the *Divine Comedy*, they were "only insofar afflicted, that without hope we live in desire."[68]

Aquinas' mild judgment on babies dead without baptism became the accepted teaching of the medieval Church. Only one prominent theologian in the late Middle Ages, Gregory of Rimini, resisted it, and he came to be known as the *tortor puerorum*, the "torturer of children."

No less remarkable is the emergence, from the twelfth century, of a widespread devotion to the Child Jesus. The texts from the early Middle Ages which treat of the Christ Child–notably the "Book on the Origins of Mary and the Childhood of the Savior" falsely attributed to the evangelist St. Matthew–present Christ as a miniature wonder worker, who miraculously corrects Joseph's mistakes in carpentry, tames lions, divides rivers, and even strikes dead a teacher who dared reprimand him in class.[69] All-knowing and all-powerful, he is the negation of the helpless, charming child. A new picture of the Child Jesus emerges, initially under Cistercian auspices, in the twelfth century. For example, between 1153 and 1157 the English Cistercian Aelred of Rievaulx composed a meditation, "Jesus at the Age of Twelve." Aelred expatiates on the joy which the presence of the young Christ brought to his elders and companions: ". . . the grace of heaven shone from that most beautiful face with such charm as to make everyone look at it, listen to him, and be moved to affection. See, I beg, how he is seized upon and led away by each and every one of them. Old men kiss him, young men embrace him, boys wait upon him. . . . How do the old women complain when he lingers a little longer with his father and his companions? Each of them, I think, declares in his inmost heart: 'Let him kiss me with the kiss of his mouth'"[70]

Aelred goes on to speculate concerning the intimate details of the domestic life of the holy Child during the three days he was separated from his parents in Jerusalem: "Who provided you with food and drink? Who made up a bed for you? Who took off your shoes? Who tended your boyish limbs with oil and baths?" Passionate and sensuous, these meditations are the more remarkable as they come from a monk vowed to celibacy and asceticism.

Doubtlessly, the special characteristics of Cistercian monasticism were influential here. Like other reformed orders of the twelfth century, the Cistercians no longer admitted oblates, the boys placed in the monastery at tender ages, who grew up in the cloister with no experience of secular life.[71] The typical Cistercians– St. Bernard of Clairvaux and his brothers, for example– were raised within a natural family, and many were familiar with the emotions of family life. Grown men when they entered the monastery, they carried with them a distinct mentality–a mentality formed in the secular world and open to secular values. Many doubtlessly had considered and some had pursued other careers before electing the monastic life; they presumably had reflected upon the emotional and spiritual rewards of the married state and the state of parenthood. While fleeing from the world, they still sought in their religious experiences analogues to secular and familial emotions. In numerous commentaries on the biblical Song of Songs, they examine the love which joins bridegroom and bride and the mystical parallels to it offered in religion. In celebrating the joys of contemplating a perfect child, they find in their religious experience an analogue to the love and satisfaction which parents feel in observing their growing children. The Cistercian cult of the Child Jesus suggests, in other words, that lay persons, too, were finding the contemplation of children emotionally rewarding.

In the thirteenth century, devotion to the Child Jesus spread well beyond the restricted circle of Cistercian monasticism. St. Francis of Assisi, according to the *Legenda Gregorii*, set up for the first time a Christmas crèche, so that the faithful might more easily envision the tenderness and humility of the new-born Jesus.[72] St. Francis, the most popular saint of the late Middle Ages, was thus responsible, at least in legend, for one of the most popular devotional practices still associated with Christmas. St. Anthony of Padua, who died in 1231, was observed one day in the quiet of his room embracing and kissing an angelic child. This legend, to be sure, appears more than a century after Anthony's death but gains wide popularity in the late Middle Ages.[73]

Saints of lesser renown also sought and were favored with visitations from the Christ Child. A widow of Florence, Umiliana dei Cerchi, who died in 1246, prayed that she might see "the infant Jesus as he was at three or four years of age."[74] She returned to her room one night to find a delightful child playing; simply from watching this child at play, she drew ineffable joy. A similar story, told of St. Agnes of Montepulciano, who died in 1317, ends with a bizarre twist. She too prayed for the special favor of holding and fondling the infant Jesus. One night in her convent cell, the Virgin gave her the sacred child; when Mary returned at dawn to reclaim the infant, Agnes, captivated by his charm, refused to give him back. The women argued, and their "loving and pious dispute," in the words of Agnes' biographer, aroused the convent.[75]

This cult of the Christ Child implies an idealization of childhood itself. "O sweet and sacred childhood," another Cistercian, Guerric of Igny, writes of the early years of Christ, "which brought back man's true innocence, by which men of every age can return to blessed childhood and be conformed to you, not in physical weakness but in humility of heart and holiness of life."[76]

How are we to explain this celebration of "sweet and sacred childhood"? It closely resembles other religious movements which acquire extraordinary appeal from the twelfth century—the cults of poverty, of Christian simplicity, and of the apostolic life. These "movements of cultural primitivism," as George Boas might call them, point to a deepening psychological discontent with the demands of the new commercial economy.[77] The inhabitants of towns in particular, living by trade, were forced into careers of getting and spending, in constant pursuit of what Augustine had called "deceitful riches." The psychological tensions inherent in the urban professions and the dubious value of the proffered material rewards seem to have generated a nostalgic longing for alternate systems of existence, for freedom from material concerns, for the simple Christian life as it was supposedly lived in the apostolic age. Another model for an alternate existence, the exact opposite of the tension-ridden urban experience, was the real or imagined life of the child, who was at once humble and content, poor and pure, joyous and giving joy.

The simple piety of childhood remained an ideal of religious reformers for the duration of the Middle Ages. At their close, both Girolamo Savonarola in the south of Europe and Desiderius Erasmus in the north urged their readers to look to pious children if they would find true models of the Christian life.[78] Erasmus, in his *Colloquies*, after a pious child tells him of his religious practices, affirms his intent of following the child's example.[79]

Moreover, the medieval cult of childhood extends beyond religious movements and informs secular attitudes as well. In the French allegorical poem of the thirteenth century, *The Romance of the Rose*, youth is presented as a young girl "not yet much more than twelve years old."[80] The poet remarks on her innocence: she "did not yet suspect the existence of evil or trickery in the world." She smiles continuously, for "a young thing is troubled by nothing except play." She is also free from adult hypocrisy. Her sweetheart, described as a young boy of the same age, kisses her when he pleases. "They were never ashamed . . . ," explains the poet, "rather you might see them kissing each other like two turtle doves." Later in the Middle Ages, a Florentine citizen and merchant named Giovanni Morelli, reflecting on his own life, calls childhood "nature's most pleasant age."[81] In his *Praise of Folly*, Erasmus avers that the simplicity and unpretentiousness of childhood make it the happiest time of life. "Who does not know," Folly asks her audience, "that childhood is the happiest age and the most pleasant for all? What is there about children that makes us kiss and hug them and cuddle them as we do, so that even an enemy would help them, unless it is this charm of folly?"[82] Clearly, we have come far from Augustine's opinion, that men would prefer eternal death to life again as a child.

The history of medieval children is as complex as the history of any social group, and even more elusive. This essay has attempted to describe in broad outline the cultural attitudes which influenced the experiences of medieval children, as well as the large social trends which touched their lives. The central movements which, in this reconstruction, affected their fate were the social and economic changes widely evident across Europe from the twelfth century, most especially the rise of a commercialized economy and the proliferation of special skills within society; and the worsening health conditions of the late Middle Ages, from the second half of the fourteenth century. The growth of a commercialized economy made essential an attentive pedagogy which could provide society with adequately trained adults. And the deteriorating conditions of hygiene across the late Middle Ages heightened the concern for, and investment in, the health and survival of the very young. Paradoxically, too, the growing complexities of social life engendered not truly a discovery but an idealization of childhood: the affirmation of the sentimental belief that childhood is, as Erasmus maintains, a blessed time and the happiest moment of human existence.

We have sought to identify patterns in the complex experiences of medieval children, but we recognize that the model we propose doubtlessly remains too simple. But this much can safely be affirmed:

the Middle Ages developed and sustained a broad spectrum of prejudices and beliefs regarding children, some of them destined to influence the subsequent centuries of Western history, some of them living today.

NOTES

1. "A, a, a, je ne scey parler; / Enfant suis, j'ay la langue mue / Hier naquis, huy m'en fault aller / Je ne faiz qu'entree et yssue" (Jean Gerson, "La Danse Macabre," in *Oeuvres complètes*, ed. P. Glorieux [Paris and New York: Desclée, 1966], p. 7:298).
2. ". . . car enfance est li fondemenz de vie, et sor bons fondemenz puet on bastir granz edifiz et bons" (*Les quatre ages de l'homme: Traité moral de Philippe de Navarre*, ed. Marcel de Fréville [Paris: Firmin Didot, 1888], p. 27).
3. *L'enfant et la vie familiale sous l'ancien régime* (1st ed., Paris: Plon, 1960; 2nd ed., Paris: Editions du Seuil, 1973); pp. 23–41 of the first edition form the chapter entitled "La découverte de l'enfance." The work is translated as *Centuries of Childhood: A Social History of Family Life*, trans. Robert Boldick (New York: Alfred Knopf, 1962).
4. *L'enfant et la vie familiale*, p. 460. George Boas, *The Cult of Childhood* (London: Warburg Institute, 1966), p. 21, finds "the beginnings of the cult of childhood in the scepticism of the sixteenth century." Boas does not seem to be aware of Ariès' earlier publication on the history of childhood.
5. "The Child as Beginning and End: Fifteenth and Sixteenth Century English Childhood," in *The History of Childhood*, ed. Lloyd de Mause (New York: Psychohistory Press, 1974), p. 229.
6. Ibid., p. 252; and Ivy Pinchbek and Margaret Hewitt, *Children in English Society* (London: Routledge and Paul, 1969), 1:41.
7. *History of Childhood*, ed. De Mause, p. 407.
8. Ibid., pp. 1–74. See also his reply to criticisms of his views in idem, "The Formation of the American Personality through Psychospeciation," *Journal of Psychohistory* 4 (1976): 1–30.
9. *History of Childhood*, ed. De Mause, p. 52.

10. Ibid., p. 54.
11. Christian Bec, *Les marchands écrivains: Affaires et humanisme à Florence, 1376–1434* (Paris and The Hague: Mouton, 1967), pp. 286–299; Christiane Klapisch, "L'enfance en Toscane au début du XVe siècle," *Annales de démographie historique*, 1973, pp. 99–127; Richard Goldthwaite, "The Florentine Palace as Domestic Architecture," *American Historical Review* 77 (1972): 1009–1010. For further criticism of Ariès' use of medieval iconographical evidence, see Ilene H. Forsyth, "Children in Early Medieval Art: Ninth through Twelfth Centuries," *Journal of Psychohistory* 4 (1976): 31–70.
12. Pierre Riché, "Découverte de l'enfant," in *De l'éducation antique à l'éducation chevaleresque*, Questions d'histoire (Paris: Flammarion, 1968), p. 30. Compare his remarks in his earlier, large work *Education et culture dans l'Occident barbare, VIe–VIIIe siècles*, Patristica sorbonensia, 4 (Paris: Editions du Seuil, 1962), p. 505: "Les moines ont-ils redécouvert la nature enfantine et toutes ses richesses? Disons plutôt qu'ils ont suivi les enseignements du Christ et non la tradition romaine."
13. Peter Brown, *The World of Late Antiquity, A.D. 150–750*, History of European Civilization Library, ed. Geoffrey Barraclough; (London: Thames and Hudson, 1971), p. 12.
14. See Robert Etienne, "Ancient Medical Conscience and the Life of Children," *Journal of Psychohistory* 4 (1976): 131–161, translated from the French article which appeared in the *Annales de démographie historique*, 1973; ". . . the right to commit infanticide was one of the attributes of *patria potestas*" (p. 134). See also the old but informative work of Léon Lallemand, *Histoire des enfants abandonnés et délaissés: Etudes sur la protection de l'enfance* (Paris: A. Picard, 1885), pp. 31–71. Philo the Jew seems to have been the earliest ancient writer who explicitly condemned the practice of infanticide (see *History of Childhood*, ed. De Mause, p. 28).
15. *Confessionum libri tredecim*, ed. P. Knoell and Martinus Skutella (Leipzig: Teubner, 1934), 1:9; *Confessions of St. Augustine*, trans. F. J. Sheed (London: Sheed and Ward, 1944), p. 8.
16. Ibid.

17. "Quis autem non exhorreat, et mori eligat, si ei proponatur, aut mors perpetienda, aut rursus infantia?" (*De civitate Dei*, ed. B. Dombart [Leipzig: Teubner, 1909], 21:14). In the judgment of George Boas, "in general the Ancients had a low opinion of children if they appraised them at all" (*Cult of Childhood*, p. 12).

18. *De Germania*, ed. C. Halm (Leipzig: Teubner, 1911), chap. 19: "To limit the number of children or to put any of the later children to death is considered a crime, and with them good customs are of more avail than good laws elsewhere." The translation is taken from *Medieval Culture and Society*, ed. David Herlihy (New York: Harper and Row, 1968), p. 29.

19. *Germania*, chap. 20; *Medieval Culture and Society*, ed. Herlihy, p. 29.

20. *Leges visigothorum*, ed. Karolus Zeumer, *Monumenta Germaniae Historica*, Legum Sectio I, Legum nationum germanicarum, 1 (Hanover and Leipzig: Hahn, 1902), pp. 336–337.

21. *Lex ribuaria*, ed. Franz Beyerle and Rudolf Buchner, *Monumenta Germaniae Historica*, Legum Sectio I, Legum nationum germanicarum, III, 2 (Hanover: Hahn, 1954), p. 78, "De homicidiis mulierum." *Pactus Legis salicae*, ed. Karl August Eckhardt, *Monumenta Germaniae Historica*, Legum Sectio I, Legum nationum germanicarum, IV, 1 (Hanover: Hahn, 1962), p. 92.

22. *Polyptyque de l'Abbé Irminon*, ed. Benjamin Guérard, 2 vols. (Paris: Imprimerie royale, 1844). With the aid of Mr. Larry Poos, I have prepared a machine-readable edition of the survey, and the figures cited in this article are derived from a computer-assisted analysis of the document.

23. Among those of uncertain age status, the sex ratio is even higher – 384.3, or 957 men and 249 women.

24. For a different interpretation of these high sex ratios among the children in this survey, see Emily R. Coleman, "Infanticide in the Early Middle Ages," in *Women in Medieval Society*, ed. Susan Mosher Stuard (Philadelphia: University of Pennsylvania Press, 1976), pp. 47–70. The serfs of the monastery of Farfa in central Italy, who were listed in a survey dated ca. 820, similarly show a high sex ratio among children, 136.1. The

sex ratio for the entire population is 118.1. This survey of 244 households is published in *Il Chronicon farfense di Gregorio di Catino*, ed. Ugo Balzani, Fonti per la storia d'Italia, 33–34 (Rome: Forzani, 1903), 1:261–275. The figures were calculated by Richard Ring, who will soon publish an extended study of the families of Farfa.

25. *The Hildebrandslied*, trans. Francis A. Wood (Chicago: University of Chicago Press, 1914), pp. 4–7. For a general treatment of the child in Old German literature, see Ursula Grey, *Das Bild des Kindes im Spiegel der altdeutschen Dichtung und Literatur mit textkritischer Ausgabe von Metlingers "Regiment der jungen Kinder"*, Europäische Hochschulschriften, Reihe I, Deutsche Literatur und Germanistik, 91 (Bern: Herbert Lang, and Frankfurt: Peter Lang, 1974).

26. On ecclesiastical condemnations of infanticide, see L. Godefroy, "Infanticide," *Dictionnaire de théologie catholique*, VIII, 2 (Paris: Librairie Letouzey et Ané, 1927), 1717–1726.

27. Y. B. Brissaud, "L'infanticide à la fin du moyen âge," *Revue historique de droit français et étranger* 50 (1972): 229–256.

28. The Council of Elvira, ca. 300, alludes to women who suffocate their babies in order to conceal their sins. The Council of Toledo, 589, mentions parents who kill their babies in order to escape the burden of feeding them; see Godefroy, "Infanticide," p. 1723. Some early penitentials assign lighter penances to women who kill their children because of poverty, see *Die Canones Theodori cantuariensis und ihre Überlieferungsformen*, ed. Paul Willem Finsterwalder (Weimer: H. Böhlaus Nachfolger, 1929), p. 280: "Mulier paupercula si occidit filium suum homicida sit x. annos peniteat." The usual penance was twelve years.

29. Matt. 18:1–5; see also Matt. 19:33–37, Luke 9:46–48.

30. "Sancte, sis dux, Rex puerorum intactorum"; cited in Ernest Semichon, *Histoire des enfants abandonnés depuis l'antiquité jusqu' à nos jours* (Paris: E. Plon, 1880), pp. 290–292.

31. Cited in Riché, *Education antique*, p. 31, from Leo's "Sermon on the Epiphany."

32. "Vita Memorii presbyteri et martyris," in *Passiones vitaeque sanctorum aevi merovingici et antiquiorum aliquot*, ed. Bruno

Krusch, *Monumenta Germaniae Historica*, Scriptores rerum merovingicarum, 3 (Hanover: Hahn, 1916), p. 102. The angel instructs the bishop: "Surge, fidelissime sacerdos Christi, iube perquirere duodecim innocentes et eos baptiza . . ."

33. See Jean Delalande, *Les extraordinaires croisades d'enfants et de pastoreaux au Moyen Age: Les pèlerinages d'enfants au Mont Saint-Michel* (Paris: Lethielleux, 1962).

34. This is essentially the thesis of P. Riché, *Education et culture*, cited in n. 12 above.

35. Ibid., p. 505, citing the *Regula Benedicti*, chap. 3, "Saepe juniori dominus revelat quod melius est."

36. Ibid. St. Columban writes, "Infans humilis est, non laesus meminit, non mulierem videns concupiscit, non aliud ore aliud corde habet."

37. A. M. Jacquin, "La prédestination d'après Saint Augustin," in *Miscellanea Agostiniana* (Rome: Tipografia Vaticana, 1931), p. 868.

38. "Ecce exposuit tibi quid sit regnum, et quid sit ignis aeternus; ut quando confitearis parvulum non futurum in regno, fatearis futurum in igne aeterno" (Sermo 294, chap. 3, cited in ibid., p. 912).

39. *Conf.* 1:7; *Confessions*, trans. Sheed, p. 7.

40. *De civitate Dei*, 22:22: "Nam quis ignorat cum quanta ignorantia ueritatis, quae iam in infantibus manifesta est, et cum quanta abundantia uanae cupiditatis, quae in pueris incipit apparere, homo veniat in hanc uitam, ita ut, si dimittatur uiuere ut uelit et facere quidquid uelit, in haec facinora et flagitia . . . uel cuncta uel multa perueniat."

41. *Les quatre ages de l'homme*, p. 10: "Après, si doit l'an as anfanz apanre tel mestier qui soit a chascun androit soi; et doit on commancier au plus tost que on puet. Car cil qui est par tems et longuement deciples doit après etre miaudres maitres de ce que l'an li avra apris . . ."

42. "Liber contra doctrinam retrahentium a religione," in *Opera omnia iussu Leonis XIII P. M. edita*, LXI, pars. B–C (Rome: Ad Sanctam Sabinam, 1969), col. 44: "Hoc manifeste apparet, secundum quam homines a pueritia applicantur illis officiis vel artibus in quibus vitam sunt acturi; sicut qui futuri sunt clerici

mox a pueritia in clericatu erudiuntur; qui futuri sunt milites opportet quod a pueritia in militaribus exercitiis nutriantur, sicut Vegetius dicit in libro De re militare; qui futuri sunt fabri fabrilem artem a pueritia discunt. . . . Quinimmo necesse est ut quanto aliquid est difficilius, tanto ad illud portandum homo a pueritia consuescat."

43. *Doctrine d'enfant: Version médiéval du MS Fr 22933 de la B. N. de Paris*, ed. Armand Llinares (Paris: C. Klincksieck, 1969), p. 170: "Plus seure richece est enrichir son filz par aucun mestier. . . . Il n'est pas mestier qui bons ne soit." For the comparison of the world with a wheel, see ibid., p. 171. Raymond wrote this tract originally in Catalan, but this French translation was made soon after the original.

44. *Regola di cura familiare*, ed. D. Salvi (Florence: A. Garinei, 1860), p. 183: ". . . e non saranno costretti, come son molti, di mendicare o tor quel d'altri, porsi per famigli, o fare quel che non si conviene."

45. *Self and Society in Medieval France: The Memoirs of Abbot Guibert of Nogent*, ed. John F. Benton (New York: Harper and Row, 1970), p. 17. Guibert himself in his memoirs gives a long account of his childhood experiences, which are perceptively interpreted by Benton in his Introduction to the cited translation. Guibert's interest in his own childhood may well reflect this new social concern with the moral and cultural formation of children.

46. *Cronica di Giovanni Villani* (Florence: Magheri, 1823), 6:183–184: "Troviamo che' fanciulli che stanno ad imparare l'abbaco a algorismo in sei scuole, da mille in mille dugento. E quegli che stanno ad apprendere la grammatica e loica in quattro grandi scuole, da cinquecento-cinquanto in seicento." E. Fiumi, "Economia e vita privata dei Fiorentini nelle rilevazioni statistiche di G. Villani," *Archivio Storico Italiano* 111 (1953): 207 ff., estimates that the school-age population of the city of Florence was at that time only about 9,000 persons, but his estimates of the size of the city (93,000 persons) and of the proportion of school-age children within it (10 percent) are probably low. If we estimate that Florence then contained 120,000 persons, and that the school-age children formed 16.3 percent

of the total (the proportion prevailing in 1427, according to a census of the city taken that year), their numbers would have been about 15,000.

47. On the history of orphanages in the Middle Ages, see Fiorenzo Romita, *Evoluzione storica dell' assistenza all' infanzia abbandonata* (Rome: Desclé, 1965).

48. One of the most important of the new orders was that of the Holy Spirit, founded at Montpellier in 1178; see Paul Brune, *Histoire de l'Ordre Hospitalier du Saint Esprit* (Paris: Lons-le-Saunier, 1892).

49. *Cronica*, 6:185.

50. *"L'Istoria di Firenze" di Gregorio Dati dal 1380 al 1405 illustrata e pubblicata secondo il Codice inedito stradiniano*, ed. Luigi Pratesi (Norcia: T. Cesare, 1905), p. 119: "V'è ancora più Ospedali i quali ricettano i fanciulli nati celatamente, de' quali l'uno è di Santa Maria della Scala; l'altro è quello di San Gallo, e quello che è in sulla Piazza de' Servi titolato Spedale Nuovo; e questi tali danno ricetto a ogni fanciullo o fanciulla e tutti gli mandano a balia e nutriscono, e quando le femmine sono grandi tutte le maritano e i maschi pongono ad arte, che è una cosa stimabile. La spesa che i detti Spedali hanno l'anno e qualunque di questi sarebbe in se una città . . ." The date when Dati wrote is uncertain, but it must be later than 1421, when the Hospital of the Innocenti, to which his Spedale Nuovo surely refers, was founded at Florence. On the question of abandoned children at Florence, see the recent study by Richard C. Trexler, "The Foundlings of Florence, 1395–1455," *History of Childhood Quarterly* 1 (1973): 259–284.

51. *La carità cristiana in Roma*, ed. Vincenzo Monachino, with the collaboration of Mariano da Alatri and Isidoro da Villa Padierna, Roma Cristiana, 10 (Bologna: Cappelli, 1968), p. 142. The rule dates from 1228–1250, and its most recent edition is by Ottavio De Angelis, *Regula sive statuta hospitalis sancti spiritus: La più antica regola hospitaliera di Santo Spirito in Saxia* (Rome, 1954).

52. *Carità cristiana*, p. 142, which also recounts the legend of the hospital's founding by Innocent III.

53. Umberto Rubbi and Cesare Zucchini, "L'ospizio esposti e l'asilo

di maternità," in *Sette secoli di vita ospitaliera in Bologna*, pp. 401–417 (Bologna: Cappelli, 1960); Casimira Biglieri, "L'Ospedale degli Esposti di Pavia," *Studi di Storia Ospitaliera* 3 (1965): 139–156.

54. Semichon, *Enfants abandonnés*, p. 80; Lallemand, *Enfants abandonnés*, p. 121. A royal letter patent of 1445 reads as follows: "Moult de gens feroient moins de difficultés de eux abandonner à pécher quand ils verroient qu'ills n'auroient pas la charge première ni la sollicitude de leurs enfants . . ."

55. On the care of abandoned children in France in the late Middle Ages, see Lallemand, *Enfants abandonnés*, pp. 120–130. For England, see Rotha Mary Clay, *The Medieval Hospitals of England* (London: Methuen, 1909), esp. pp. 25–34, "Homes for Women and Children."

56. This seems to have been characteristic of the plagues which struck the city of Florence during the late Middle Ages. See the analysis of age-specific mortalities at Florence in the forthcoming book by David Herlihy and Christiane Klapisch, *Les Toscans et leurs familles: Une étude du Catasto florentin de 1427*.

57. *Oeuvres complètes*, ed. Glorieux, 7:322: "Vrai est que ce qui seult aggrever fort la douleur et la tristesse d'aulcuns, especialement des nobles gens, est quant par la mort de leurs enfants leur lignie fault et deschiet, et que nulz heritiers ne leur succedent en droite ligne; et par ainsi leurs armes perissent et leur nom va a oubliance quant au monde."

58. *De eruditione filiorum nobilium*, ed. Arpad Steiner (Cambridge, Mass.: Medieval Academy of America, 1938; repr., New York: Kraus, 1970). Vincent includes the same instructions in his "Speculum doctrinale," published in the third volume of the *Biblioteca mundi Vincentii Burgundii* (Douai: B. Belleri, 1624). On Vincent's educational philosophy, see Astrik L. Gabriel, *The Educational Ideas of Vincent of Beauvais*, Texts and Studies in the History of Medieval Education, ed. A. L. Gabriel and J. N. Garvin, 4 (Notre Dame, Ind.: Medieval Institute, University of Notre Dame, 1956). Vincent's remarks on the physical care of the infant are in his "De arte medicina," Liber 12 of the Speculum doctrinale, *Biblioteca mundi*, 3:1088–1093. For a recent survey of medieval medical literature relating to children,

see Luke Demaitre, "The Idea of Childhood and Child Care in Medical Writings of the Middle Ages," *The Journal of Psychohistory* 4 (1977): 461–490.

59. *Doctrine d'enfant*, p. 203: "De la maniere su laquele home doit nourir son fiuz." Raymond stresses the need for close but affectionate attention to the child: "Amable fiuz, tout home doit chier tenir son enfant . . ." (p. 204).

60. In the thirteenth book, addressed to nurses, of his *Reggimento e costumi di donna*, ed. G. E. Sansone, Collezione di "Filologia romanza," 2 (Turin, 1957). On Francesco's sources, see G. B. Festa, *Un galateo femminile italiano del Trecento*, Biblioteca di cultura moderna, 36 (Bari: G. Laterza, 1910).

61. "Ingenia tamen puerorum nimia emendationis severitate deficiunt: nam et desperant, et dolent, et novissime oderunt; et quod maxime nocet, dum omnia timentur, nihil conantur" (*Biblioteca mundi*, 3:487).

62. *Della Vita civile: Trattato di Matteo Palmieri cittadino fiorentino*, Biblioteca scelta di opere italiane antiche e moderne, 160 (Milan: G. Silvestri, 1825), p. 34: "Quegli che hanno il padre ed il maestro disposti e solleciti a fargli buoni, non mi piace abbino busse, prima, perchè pare cosa non benigna, ma piuttosto contra natura, ed atta a fare gli animi servi, ed alla volta poi, cresciuti, se lo reputano ad ingiuria, onde se ne scema l'affezione del natural amore." Maffeo Vegio da Lodi, *De educatione liberorum et eorum claris moribus*, ed. Sister M. Walburg Fanning and A. Stanislaus Sullivan (Washington, D.C.: Catholic University of America, 1933–1936), p. 19.

63. *Doctrine d'enfant*, p. 206: "Saches, fiuz, que plus sage est nature a norrir les enfanz que n'est ta mere."

64. *Cura familiare*, p. 182. Like Lull, Dominici affirms that education must conform to the nature of the child: "'. . . però che la natura aiuta l'arte, e arte pressa contra natura non s'impara bene."

65. Ibid., p. 183: ". . . le terre sarebbono rette bene, le mercantanzie si farebbono iustamente, e l'arti procederebbono ordinate; goderebbe la repubblica nella pace e abondanzia grassa, felice in tutti i fatti suoi."

66. *Oeuvres complètes* 7:322: ". . . pour avencier leurs prochains es honneurs et pompes de ce monde mettent toute leur cure et

entente et n'en prennent repos ne nuit ne jour et en deviennent souvent tres avaricieux." The entire passage makes clear that the sense of "prochains" is "children."

67. J. Bellamy, "Baptême (Sort des enfants morts sans)," *Dictionnaire de théologie catholique*, II (1905), cols. 364–378. A. Gaudel, "Limbes," ibid., IX, 1 (1926), cols. 760–762.

68. *Inferno*, Canto IV; *The Divine Comedy: The Carlyle-Wicksteed Translation Unabridged* (New York: Random House, 1950), p. 27.

69. "Liber de ortu beatae Mariae et infantia Salvatoris, a beato Matthaeo evangelista hebraice scriptus et a beato Ieronomo presbytero in latinum translatus," in *Evangelia apocrypha*, ed. Constantin von Tischendorf, 2nd ed. (Leipzig, 1876), pp. 51–105. See p. 104 for the taming of the lions; p. 106 for divine aid in the carpentry shop; and p. 107 for the incident in the classroom.

70. *The Works of Aelred of Rievaulx*, vol. 1: *Treatises: The Pastoral Prayer*, Cistercian Fathers Series, 2 (Spencer, Mass.: Cistercian Publications, 1971), p. 9. St. Bernard also urges Christians to imitate the simplicity and humility which the baby Jesus and all young children manifest; see his sermon in *Patrologia Latina*, ed. J. P. Migne (Paris: apud Garnier Fratres, 1853), vol. 183, col. 152: ". . . primo omnium Christus appareat puer cum Virgine matre, ut simplicitatem et verecundiam ante omnia quaerendam nobis doceat esse. Nam et pueri simplicitas naturalis, et cognata virginibus verecundia est. Omnibus ergo nobis in conversationis nostrae initio nulla magis virtus necessaria est, quam simplicitas humilis et gravitas verecunda."

71. J. H. Lynch, "The Cistercians and Underage Novices," *Cîteaux* 23 (1973): 283–297. The Carthusians, Grandmontines, and Templars also refused to accept children as novices.

72. *St. Francis of Assisi According to Brother Thomas of Celano*, ed. H. G. Rosedale (London: J. M. Dent, 1904), p. 67: "De presepio, quod fecit in die natalis domini." The legend says of the crib and child: "Honoratur ibi simplicitas, exaltatur paupertas, humilitas commendatur . . ."

73. The story is first recounted in the *Liber miraculorum*, which was written about 1370. *Acta Sanctorum, Junii II* (Antwerp: apud

viduam et heredes Henrici Thieullier, 1698), p. 729: ". . . vidit per fenestram amplectentem latenter quemdam puerum, in brachiis S. Antonii, pulcherrimum et jucundum: quem sanctus amplexabatur et osculabatur, indesinenter ejus faciem contemplado."

74. *Acta Sanctorum, Aprilis II* (Antwerp: apud Michaelem Cnobarum, 1675), p. 397: ". . . puerum Iesum aetate quatuor annorum vel trium . . . talem quidem qualis erat tempore infantiae suae."
75. Ibid., p. 797: ". . . caritativa concertatio et pia."
76. *Liturgical Sermons*, Cistercian Fathers Series, 8 (Spencer, Mass.: Cistercian Publications, 1970), p. 38.
77. Arthur O. Lovejoy and George Boas, *Primitivism and Related Ideas in Antiquity* (New York: Octagon Books, 1965); Boas, *Cult of Childhood* (see above, n. 4).
78. For the "cult of childhood" at Florence and the bands of young boys which aided Fra Savonarola in his reform of the city, see the informed if somewhat discursive study of Richard C. Trexler, "Ritual in Florence: Adolescence and Salvation in the Renaissance," in *The Pursuit of Holiness in Late Medieval Religion: Papers from the University of Michigan Conference*, ed. Charles Trinkaus and H. A. Oberman, Studies in Medieval and Renaissance Thought, 10 (Leyden: Brill, 1974), pp. 200–270. On Erasmus' admiration of the piety of childhood, see his "The Child's Piety," from the Colloquies, *Essential Works of Erasmus*, ed. W. T. H. Jackson (New York: Bantam Books, 1965), pp. 186–197.
79. *Essential Works of Erasmus*; ed. Jackson, p. 197: "Erasmus: But without jesting, I'll try to imitate that course of life."
80. *The Romance of the Rose by Guillaume de Lorris and Jean de Meun*, trans. Charles Dahlberg (Princeton: Princeton University Press, 1971), pp. 47–48, lines 1259–1278.
81. *Ricordi*, ed. Vittorio Branca (Florence: Felice le Monnier, 1969), p. 498: ". . . ne' tempi piu dilettevoli alla natura." In fact Morelli's own childhood was singularly unhappy, through the early death of his father.
82. *Essential Works of Erasmus*, ed. Jackson, p. 369.

The Invention of
the State

Fredric L. Cheyette

"Man is born free, and everywhere he is in chains. Many a man believes himself to be the master of others who is, no less than they, a slave. How did this change take place? I do not know. What can make it legitimate? To this question I hope to be able to furnish an answer."[1] Thus recasting an ancient Stoic sentiment, Jean-Jacques Rousseau laid bare the modern problem of "the state": the state as Other, as coercive Other, opposed to the free-willing self. If nature is good and naturalness the touchstone of virtue, how can the state be anything but evil? How can coercion of the self by what is not the self be justified? This concentration on coercion, on the exercise of power over the free will of the individual self, distinguishes Rousseau and all modern political philosophers from the ancients from whom they otherwise draw so much.

Not that the ancients were unaware of the anguish that wells up when one's selfhood and the demands of the *polis* collide. Crito, urging Socrates to escape on the eve of his execution, is its eloquent spokesman. But Socrates, though he calls himself the slave–and child –of the law, cannot conceive of the laws as chains. Quite the contrary: "Did we [the laws] not bring you into existence," he has them say. "[Do you object] to those of us who after birth regulate the nature and education of children, in which you also were trained?"[2] Indeed the very otherness of the state was alien to Plato, whose principal task in his "political" dialogues was to describe the state in which no such conflict would appear. Aristotle might have considered the issue in his discussion of slavery, but he chose to answer the implicit question of why the slave should obey his master with the lapidary answer: Because it is good for him.[3] Tyranny appears in the *Politics* as a disease of the political body and a practical problem for the tyrant, but not—as it would for lawyers and publicists of late medieval Europe and for centuries of their successors—as a problem of obedience and legitimate resistance.[4]

For Plato and Aristotle, as for the Stoics of later antiquity, the naturalness of the political community or of law was less the solution to the problem of obedience than the reason why it cannot arise. If the community or just law is analytically prior to the individual, the demands of the community or of the law cannot be coercive. Even though poets and sophists argued that it was the function of law to inspire fear—and the Greek laws that have survived seem to assume the same function—the ultimate justification for that fear was justice, meaning harmony and virtue, a state of political health.[5] Only those who believe the laws to be mere convention or brute force might have argued otherwise.[6]

> Then no man on earth is truly free.
> All are slaves of money or necessity.
> Public opinion or fear of prosecution
> Forces each one, against his conscience,
> To conform.
> (Euripides, *Hecuba*, 11.864–867)[7]

The sentiment with which Rousseau opened his *Social Contract* could only have introduced among the ancients a discussion of the right relationship of reason to will or, later, among Christian philosophers, of the right relationship of the soul to God. For Rousseau it expressed the problem of all political communities.

I

Why did the modern West come to view the state in these peculiar terms? Why in consequence did it come to think of law, human law, as essentially coercive, and of political organization, of which law is a functional component, as essentially an apparatus, the human embodiment of that Other? What happened between antiquity and the modern world to make this difference?

We now know much of the history of the words and concepts with which modern discussions of state, law, and politics are carried on. Once believed to be novelties of the sixteenth century, the direct reflection of the assumed changed conditions of political life, these terms in fact have long medieval pedigrees. Common utility was a political argument already used in the twelfth century. Corporate concepts, applied not only to ecclesiastical bodies but also to villages, cities, and kingdoms were being elaborated in the twelfth and thirteenth centuries. Sovereignty was a commonplace of political and legal argument by the turn of the fourteenth century.[8]

For most of these words and concepts, the twelfth and thirteenth centuries seem to have been the great arsenal. What gave this extraordinary inventiveness to these centuries? The answer seems almost automatic: it must have been the rediscovery of Roman Law followed by the rediscovery of Aristotle. And yet the conclusions that medieval professors and politicians drew from both these sources would never have been recognized in antiquity; nor was the system of states that resulted a replay of either the Greek *polis* or the Roman *res publica*. Could these texts alone have been the cause of what occurred in the twelfth and thirteenth centuries? One's readiness to ascribe such effects to them must surely be qualified. Aristotle and the Roman Law seem rather to have been rediscovered within a conceptual world that had already altered fundamentally. And this alteration called forth both the new interest in ancient law and political philosophy and the political inventiveness that followed. When did this change occur and what was its nature?

An older view would have rejected outright the notion that the state was invented afresh in the Middle Ages. For if the history of the centuries between the Carolingian Empire and the rise of Western monarchies was essentially a "battle between the central power and particularism," as Heinrich Mitteis argued a generation ago, the state in some sense was always there.[9] It had to be neither invented nor reinvented but only brought to fruition from its inchoate germ. It was there in desire, even if the apparatus and, perhaps, the conscious idea itself were wanting. This view was shared by those who imagined the state in its first form as a feudal monarchy emerging from the feudal customs of an earlier age.[10] What existed was potentially a state, a not-yet-state, waiting for the mighty figures of the twelfth and thirteenth centuries to bring it forth. Historians could thus speak easily of the "fragmentation of public powers" in the tenth and eleventh centuries, of the "passing of public powers into private hands" when castellans spread their might across the land.[11] Such judgments were made all the more easy by the language of the twelfth- and thirteenth-century documents themselves, which spoke often enough of "usurpation" of regalian or ecclesiastical rights, while publicists in France and the Empire laid claim to a strict continuity between Charlemagne and the reigning king or emperor.

We can now see how strongly these historical attitudes of previous generations were shaped by the application of modern legal terms and even more by the imposition of nineteenth-century liberal political ideals to medieval phenomena. As we watch the nation-state gradually fade from its glory as the ultimate goal of all historical experience, we begin to understand that such concepts as "public," "private," "central power," and "particularism" are themselves the value-laden products of historical development and not atemporal categories of human thought. The most basic categories of constitutional and legal history, categories that assume these concepts or their equivalents, in consequence become problematic.[12] They cannot be the starting point for historical analysis or description, because they are themselves history-bound: "public," "private," "particularism," and all the remaining vocabulary of constitutional history, scientific and judgmental, had their particular origins and their particular developments. Their appearance, like the appearance of the state as their summation, was part of a larger process, and they cannot appropriately be used to talk about the world before they appeared, when they did not exist. To ask when the state began is therefore to ask a meaningful and important question.

In 1970 Joseph Strayer answered this question, dating the invention to a full half-millennium, 1100 to 1600, and ascribing it to "the formation of impersonal, relatively permanent political institutions." These institutions, which could "survive changes in leadership and fluctuations in the degree of cooperation among subgroups," and which were quite different from the officials who "simply protect the private interests of the wealthy and the powerful," grew in "prestige and authority" and finally gained "a moral authority to back up [their] structure and [their] theoretical legal supremacy." The state was thus an invention but a slow one, an accumulation, or even an accretion, of a multitude of changes.[13]

By pointing to institutions, Strayer brings us directly to the core of our problem. For what are institutions, of whatever kind, if not the very embodiment of that Otherness that so troubled Rousseau? And to the extent that these institutions in the Middle Ages were essentially fiscal and judicial, they were the very embodiment of coercive Otherness. They were, furthermore, an Other, an alien being, not just to those whom they taxed and judged: to the degree that they were truly impersonal and relatively permanent, to the degree that they truly survived changes in leadership (and membership), they were also definably something other than the individual persons who temporarily embodied them or filled the posts within them. "A bishop has two persons," wrote the fourteenth-century jurist Cinus, "one in so far as he is bishop, another in so far as he is Peter or Martin." His near contemporary Bartolus expressed it in corporate language: "universitas repraesentat unam personam, quae est aliud a scholaribus seu ab hominibus universitatis." [A corporation manifests itself as a single person, which is other than the students (of a university) or the men of a corporation.][14] Institutions assumed a distinction between person and institution as much as they assumed a coercive relationship between institution and subject. Their invention thus found a world *already* face to face with the problem of the modern state.

Strayer would argue, of course, that there is more to the modern state than institutions. There are the attitudes of loyalty, the acceptance of legitimacy, the complex of moral and political judgments that over the centuries the state has gathered around itself. However, as he himself states, these attitudes and ideas have adhered to institutions.[15] His argument thus becomes circular: the modern state was created by institutions which themselves conceptually presupposed the nature of the modern state. How can we escape this circularity? We cannot begin the history of the state with the growth of institutions because that is already within the conceptual world of our own political culture.

It is only by transcending that conceptual world that we can observe the state in the process of becoming.

Yet how difficult it has been even for sociologists and anthropologists – those very professionals who make it their task to transcend the narrow bonds of Western concepts– to go beyond the limits of the state, to think away the category of institution. Strayer's developmental categories are strikingly parallel to the analytical categories with which Max Weber defined the sociological realm of law. "An order will be called *law* if it is externally guaranteed by the probability that coercion . . . will be applied by a *staff* of people holding themselves specially ready for that purpose."[16] Although Weber extended the notion of "staff" to include the clan and the notion of coercion to include feud, he admitted that these were marginal cases.[17] One is surely justified in believing that institutional officials are peeping out from behind the purposely vague term *staff* (for what otherwise would be marginal about clan enforcement and the feud?). And, indeed, no matter where one turns– to legal anthropology, political anthropology, or philosophy of law– the controlling image of the modern state is often not far, sometimes making primitive peoples lawless by definition and frequently leading to bitter struggles over the definition of fields of ethnological endeavor.[18]

These discussions, of course, will not answer the historical question that I have posed. Conceptually, however, the problem faced by ethnologists seeking the realm of law or political organization in a primitive society is identical to the problem faced by the historian looking for the origins of the modern state. Before the modern state, there must have been something else. What was that something else? How did it turn into what we know? Before there was law in the modern sense, was there something lawlike, potentially law, not-yet-law? Before there were institutions in the modern sense, were there forms that were institutionlike? Before there was a state, was there an organization of society that was statelike, potentially a state, a not-yet-state? Or is a culture without a state, was Europe before the state, fundamentally different and thus difficult– or impossible– to analyze by these terms? This is the path of inquiry we must follow to see the invention of the modern state.

II

It is with good reason that those who have written about the theory or history of the state have not tried to define it. The range of its manifestations appears too vast. Behind the idea, however, and above all behind its manifestations as institutionalized social control, permanent and impersonal, lies a small number of fundamental distinctions, so fundamental we tend to take them for granted. One need only enunciate them to recognize immediately their power and importance. They define what we might call the realm of discourse of the modern state.

These distinctions are five:

office/person
the rule of law/the rule of man
public/private
authoritative/nonauthoritative
artifice/naturalness

To these we may add a basic definition, obvious, perhaps, but worth pointing to: law is a set of verbalized rules.

It is difficult for us to imagine a world in which these distinctions did not exist, so readily do they come to our lips when we begin to talk about law or government. Yet there was an era when a few intellectuals thrust them impetuously into the stream of European thinking about society, its laws, and its organization, and imposed them upon a society that found these distinctions strange, difficult to manipulate, uncertain in their consequences. That era was the late eleventh century. We must now try to enter into the culture that Europeans shared when those distinctions were not yet commonplace.

It was not a state of nature. Europeans lived in a society whose organization may seem excessively simple compared with ours, but it was organized. They shared certain mores, certain patterns of accepted behavior, certain ideals, and a store of acquired techniques. The mores they shared, their patterns of accepted behavior, their ideals and techniques were transmitted orally. Technically speaking, it was not a "primitive" society. It was, however, a nonliterate society dependent essentially on memory for the transmission of all except clerical culture. The term *nonliterate* rather than *preliterate* is appropriate because this society contained a small group of people who shared a craft literacy–the clergy. The invention of the state is the story of how this small minority of literate men slowly imposed upon the nonliterate their special ways of thinking about politics and law.

Around the year 1000 the vast majority of lay society shared an exclusively oral culture. How do we know that this was the case? There is, first of all, the simple quantitative testimony of what has survived. It is one of the curiosities of medieval history that there exists less archival documentation for the tenth century than for the ninth, and that, in many areas of Europe, this decline continues on into the eleventh century. For just this reason the early stages of medieval economic development remain so impenetrably obscure. For much the same reason so many regional studies of medieval society begin only in the eleventh century. The reason seems obvious enough: fewer written documents survive because fewer were produced. There is no reason to believe that time would have dealt more severely with tenth-century charters than with documents of the ninth or the twelfth.

Some, of course, do survive. These, however, are largely the products of a few centers: Rome; a few major monasteries and cathedrals (for example Regensburg, St. Gallen, Liège, Fleury); the Imperial court; and, rather oddly, the very fringes of the European world–Anglo-Saxon England and the kingdoms of the Hispanic frontier, fringes to which we will have to return. On the Continent there were scarcely enough documents to maintain a literate transmission of even a simple social and political culture from generation to generation.

Monks, to be sure, were required by their rule to read and write. But writing was a labor; how laborious an occasional voice sighing at the end of a manuscript lets us know. "The act of writing is difficult. It tires the eyes, breaks the back, and cramps the arms and legs." "The end has come. Give me a pot of wine." "Give the poor scribe a pretty girl."[19]

Nor was learning one's letters a task to elate the youthful spirit. Here, for example, are the memories of Guibert Nogent, who was learning to read and write in the early 1050's.

There was still in my youth such a scarcity of teachers that hardly any could be found in the towns . . . and those who by good chance could be discovered had but slight knowledge. The man in whose charge my mother decided to put me had begun to learn grammar late

in life, and he was the more unskilled in the art through having im-
bibed little of it when young. . . . He worked me hard. . . . [But] he was,
in fact, utterly unskilled in prose and verse composition. Meanwhile
I was pelted almost every day with a hail of blows and harsh words
while he was forcing me to learn what he could not teach.[20]

Among the clergy, the physical act of writing was, furthermore, an
art form. There were local schools of handwriting, as there were local
schools of manuscript illumination or sculpture. Because there were
local schools, writing as a means for transmitting information or instruction over long distances was occasionally an impediment rather
than a handmaid to communication. Two different chronicles from
the eleventh century tell stories of bishops unable to read the so-called
curial script of the Roman court; one of these bishops even claimed
that the papal letter was false because he was unable to read it.[21]

For writing to serve as a vehicle to transmit mores, ideals, patterns
of behavior, and techniques from generation to generation it must,
first of all, be fairly widespread. It clearly was not widespread in the
tenth and eleventh centuries. Writing to serve this purpose must also
contain those mores, ideals, and patterns. Continental literate produc-
tion in fact contained principally religious literature: the Bible, the
Fathers of the Church, and books of church ritual. Only England,
with its remarkable series of vernacular laws and its equally remarkable vernacular poems and chronicles, stands out as an exception in
the tenth and eleventh centuries. Yet even there–at least as far as
poetry was concerned–what was written had been composed and long
transmitted orally.

> Listen! [the *Beowulf* poet enjoins]
> We have heard   of the glory of the Spear-Danes
> in the old days,   the kings of tribes–
> how noble princes   showed great courage![22]

Although England could boast of its King Alfred, its Dunstan, and
even an occasional literate nobleman, centers of literate culture there
in the tenth century were few and fragile.[23] The strength of its vernacular tradition was testimony not just to the lasting impulse giv-
en it by the great Wessex king but equally to the dearth of clergy

trained in Latin, whose own instruction therefore depended heavily on works glossed or translated into Old English.[24]

Here and there, other kinds of documents were produced that might have served to record for posterity a few, at least, of the accepted patterns of social life. Those that survive are extremely rare, and they— like *Beowulf* and *Widsith*—likewise betray an essential nonwritten culture. They betray it in their physical form itself.

One of the many reforms undertaken at the court of Charlemagne was the reform of handwriting. Of the many aspects of this reform probably the most far-reaching was the decision to separate individual words by blank spaces rather than running all words together or placing spaces randomly as one lifted his hand or re-inked his quill. This made it possible for the first time to read an unknown text with ease and to transmit new information or commands visually, rather than using the written text as an *aide-memoire*. The Carolingian minuscule became the court hand of the ninth and tenth centuries. But what was being produced away from the major centers of learning? The documents reproduced in Figures 1 and 2 come from the archives of the Abbey of LaGrasse, just north of the Pyrenees; they are thus also examples of monastic writing.[25] Although the Carolingian handwriting was by this time a century or more old (Fig. 1 is dated 893, Fig. 2, 957), it had not yet reached this house. Spaces are arbitrarily placed, usually in the middle of words, rather than between them; letters are unevenly formed. The scribes were apparently not very used to holding the quill. In Figure 1, the donor, a priest, has signed his own name—an indication of minimal literacy, to be sure, but he clearly has not mastered the craft of writing.

Early contracts, donation, quitclaims, and other land transactions likewise betray a predominantly nonwritten culture. The wording of some suggests that they were recording an oral procedure that had taken place sometime before the actual writing of the document, that they were not the acts themselves but only their confirmation, their record.[26] In England the picturesque alliterative couplets of Old English law—*sacu* and *socn*, *toll* and *team*—represent the intrusion of colloquialisms of the countryside into the language of royal donations.[27] Even on the shores of the Mediterranean, where late Roman notarial traditions remained strong and even humble peasants kept written contracts in their huts, one suspects that scribes drew up their documents following a craft tradition that prescribed only a few fixed forms, with the result that what they wrote may have corresponded only distantly to the actual relations between the parties involved. How else is one to understand the degradation of distinctions between sale, gift, and quitclaim—as charter after charter in the eleventh century used these terms synonymously—except as the attempt of scribes to place into the mold of fixed formulae exchanges of land and money that in fact were technically neither sales, nor gifts, nor quitclaims?[28] How, likewise, is one to explain the appearance of Roman legal technicalities in Latin charters a full half-century before they appear in vernacular charters in the same region[29] or, even in the twelfth century, the enormous differences in technical quality between charters drawn up in major centers and those drawn up by hill-village scribes[30] except as the consequence of the variable force of purely craft learning only partially in touch with social forms maintained by oral tradition?

In the Mediterranean region scribes occasionally did record the oral act itself, the words the parties said to each other. When this occurred the resultant documents took a very special and peculiar form. The most remarkable of these were the oaths that southern fighting men took to their lords when they were given possession of fortifications or that great men took to each other when they entered into a peace treaty or other important agreements. These oaths often contained a mixture of Latin and vernacular words which when pronounced aloud sound out a peculiar rhythmic or rhyming chant suggestive—like the alliterations of Old English Law—of the oral tradition that passed these oaths from generation to generation. Rhythm and rhyme sit more solidly in the memory.[31]

De ista hora in antea ego [name] te [name] non vos decebrei, ne vos nols tolrei, ne nols vos devedarei lo castel de [name], las fortezas que hodie in illis sunt. . . .

Non decebra [name] de sua vita ni de sua membra que in suum corpus portat, per que o perda, ni non engenera sua persona suo damno suo sciente.[32]

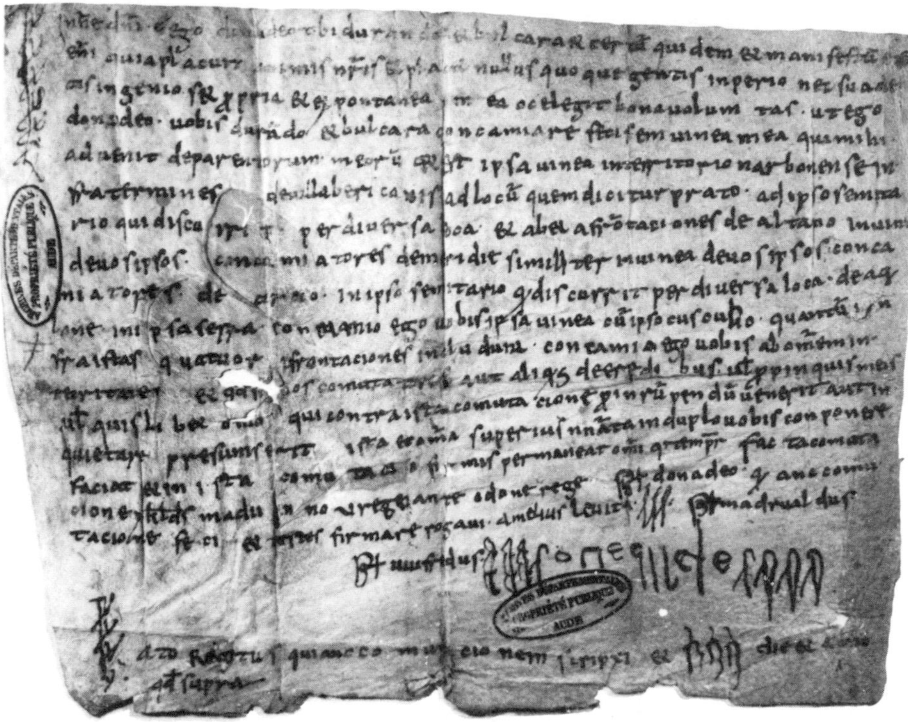

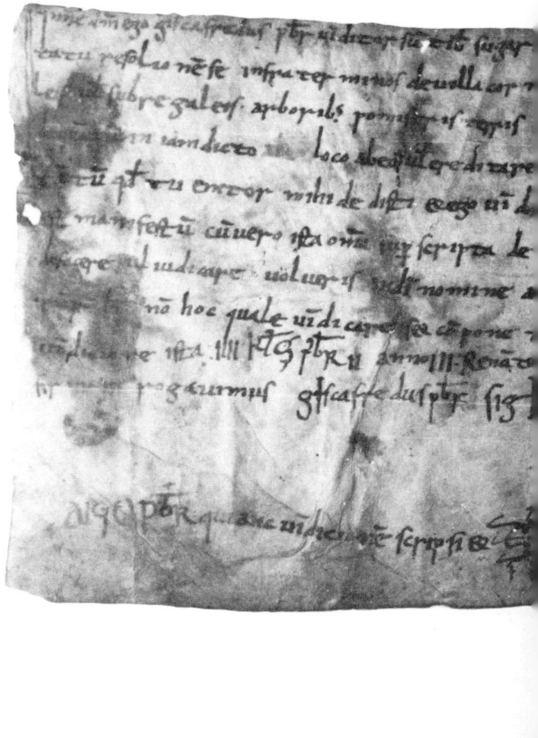

et hanc se[...] que udicio nos me uendo tibi alode mm̄ q̄ abes mea um
uente mihi q̄ aparacio nū iſta om̄a uēdo tibi, idē caſales cuᵽ tales ortalſ̃ q̄ eᵹa
racioneſ ut t_ in tueſ ſ cū omni uoce opoſitoriſmc ; & cuiuſ uſ cuᵽ ſueſſ̃ queſ
ū q̄ uoce ſic uendocit ab omnē iura gⁱe tace aᵽt fctū ſt diſᵽꝫ ii
manibꝫ mſᵽe ct pⁱ cꝫdeſ ipſo fcio apuꝫ te Ortoᵽe nihil remiſſ fciⁱ
cuo tᵽado do miⁱno poteſtate . cuᵽqꝫꝫuſ ut pⁱegreſſeſ euꝰū et quiquiꝫ q̄ē
eſ gꝰ ſi ego uꝫdi tuᵽ aut ullꝰ homo qᵘ cōtᵽa iſta om̄a uenᵽe pⁱt adimꝫ
n duplo ꝙmaᵽ tea iſta om̄a cū tecta firma pᵐmaneaꝫ ꝗfacta capra
ſꝫ filiolouꝫde uici ſic iiⁱ q̄ſcafꝫedeſ qui ane uꝫdicioⁱe fecimuſ et eſ ſ
ſigt̄ nipᵽ meipiuſ · ſigt̄ inᵃᵗ meſueſ

annoqꝫ ſꝫupra x

Unlike other written acts of the eleventh and twelfth centuries whose formulae changed significantly over time, these oaths and the documents that contained them kept rigidly to this highly archaic speech through the entire period–even to the extent of naming the persons who gave and received the oaths by their given names and *the names of their mothers* while in all other documents people identified themselves through the early eleventh century by patronymic and then gradually by family name.

Early written charters thus present the historian with a difficult and troubling problem. Do they really contain the act as it was performed? Or are their verbal contents dictated mainly *by a tradition of how acts were to be recorded*? Many things about these early acts suggest that the latter is the correct answer. If so, these charters *do not* precisely record the accepted patterns of social life as it was lived and experienced.

In the tenth and eleventh centuries there seems to have existed side by side a literate craft culture of the clergy, a culture devoted almost exclusively to ritual and to spiritual learning; a modest craft culture; especially in Anglo-Saxon England and in lands that had been heavily Romanized, devoted to the recording of certain very special social arts and occasionally to recording oral literature; and the oral culture of the rest of society.

III

The society of the tenth and eleventh centuries differed from ours in two ways. It was largely an oral culture, and it lacked the realm of discourse, the set of distinctions, that are the foundation of the modern state. How were these two connected? For greater clarity, let us turn the problem over. Did the creation of a dominant literate culture side by side and occasionally in conflict with oral culture lead to the invention of the state?

In some ways, the answer is very easy. Increasing literacy meant improved record keeping and easier transmission of administrative orders and by these means the creation of a more efficient administrative apparatus. The administrative history of the medieval state, however, as I have argued, is not conceivable without the prior in-

vention of a realm of discourse that made something called adminis-
tration possible and legitimate. Let us therefore return to this oral
culture and ask what constraints orality placed on the way men
thought about politics, law, and social organization.

Obviously, this society, in order to transmit its mores, its accepted
habits, and its ideals from generation to generation, had to rely on the
human memory. So ingrained in this culture was the social value of
memory that, long after writing became the dominant form of transmission, reliance on memory and oral performance continued to play
an important role. Think only of those professorial *virtuosi* in the
thirteenth and fourteenth centuries who committed the entire corpus
of Roman Law to memory; or of the continued importance of oral dis-
putation in the medieval schools. Literary scholars in recent years
have even found evidence for the continuing literary influence of an
oral tradition as late as the sixteenth century and have reminded us
that the training of memory was an important part of Renaissance
humanistic learning.[33]

What was it, then, that nonliterate people of eleventh- and twelfth-
century Europe stored in their memories? In what form was it organized? Undoubtedly, much of it was composed of motor skills–the techniques of the artisan; the way to plough, hoe, sow, and harvest for the
peasant; the wielding of sword and lance for the nobleman; spinning
and weaving for women of every class. These were learned in games or
by working alongside the masters of the craft. Other pieces of knowledge combined motor skills with verbal instructions–one thinks of
those folklore jingles that aided the remembrance of time to plant and
time to reap or that transmitted peasant medicine from mother to
daughter.

But much of the apparatus of society can be transmitted only in
verbal form. Ideals of behavior are of this kind, whether etiquette or
that vast ground encompassed in our own culture within the bounds
of law and politics: the ways property can be transferred, for example,
or relations of authority and dependence. These are neither motor
skills nor discrete items of information. They "exist" only in so far as
they are known–which means, in an oral culture, remembered. They
exist only in so far as they can be expressed and remembered by words
or by gestures accompanied by words. They are language-bound.[34]

It is therefore of considerable importance that, with the exception of an Anglo-Norman work called the *Leges Henrici Primi*, Europe produced no treatises on secular law before the late twelfth century. It is of considerable importance that historians should have difficulty reconstructing the rules of political or legal organization before such treatises appeared. For treatise and rule are special kinds of discourse, special ways of organizing words. Their presence indicates a particular way of thinking about society. Their absence is significant, despite one's normal hesitance in arguing *ex silentio*. Rules were not expressed, and therefore not thought of, in the same way before the twelfth century as they were from that time on.

How did people think of them? What was the discourse that contained them? In an oral culture such discourse is created and transmitted under two constraints. First of all, it must be *composed* orally. Second, it must be *memorizable*. And the most important parts of that culture, the ideals and habits most necessary for society's daily functioning, must be memorizable *by the average mind*. They therefore take particular forms: mnemonic jingles, narratives (often poetic, for the rhythm helps the memory), formulae, and fixed rituals. And so it was in the oral culture of the Middle Ages. Mores, ideals, and the standards, techniques, and instruments of social behavior were expressed, first of all, in oral formulae and gestures that people used, for example, to transfer land or reach agreements to end vendettas. We can occasionally see them vividly in medieval chronicles, as in the numerous oath-taking scenes described by Galbert of Bruges, or the *exfestucatio*, or more bizarre rituals, such as the magical dinner on the tomb of the dead Count Charles.[35] These formulae and gestures lie somewhere behind or outside the narrow confines of the Latin charters of sale, donation, mortgage, marriage, and other agreements that are the substance of early archives. They were expressed, secondly, in the vernacular *chansons de geste*–the popular literature of the twelfth-century aristocracy–and undoubtedly in much oral literature that has forever disappeared.

These forms of discourse have two qualities that we must insist on. They are *narrative*. They are *exclusively concerned with individuals*. To say that twelfth-century vernacular epics were narrative is to insist upon the obvious. It is worth noting, however, that these texts were narrative to their didactic core. They present the audience with ideals and with admonitions to seek those ideals by describing the actions that heroes and villains perform and the consequences of those actions. Rarely, except in formulaic epithets, does the poet categorize his characters or step more than briefly outside his tale to instruct his audience directly.

The old formulae and gestures that people used in their ordinary transactions were also narratives. They were visible performances. This visibility was their critical quality–public, witnessed. It seems, indeed, that written records of these transactions may have served in some parts of Europe primarily to list the witnesses.[36] They were also, probably, ritualized performances: not only those that one might immediately think of–the taking of homage, kneeling, hands between hands, or the investing of a bishop with his ring and staff, or the formalities of arbitration, duel, and ordeal–but also more commonplace rituals, such as passing a stone to confirm the sale of land, or the ritual dinner that followed a quitclaim, or the annual placing of a symbolic rent on the altar of a church.[37]

To say that these are all forms of discourse exclusively concerned with individuals may seem less clear and more arbitrary. The figures who strut across the stage not just of the epic poems but of many chronicles as well may appear to us to be characters rather than individuals. They lack the rounded opacity and ambiguity of real human beings; their actions, larger than life in virtue or vice, consciously exemplary, do not have the multitude of referents that we experience in real human actions. They seem to exist only within the narrative, to come into being at its beginning and to end with the last strophe. Yet, though these characters may often seem two-dimensional, they are not personified abstractions. They are not Everyman or the Perfect Knight. And, whether their tales were told in epic or in chronicle, there is no evidence that singers, writers, or audience were particularly aware of them as *fictions*.[38] Concerning the major figures of the epics, there were enough stories current to give them a life beyond the narrative of any given poem. And learned monks, even in the twelfth and thirteenth centuries, were only too willing to confuse historical patrons of their monasteries with the figments of epic imagination.[39]

Furthermore, poets and chroniclers often called on their audience to emulate their heroes and learn from the example of their villains.[40] Was their advice followed? Were these figures emulated? Louis VII apparently insisted on following the "route of Charlemagne" to Constantinople in 1147.⁴¹ And in that curious play between "reality" and "fiction" which makes the reader of any medieval writing wonder when and where to suspend his disbelief, King Louis' crusade may very well have been the historical model for the poem *La Pélérinage de Charlemagne*.⁴² A generation later, at the other end of the social scale, Peter Waldo may have converted to the life of poverty after hearing the story of St. Alexis.⁴³ Yet when we read these accounts in seemingly serious chronicles we must wonder what in fact we are being told. Were Charlemagne and St. Alexis merely *topoi*? Were the references to them meant only to create a moral or political response in the audience? Peter Waldo himself may indeed be a fiction. The question of emulation leads us quickly into the long-standing controversy over the functional relationships of epics to the society that found them so appealing.⁴⁴ It would be prudent to tread no further upon this battlegound.

The transactions of real life do not pose such difficult problems of literary sensibility and the relationship of literature to life. It was in real life that the obstinate ambiguity of real people and the multiple referents for their actions dominated perceptions.

How were people imagined when they engaged in social action? What did the witnesses see? Did they witness abstract vendors and purchasers, donors and donees? Or did they see particular people, members of particular families, solidarities, neighborhoods, or ecclesiastical groups, individuals embedded in the full complexities of their social relations? The texts of the charters themselves, in the tenth and eleventh centuries as later, would suggest the former. The participants tell us directly, "Ego Diaz faemina, et vir meus Isimbertus consentiens nos simul in unum venditores Rostagno abbate emptore." [I, Diaz, a woman, and my husband, Isimbertus, consenting to this, we as one are vendors to Rostagnus, the abbot purchaser.]⁴⁵ But how seriously are we to take this? Many other clauses in these charters are commonly considered purely formulaic: penalty clauses that promise payment in gold, for example.⁴⁶ So, too, one must question the meaning that *venditor* and *donator* had for those who were made to name themselves in that way, when "donors" are shown receiving payments for their "gifts."⁴⁷

If texts are ambiguous, the consequences of such acts speak with a more straightforward voice. When acts of donation or sale came into

dispute, what occurred? Before the late twelfth century, the consequence was most likely to be violence followed by arbitration or compromise, solutions in which two results were important: that both
sides agreed and that neither left without compensation.[48] That is to
say, disputes were settled, not by considering the parties as vendors
and purchasers, donors and recipients, and applying rules appropriate
to those categories, but rather by the search for a resolution in which
the status and self-esteem of both parties would be saved and a continuing social relationship created or renewed. No differently did men
imagine the consequence of oaths of homage and fealty. Far from
creating identical obligations on all vassals and lords, in the eleventh
century such oaths–even within the confines of a small region–could
place one man in the bonds of strictest obedience, while for another it
was but the affirmation of a treaty of peace or an obligation of nothing
more than the gift of a candle.[49] Oaths and acts were embedded in
the totality of the social network; they were indeed expressive of that
network. They were the actions of individuals in all their complexity
as men of wealth, family, status, friendship, and title.

It was for this reason that most notions of law, ideals of behavior,
political rules, and social mores were remembered in the form of statements about particular persons or members of defined social group-
ings *doing* things, statements with active verbs in the present or past
tense, statements about actions that were visible and had visible consequences. When Anglo-Saxon kings set out the compensations to be
paid for personal violence it was in this form:

*If, when men are drinking, one draws his weapon but inflicts no
injury with it, he shall pay* 1s. *to the householder and* 12s. *to the
king.*

*If a man coming from afar, or a stranger, leaves the highway and
neither calls out nor blows a horn . . .*[50]

Even in the thirteenth century, French witnesses that were asked to
tell who had the right to administer justice in a place would recount
what people had done: ". . . for forty years and more he saw that the
archbishops of Reims had high justice in the borough . . . and never
saw the king or any other temporal lord get involved in it."[51] This was

surely the source of the rigorous connection throughout the Middle Ages between deed and right.

We can immediately see the difference between this mode of thinking about laws and mores and our own. Our mode, like that of Greek philosophers after Plato and of European literate intellectuals from the twelfth century on, is dominated by atemporal statements making large use of the copula "to be." The entities which this atemporal predicate serves are not individuals but categories. They are statements essentially about invisibles. Because they are about abstract categories, we can test them for logical consistency. Because they are atemporal, we can use a two-hundred-year-old document not only as the foundation but also as a constant referent for our government. For that part of medieval European culture which depended on memory, such categorical thinking, such logical testing, such precise reference to the past would not have been possible. It required that individual rules be formulated in the abstract way we formulate them; but such rules were remembered instead in the form of actions by particular persons or social groups: actions that received praise and thus were to be emulated or actions that brought shame, harm, or vengeance and were thus to be avoided. This is why we have the impression that the people of earlier medieval Europe lived according to a "cake of custom" in which the distinctions we are used to– between law and morality, between private and public rules– were not made. For such distinctions are the very stuff of abstraction.

IV

To see people acting as vendors or debtors, rather than as the particular persons we know them to be, or to see them acting as officials, as persons with institutional roles, requires a special and peculiar act of the imagination, one which reduces the individual to a single role specified by a rule or a set or rules. To be a vendor means to have the obligations defined by rules concerning vendors, rules that take nothing into account except for the characteristics that define what a vendor is. Similarly, to be an official is to have the duties and obligations defined by rules concerning that kind of official and to be considered as an official only within the confines of those rules. Whatever lies outside the rules is irrelevant, whether it be status, character, family, or wealth. It is precisely the relation to rules, atemporal and impersonal, that makes these roles themselves permanent, impersonal, and abstract. When we speak of institutions or of political organization distinct from the structure of society, when we speak of a legal order, we assume this act of the imagination.

In the late eleventh century this way of thinking was discovered or rediscovered by clerical polemicists arguing the issues of the Investiture Controversy or seeking a compromise to quiet the furies and bring harmony once again to the Church. They discovered it in the very attempt at reform, as they endeavored to impose upon Europe a set of institutions whose justification they found in ancient texts and whose realization required the destruction of the status quo of custom and habit: to impose a literate conception of good order on an oral culture and its own far different way of conceiving of what was proper. The form they gave to their discovery was to distinguish between person and office, artifice and naturalness, authoritative and nonauthoritative, the rule of law and the rule of man. The distinction between public and private came soon after. Before a generation had passed, a Bolognese monk began to elaborate the law of the Church as a consciously constructed system of verbalized rules. These clerical intellectuals had invented the world of discourse of the modern state.

Our long fascination with the Investiture Controversy as the start of the conflict of Church and state (a setting that obviously derives from the secularization controversies of the nineteenth century) might incline us to place the invention of the state as a reaction to the Church, an attempt to restructure secular rule on a new foundation in response to Gregorian claims of supremacy and the collapse of what Ernst Kantorowicz has called "Christ-centered kingship."[52] This would hide, however, the more important invention of the state within the Church itself, the Church as a political, institutional body.

If we would see the old and the new side by side, the mental habits of nonliterate politics intertwined with the threads of literate institution building, we can turn nowhere better than to the work of Pope Gregory VII himself, and especially to the text that enunciated the major features of his program, the *Dictatus Papae*. In March 1075 twenty-seven statements concerning the powers and rights of the

The Invention of the State · 163

pope were inserted into Gregory's register under this title, immediately following the acts of the Lenten synod that had suspended six bishops, deposed another, anathematized the Duke of Apulia, and threatened Philip I of France and five members of the Imperial council with excommunication. The *Dictatus* is now taken by most scholars to comprise the chapter titles or heads of argument for a collection of justificatory texts.[53]

Most of the statements in the *Dictatus* enunciate general rules that define the range of papal action, such as:

5. That the pope may depose the absent.
7. That he alone may establish new laws according to the needs of the time.

But one of them must make any modern reader stop short:

23. *Quod Romanus pontifex, si canonice fuerit ordinatus, meritis beati Petri indubitanter efficitur sanctus testante sancto Ennodio Papiensi episcopo ei multis sanctis patribus faventibus, sicut in decretis beati Symachi pape continetur.*

[*That the Roman Pontiff, if canonically ordained, is undoubtedly rendered holy by the merits of Saint Peter; of this Saint Ennodius, Bishop of Pavia, gives witness with the accord of many holy fathers, as is found in the decrees of Saint Symmachus, Pope.*]

What did this mean, and why was it included? On the answers to these questions there is little agreement. To some the phrase "meritis . . . efficitur sanctus" argues a mystical union between St. Peter and the pope. To Walter Ullmann it asserts identity only "as regards the objective totality of powers . . . that is, as regards office or status."[54] Ullmann is surely correct in judging the first of these explanations "a not particularly happy formulation of a profound idea."[55] For not only is it almost as obscure as the text it glosses, but also Gregory at crucial moments is too urgently aware of the distance that separates him from St. Peter.[56] Ullmann's own explanation, however, is contradicted by the texts themselves.[57] And neither of these modern glosses explains clearly why this statement is included as a separate chapter heading rather than as a justificatory text for one of the others. What meaning, then, did this text have for Gregory?

Gregory came back to Ennodius of Pavia and Pope Symmachus again in March 1081 in his letter to Bishop Hermann of Metz justifying his second deposition of the Emperor Henry IV.[58] In contrast to the *Dictatus Papae*, where the assertion stands alone, Gregory here placed it in a context from which we can infer how he understood it.

The argument of this letter falls into two parts. The first presents a multitude of what Gregory calls *documenta* – pieces of written statements by early popes, and examples of excommunications and depositions of kings and emperors. Before this first part comes to an end, Gregory introduces the second: a comparison of the powers of the clergy. This comparison is made partly in moral terms: "Who does not know that kings and princes derive their origin from men ignorant of God who raised themselves above their fellows by pride, plunder, treachery, murder." But the thrust of the argument lies on the other side of the comparison, in the powers given the clergy. Clerical power, he argues, from the bottom to the top, from exorcist to pope, is superior to all forms of earthly dominion. This superiority derives from the clergy's power to command the invisible world: to cast out demons, perform the grace-giving sacraments, ordain, and depose. This whole system, furthermore, is arranged in strict hierarchy. Since these sacramental powers derive from ordination, from the grant of indelible character to the clergy, ordination (though never mentioned) is the fundamental assumption behind this part of Gregory's argument, as it is the recurring argument in the *Three Books against the Simoniacs* by Gregory's contemporary Cardinal Humbert.[59]

Gregory then turns to a comparison of the moral corruption of earthly rule with the holiness of spiritual rule.

From the beginning of the world to the present day we do not find in all authentic records [seven] emperors or kings whose lives were as distinguished for virtue and piety as were those of a countless multitude of men who despised the world. . . .

Whereas in one single chair of successive bishops – the Roman – from the time of the blessed Apostle Peter nearly a hundred are counted among the holiest of men.

It is at this point, to cap his argument, that Gregory quotes Ennodius of Pavia at length.

What we have said above is thus stated in the decrees of the blessed pope Symmachus—though we have learned it by experience: "He, that is St. Peter, transmitted to his successors an unfailing endowment of merit together with an inheritance of innocence"; and again: "For who can doubt that he is holy who is raised to the height of such an office, in which if he is lacking in virtue acquired by his own merits, that which is handed down from his predecessor is sufficient. For either he [Peter] raises men of distinction to bear this burden or he glorifies them after they are raised up."

In phrasing this text for the *Dictatus Papae*, Gregory had been careful to note that this transformation of the pope by the merits of St. Peter occurred on ordination. In the context of the letter to Hermann of Metz this precision takes on its full significance. Just as ordination gives an indelible character to a priest so that, no matter what his personal moral worth, he has the power to perform the sacraments, to command the supernatural, so the papal ordination gives the pope his indelible character, the "unfailing endowment of merit" and the "inheritance of innocence" transmitted from St. Peter, which allows him to command the supernatural, to bind and loose in heaven as on earth. The powers of the pope do not refer to a set of rules, they do not constitute an office in a rule-referential context, they are the effluence of character supernaturally transformed by the ritual of ordination.

How vital this conception was to Gregory can be seen in the greeting formulae of his letters.[60] Elected on April 22, 1073, not until June 30, after his ordination, did he begin in his letters to offer his apostolic benediction. As Pope-elect he could make decisions concerning marriages, write to French barons concerning a campaign in Spain, attend to the rights of St. Peter in Imola, that is, carry out the earthly duties of the pope, but it was only as pope ordained that he could command the invisible world of the Holy Spirit.[61]

This insistence on sacred character as the source of power is hardly surprising, for the sacred character of each level of the hierarchy was a leitmotif of most of the Gregorian reformers' polemics against the "simoniacs." Though one could pick among them almost at random to find a text where this proposition forms the starting point, it is perhaps most striking in Cardinal Humbert's argument against those who would distinguish between *consecratio* and *res ecclesiae* (note he does not say "office" and goods) in Book 3 of his treatise *Against the Simoniacs*.[62] The distinction, of course, was the one that finally allowed the Concordat of Worms in 1122. Those who say they have not bought the "invisibilem Spiritus sancti gratiam," the invisible grace of the Holy Spirit, but only the visible goods of the Church, "visibiles ecclesiarum res," are none the less heretics, Humbert asserts, because in so doing they lay claim to the name of the bishop and thus to consecration. The episcopal dignity contains the goods made holy to God. Thus, in the selling of consecrated goods it is the sanctification, the grace of the Holy Spirit, that is sold. Those things are *sancta* which serve sanctuaries and altars. If they are *sancta* they have the Holy Spirit in them.[63]

The reformers' insistence on the ritual of consecration and the inner dwelling of the Holy Spirit was, of course, deeply dependent upon a thousand-year-old literate tradition. Yet in their insistence on character rather than on rules as the source of power, in their insistence on transformation of persons and property by the ritual of consecration, the arguments of Gregory, Humbert, and their fellows were perfectly congruent with the political conceptions of the nonliterate world around them. Though the reformers laid claim to a literate tradition, the conceptual world within which they placed their texts, the basic structure of their argument was no different from those who likewise imagined power to be the effluence of personality and the totality of relations within which men were placed. It is probably for this reason that the *Dictatus Papae* seems to us so unorganized and the *documenta* that Gregory presents in his letter to Hermann of Metz so haphazardly arranged. We find them unorganized because we expect them to compose a logical structure of rules. But for Gregory these were emanations of a character and not a structure of rules and precedents. To see them as rules required a far different way of imagining both bishops and property, a way with which Gregory and Humbert would have been totally out of sympathy.

Yet Gregory's very act of assembling the *Dictatus*, the very notion of collating ancient texts to justify an assertion of power, contained the germ of that new imagining. It assumed that somehow these diverse texts and reported actions "meant" the same thing, that they were rationally coherent, that from them could be drawn certain conclusions, that they were capable of rational elaboration. What was required was for men to visualize these texts as a coherent system of rules, or potentially such a system, and to agree that it defined the powers and rights of clergy and the nature of ecclesiastical property. That is, they had to see office and property not as having character but as impersonal and abstract because derived from an impersonal and abstract body of rules.

It would take a lengthy investigation of the corpus of late-eleventh-century polemics to discover by what stages and in what minds this new conceptual world appeared. Since the early reformers' insistence on consecration allowed no compromise in the conflict with secular rulers and the possessors of private churches, no compromise would have been possible without this act of imagination. It is in the work of one of the early moderates within the reform movement that we can see it already accomplished.

When Ivo of Chartres wrote to Archbishop Hugh of Lyons in 1097 to defend the election of Archbishop Daimbert of Sens against charges of simony (for he was accused of having received investiture from the hands of King Philip I), he turned for support to a text of St. Augustine that said it all:

By what law do you lay claim to estates of the church? By divine law or human? We find divine law in the Scriptures and human in the laws of kings. By what right does a man possess what he possesses? Is it not by human law? For by divine law, "The earth is the Lord's and the fullness thereof." But by human law it is said, "This estate is mine; this house is mine; this slave is mine." Take away the laws of the emperors and who would dare say, "This estate is mine; this slave is mine; this house is mine"? . . . Don't say, "What is the king to me?" For in that case what are possessions to you? By the law of kings possessions are possessed. You said, "What is the king to me?" Don't then speak of your possessions, because you have renounced the rights you had according to human laws by which possessions are possessed.[64]

Goods of the Church were not made *sacra* by their donation. As property, as *meum* and *tuum*, by their very nature they existed only by virtue of human law, for possession is itself a category of human law. By extension, the bishop as holder of property, as *possessor*, is also a category only of human law. In contrast, and by implication, the bishop as performer of spiritual actions must be a category of divine law. It is for this reason that Ivo can treat the grant of the pastoral staff as merely a symbol of assent or conferral. Humbert had found such usage heretical because the objects of investiture were the very vehicles by which the Holy Spirit passed.[65] Once power ceased to emanate from character, however, and was made rule referential, the ritual of investiture became nothing more than placing a person in the context of those rules. The ritual became merely symbolic.

Ivo thus had already made, or discovered in Augustine, the crucial distinction between person and office—the person of flesh and character, the office as an abstract category of law. He likewise had made the distinction between nature and artifice, or in this case, between what is given by God and is thus unalterable and what is created by man and thus mutable. By implication, since power was to be viewed as a category of law, he had also made the distinction between the rule of law and the rule of man—and indeed the preceding portion of the letter, accusing Hugh of altering the old law regarding consecration with "privatis legibus et novis traditionibus" is an explicit appeal to that distinction.[66]

These distinctions were still in embryo at the end of the eleventh century. In many ways the course of Western political thought from that moment until now may be considered the complex development of the genetic material they harbored. We have seen that they first emerged as a consequence of literate thinkers reassessing, regrouping, and redefining the remembered actions of an oral culture in the light of their texts. The reformers of the mid-eleventh century, and especially Pope Gregory VII, conceived their divinely ordained task to be the reordering, the purification, the "re-formation" of the Church, a return of the Church to its form in the days of the Fathers. This was a wholly literate suggestion and could have occurred only in a literate community, for it depended not on oral memory but on texts, against which Gregory and his fellow reformers judged their contemporary world. In one of the more striking letters of this entire controversy, Gregory cited an ancient dictum of St. Cyprian to answer the charge that by his demands for reform he was overturning the accepted customs of the Church. "Scire debes creatorem tuum dixisse: Ego sum veritas, non autem usus vel consuetudo." [You ought to know that your creator has said: "I am truth," not "usage" or "custom."][67]

This insistence that "truth" was to be found in texts and not in what people did proclaimed the atemporal, abstract nature of those texts. But it also posed directly the question, Who is to interpret those texts and by what right? And who is to supplement them when they are found wanting? Was it men who by the saintliness of their lives or their trained wisdom earned the right to interpret those texts? Or was it someone else? For years the clerical intellectuals of Europe struggled with this question. Indeed it was never really satisfactorily solved, for it returned again to haunt the clergy during the period of the Great Schism in the fifteenth century. But it posed directly the problem of authority. That authority was finally defined in terms of office: the papal office, first of all, and then other offices both clerical and lay claiming their share of authority in Church and secular government as the twelfth and thirteenth centuries progressed. It was around the concept of office that the distinction between public power and private right finally emerged, and with it the analysis of which rights belonged to an office by human design and which belonged to it by nature or by divine grace.

Law and the state were from the very first an instrument to combat what we might call "habit" and "custom," an abstract, impersonal, literate structure of coercive force. The Gregorian reformers appealed beyond what men remembered to rules preserved in writing, rules with atemporal force, abstracted from the immediacy of daily life, from the obstinate opacity, the multiple referents, of individual lived experiences. By this act they forced themselves and all those who followed in their footsteps–first their opponents, then the dominant literate intellectual tradition–onto the abstract plane where dwells the state.

The men of the eleventh and early twelfth centuries did not take this change easily. Bishops, in the name of custom, stoutly resisted the claims of the papacy. When secular adjudication began to depend on words and their manipulation, even literate men were frightened.

Here, for example, is the worried account of a Flemish chronicler of 1124; a clerk, a professional notary:

Thanks to this boon of peace, men governed themselves in accordance with laws and justice, devising by skill and study every kind of argument for use in the courts. . . . Rhetoric was now used both by the educated and by those who were naturally talented. But, on the other hand, because these by their deceits brought action in the courts against the faithful and the lambs of God, who were less wary, God, who sees all from on high, did not fail to chastise the deceivers. . . .

Therefore God inflicted the scourge of famine and afterwards of death on all who lived in our realm.[68]

Across the Channel the compiler of the *Laws of Henry I*, a contemporary of this Fleming, wrote: "There is so much perversity in human affairs and so much profusion of evil that the precise truth of the law . . . can rarely be found, and he who does most harm to most people is valued the most highly. . . . these processes and the quite unpredictable hazard of the courts seem rather things to be avoided."[69] Such doubts took long to pass. The process by which the concepts of literate law passed into the habits of European peoples was a long one. In many ways it is still going on.

Yet so long have we dwelled on the abstract plane of the state under the rule of verbalized rules, that we now find it difficult to imagine mankind ever having dwelt elsewhere. I suspect, however, that even today, in the ceaseless flow of lived experience, we still, lawyers and laymen alike, in fact learn and remember many of our mores, our ideals, and our social behavior in the same mode as did men living in the oral tradition of the Middle Ages. Perhaps this is why so many of those problems first posed in the great medieval awakening after 1050 are still with us nine hundred years later.

1. Jean-Jacques Rousseau, *The Social Contract*, trans. G. Hopkins, ed. E. Barker (London: Oxford University Press, 1947), book 1, chap. 1, p. 240.
2. *Crito*, 50; trans. B. Jowett (New York: Random House, 1937), pp. 434–435.
3. *Politics*, 1254^{a-b}; trans. B. Jowett (New York: Random House, 1941), pp. 1132–1133.
4. Ibid., 1279^b, 1295^a, 1311^a–1315^b; trans. Jowett, pp. 1186, 1219, 1252–1262.
5. For a general survey, see J. W. Jones, *The Law and Legal Theory of the Greeks* (Oxford: Clarendon Press, 1956), chaps. 1, 3.
6. Ibid., pp. 38–39; and the classical statement by Thrasymachus in Plato's *Republic*, book 1.
7. Trans. W. Arrowsmith (Chicago: University of Chicago Press, 1959).
8. For the following discussion, only a few works can be noted among what is now a vast literature. Common utility: G. Post, "Ratio Publicae Utilitatis, Ratio Status, and Reason of State," in his *Studies in Medieval Legal Thought*, chap. 5 (Princeton: Princeton University Press, 1964); J. R. Strayer, "Defense of the Realm and Royal Power in France," in his *Medieval Statecraft and the Perspectives of History* (Princeton: Princeton University Press, 1971), pp. 291–299. Corporate concepts: Post, *Studies*, passim; E. Kantorowicz, *The King's Two Bodies* (Princeton: Princeton University Press, 1957); P. Michaud-Quantin, *Universitas: Expressions du mouvement communautaire dans le moyen-âge latin* (Paris: J. Vrin, 1970). Sovereignty in political and legal argument: my "The Sovereign and the Pirates, 1332," *Speculum* 45 (1970): 40–68.
9. H. Mitteis, *Der Staat des hohen Mittelalters* (Weimar: H. Böhlaus Nachf., 1968), esp. chaps. 14, 15.
10. Ibid., part 3; H. Mitteis, *Lehnrecht und Staatsgewalt* (Weimar: H. Böhlaus Nachf., 1958), chap. 5; R. Fawtier, *The Capetain Kings of France*, trans. L. Butler and R. J. Adam (London: Macmillan & Co., 1965), esp. pp. 60 ff.; more moderate view in F. Ganshof, *Feudalism*, trans P. Grierson (New York: Harper &

Bros., 1961), pp. 156 ff. Compare the treatment of the same theme in R. Boutruche, *Seigneurie et Féodalité* (Paris: Aubier, 1970), 2:296 ff. and esp. p. 300: "Le temps de Philippe Auguste constitue la charnière entre deux mondes: celui, sans veritable état . . . ; celui d'une monarchie féodale."

11. Classic formulation in Marc Bloch, *Feudal Society*, trans. L. Manyon (Chicago: University of Chicago Press, 1961), chap. 29; a tradition carried on in G. Duby, *La société aux XIe et XIIe siècles dans la région mâconnaise* (Paris: Armand Colin, 1953), p. 155, and in J. R. Strayer, "Feudalism in Western Europe," reprinted in my *Lordship and Community* (New York: Holt, Rinehart & Winston, 1968), esp. p. 14: "Public authority has become a private possession"; views slightly modified in Strayer, "The Two Levels of Feudalism," in *Medieval Statecraft*, pp. 63–76.

12. Classic critique by O. Brunner, "Moderner Verfassungsbegriff und mittelalterliche Verfassungsgeschichte," reprinted in *Herrschaft und Staat im Mittelalter*, ed. H. Kämpf, pp. 1–19 (Bad Homburg: H. Gentner, 1963). A more recent statement is Karl Kroeschell, *Haus und Herrschaft im frühen deutschen Recht*, Göttinger rechtswissenschaftliche Studien, 70 (Göttingen: O. Schwartz, 1968), pp. 48 ff. The result of this critique has been a very different approach to early Germanic institutional history by such scholars as Theodor Mayer, Walter Schlesinger, and their followers and students.

13. J. R. Strayer, *On the Medieval Origins of the Modern State* (Princeton: Princeton University Press, 1970), pp. 6 ff.

14. O. Gierke, *Das deutsche Genossenschaftsrecht* (Berlin: Wiedmann, 1881), 3:363 n. 34, 366.

15. Strayer, *Medieval Origins*, p. 9.

16. M. Weber, *On Law in Economy and Society*, trans. E. Shils and M. Rheinstein (Cambridge, Mass.: Harvard University Press, 1954), p. 5.

17. Ibid., p. 6.

18. For a general discussion, see L. Pospisil, *Anthropology of Law: A Comparative Theory* (New York: Harper & Row, 1971), chaps. 1, 2; and the methodological discussion by L. Nader and P. H. Gulliver in *Law in Culture and Society*, ed. L. Nader (Chi-

cago: Aldine, 1969), pp. 1–23. For similar problems in the definition of political anthropology, see M. Bloch, ed., *Political Language and Oratory in Traditional Society* (New York: Academic Press, 1975), pp. 1–5. For an example of this controlling image in legal theory that attempts to transcend the Western model, see H. L. A. Hart, *The Concept of Law* (Oxford: Clarendon Press, 1961), esp. pp. 89–90.

19. J. Stiennon, *Paléographie du Moyen Age* (Paris: A. Colin, 1973), pp. 16–17.
20. J. F. Benton, ed. and trans., *Self and Society in Medieval France* (New York: Harper & Row, 1970), pp. 45–47.
21. J. Stiennon, *L'écriture diplomatique dans le diocèse de Liège du XIᵉ au milieu du XIIIᵉ siècle* (Paris: A. Colin, 1960), p. 49.
22. *Beowulf: A Dual-Language Edition*, trans. Howell D. Chickering, Jr. (Garden City, N.J.: Anchor Books, 1977), p. 49.
23. If, that is, the ealdorman Æthelweard was really the translator into Latin of the Anglo-Saxon chronicle. See D. A. Bullough, "The Educational Tradition in England from Alfred to Ælfric: Teaching *Utriusque Linguae*," in *La scuola nell'Occidente latino dell'Alto Medioevo*, Settimane di studio del Centro Italiano di Studi sull'Alto Medioevo, 19 (Spoleto: Presso la Sede del Centro, 1972), 2:477–478.
24. Forcefully argued by Bullough, "Educational Tradition," pp. 453–494. For an earlier period, see Philip Grierson, "Les foyers de culture en Angleterre au haut moyen âge," in *Centri e vie di irradiazione della civiltà nell'Alto Medioevo*, Settimane di studio del Centro Italiano di Studi sull'Alto Medioevo, II (Spoleto: Presso la Sede del Centro, 1964), pp. 279–295.
25. Archive départementale de l'Aude, H. 102, H. 65.
26. Some original eleventh-century charters in Languedoc suffer from floating tenses, moving irregularly from present to past and back again. In other areas, because the act was oral, it was vital to have witnesses alive to testify to it. See Y. Bongert, *Recherches sur les cours laïques du Xᵉ au XIIIᵉ siècle* (Paris: A. et J. Picard, 1949), pp. 256 ff.
27. Sir Frank Stenton, *Anglo Saxon England*, 3rd ed. (Oxford: Clarendon Press, 1971), p. 497: "They were obviously taken over by

the king's writing-office from the speech of common men, and they only give the popular impression of the kind of judicial authority which generally belonged to a great lord."

28. Numerous examples may be found in almost any collection of · eleventh-century charters. See the discussion of such forms in M. L. Carlin, *La pénétration du droit romain dans les actes de la pratique provençale* (Paris: Librairie générale de droit et de jurisprudence, 1967), pp. 53 ff.

29. Ibid., p. 300.

30. Numerous examples may be found, for example, in the *Cartulaires des Templiers de Douzens*, ed. P. Gérard and E. Magnou, Collection de documents inédits sur l'histoire de France, sér. in-8, 3 (Paris: Bibliothèque Nationale, 1965).

31. See the forceful argument in E. A. Havelock, *Preface to Plato* (Oxford: Blackwell, 1963), chap. 9.

32. E. Magnou-Nortier provides several examples in "Fidélité et féodalité meridionales d'après les serments de fidélité," in *Les structures sociales de l'Aquitaine, du Languedoc et de l'Espagne au premier âge féodal* (Paris: C.N.R.S., 1969), p. 121. Many others may be found in C. Devic and J. Vaissete, *Histoire générale de Languedoc*, A. Molinier (Toulouse: Privat, 1875), passim.

33. F. Yates, *The Art of Memory* (Chicago: University of Chicago Press, 1966).

34. Those who have read them will immediately recognize my indebtedness in the argument that follows to Havelock, *Preface to Plato*, and W. J. Ong, *The Presence of the Word* (New Haven: Yale University Press, 1967).

35. Galbert of Bruges, *The Murder of Charles the Good*, trans. J. B. Ross (New York: Columbia University Press, 1960), oaths: passim; *exfestucatio*: pp. 171, 269, 278, 281; food on the Count's tomb: p. 218.

36. Bongert, *Recherches*, pp. 283 ff.

37. The use of a stone is mentioned occasionally even in the formula-ridden Languedocian charters: J. Rouquette, *Cartulaire de Béziers (Livre Noir)* (Montpellier-Paris: A & J Picard, 1918), nos. 88, 93, etc.; a ritual dinner appears to be the only plausible

interpretation of "nostrum manducare de absolutione et quir-pitione" (no. 143), or of "denariis pro manducare de venditione" (no. 152). Symbolic rents: *Cartulaires de Douzens*, A. 53.

38. See the discussion in C. S. Lewis, *The Discarded Image* (Cambridge: At the University Press, 1964), pp. 179–181.

39. See, for example, Lynette Muir's Introduction to Glanville Price, ed., *William, Count of Orange: Four Old French Epics* (Totowa, N.J.: Rowman and Littlefield, 1975), esp. pp. ix–x.

40. As Guibert de Nogent wrote, "I have undertaken to tell the tale of my fortunes and misfortunes for what help it may be to others" (Benton, *Self and Society*, p. 130; see also p. 195). This use of story and history is analyzed by Lewis, *The Discarded Image*, pp. 177–178.

41. Odo of Deuil, *De profectione Ludovici VII in orientem*, trans. V. G. Berry (New York: Columbia University Press, 1948), p. 58, n. 48. For background, see P. Alphandéry and A. Dupront, *La chrétienté et l'idée de croisade* (Paris: Albin Michel, 1954), 1:18–31, 203–208.

42. J. Horrent, "La chanson du *Pélérinage de Charlemagne* et la réalité historique contemporaine," in *Mélanges de langue et de littérature du Moyen Age et de la Renaissance offerts à Jean Frappier*, pp. 411–418 (Geneva: Droz, 1970).

43. W. L. Wakefield and A. P. Evans, *Heresies of the High Middle Ages* (New York: Columbia University Press, 1969), pp. 200–201. What is the relationship between such assertions and the common medieval *exemplum*? The question remains open; see J. T. Welter, *L'exemplum dans la littérature religieuse et didactique du moyen-âge* (Paris: Guitard, 1927).

44. The literature is now substantial. Two works have set the framework of the debate: E. Köhler, *Ideal und Wirklichkeit in der höfischen Epik* (Tübingen: M. Niemeyer, 1956); and R. Bezzola, *Les origines et la formation de la littérature courtoise en Occident*, part 2: *La société féodale et la transformation de la littérature de cour* (Paris: H. Champion, 1960).

45. O. Terrin, ed., *Cartulaire du chapitre d'Agde* (Nîmes, 1969), no. 285.

46. For one example of such opinion, see M. Castaing-Sicard, *Monnaies féodales et circulation monétaire en Languedoc*, Cahiers

de l'Assoc. Marc Bloch de Toulouse, 4 (Toulouse: Assoc. Marc Bloch, 1961), p. 66.

47. Examples can be found in any eleventh-century collection. For a discussion, see Carlin, *Droit romain*, pp. 59 ff.

48. See my "Suum cuique tribuere," *French Historical Studies* 6 (1970): 287–299.

49. Duby, *Mâçonnais*, pp. 185 ff.

50. Dooms of Hlothaere and Eadric, 12, and of Wihtread, 28; translations from C. Stephenson and F. G. Marcham, *Sources of English Constitutional History* (New York: Harper & Bros., 1937), pp. 4–8. For a discussion of the verbal texture of these laws, see D. Korte, *Untersuchungen zu Inhalt, Stil und Technik angelsächsischer Gesetze und Rechtsbücher des 6. bis 12. Jahrhunderts* (Meisenheim am Glan: A. Hain, 1974), pp. 131 ff.

51. For a discussion of these replies, see my "Custom, Case Law, and Medieval Constitutionalism: A Re-examination," *Political Science Quarterly* 78 (1963): 373.

52. Kantorowicz, *King's Two Bodies*, chap. 3.

53. E. Caspar, ed., *Das Register Gregors VII, Monumenta Germaniae Historica*, Epistolae selectae, 2 (Berlin: Weidmann, 1955), 1:201–208. For the nature of this text, see K. Hofmann, "Der 'Dictatus papae' Gregors VII als Index einer Kanonessammlung?" *Studi Gregoriani* 1 (1947): 531–537.

54. W. Ullmann discusses the various interpretations of this sentence, as well as his own, in "Romanus pontifex indubitanter efficitur sanctus: Dictatus Papae 23 in retrospect and prospect," *Studi Gregoriani* 6 (1959–61): 233.

55. Ibid.

56. As, for example, in his two depositions of Henry IV, when he addresses St. Peter, and, especially, in the second, where it is St. Peter who must make the final determination in trial by battle (Caspar, *Register*, pp. 270, 483).

57. The main reason for my disagreement with Ullmann will be apparent in what follows. There are also internal grounds for disagreement. First, his terms *objective*, *office*, and *status* in this context are filled with ambiguity. The discussion must be of the precise content of such words within Gregory's own system of understanding. Second he contradicts himself explicitly on pp.

248–249 by stating (correctly) that Gregory exercised governmental functions before his ordination but acquired his "purely jurisdictional functions" only after ordination (unless Ullmann understands a distinction here that he does not make clear). Finally, he does not discuss the text within the context of the letter to Hermann of Metz, ignoring the most important clue we have to its meaning for Gregory.

58. Caspar, *Register*, pp. 547 ff. I will quote from it in the translation by E. Emerton, *The Correspondence of Pope Gregory VII* (New York: Columbia University Press, 1932), pp. 166 ff.
59. Friedrich Thaner, ed., *Libelli de Lite, Monumenta Germaniae Historica* (Hanover: Hahn, 1891), 1:95 ff.
60. Ullmann discusses this interesting fact but, I believe, misinterprets its meaning ("Dictatus Papae 23," pp. 246 ff.).
61. Caspar, *Register*, letters 1, 5, 7, 10.
62. *Libelli de Lite*, 1:198 ff.
63. I have greatly abbreviated the argument as Humbert presents it.
64. *Libelli de Lite*, 2:645: "Quo iure defendis villas aecclesiae, divino an humano? Divinum ius in·scripturis habemus, humanum in legibus regum. Unde quisque possidet quod possidet? nonne iure humano? Nam iure divino 'Domini est terra et plenitudo eius.' Iure humano dicitur: Haec villa mea est, haec domus mea [est], hic servus meus est. Tolle iura imperatorum, quis audeat dicere: Haec villa mea est, meus est iste servus, mea est ista domus? *Item*: Noli dicere, quid michi et regi? Quid tibi ergo et possessioni? Per iura regum possidentur possessiones. Dixisti: Quid michi et regi? Noli dicere possessiones tuas, quia ad ipsa iura renuntiasti humana, quibus possessiones possidentur."
65. Ibid., 1:205–206.
66. Ibid., 2:644.
67. The text is discussed in G. B. Ladner, "Two Gregorian Letters," *Studi Gregoriani* 5 (1956): 221–242.
68. Galbert of Bruges, *Murder of Charles the Good*, p. 84.
69. L. J. Downer, ed. and trans., *Leges Henrici Primi* (Oxford: Clarendon Press, 1972), p. 99.